# BROWNSHIRT PRINCESS

Lionel Gossman is M. Taylor Pyne Professor of Romance Languages emeritus at Princeton University. Most of his work has been on 17th and 18th century French literature, 19th century European cultural history, and the theory and practice of historiography. His publications include *Men and Masks: A Study of Molière*; *Medievalism and the Ideologies of the Enlightenment*; *French Society and Culture: Background for 18th Century Literature*; *The Empire Unpossess'd: An Essay on Gibbon's "Decline and Fall"*; *Between History and Literature*; *Basel in the Age of Burckhardt: A Study in Unseasonable Ideas*; *The Making of a Romantic Icon: The Religious Context of Friedrich Overbeck's "Italia und Germania"*; and several edited volumes: *The Charles Sanders Peirce Symposium on Semiotics and the Arts*; *Building a Profession: Autobiographical Perspectives on the Beginnings of Comparative Literature in the United States* (with Mihai Spariosu); *Geneva-Zurich-Basel: History, Culture, and National Identity*, and *Begegnungen mit Jacob Burckhardt* (with Andreas Cesana). He is currently working on a study of the *Jugendstil* artist Heinrich Vogeler.

1. Heinrich Vogeler. Frontispiece for Marie Adelheid Reuß, Prinzessin zur Lippe, *Gott in mir* (1921).

Lionel Gossman

# Brownshirt Princess

*A Study of the "Nazi Conscience"*

Cambridge
OpenBook Publishers

2009

40 Devonshire Road, Cambridge, CB1 2BL, United Kingdom
http://www.openbookpublishers.com

@ 2009 Lionel Gossman

Some rights are reserved. This book is made available under the Creative Commons Attribution-Non-Commercial-No Derivative Works 2.0 UK: England & Wales License. This license allows for copying any part of the work for personal and non-commercial use, providing author attribution is clearly stated. Details of allowances and restrictions are available at:

http://www.openbookpublishers.com

As with all Open Book Publishers titles, digital material and resources associated with this volume are available from our website:

http://www.openbookpublishers.com

ISBN Hardback: 978-1-906924-07-2
ISBN Paperback: 978-1-906924-06-5
ISBN Digital (pdf): 978-1-906924-08-9


Acknowledgment is made to the following for generously permitting use of material in their possession: Archiv Böttcherstraße Bremen; Princeton Theological Seminary Library; Princeton University Library; Marquand Library of Art and Archaeology, Princeton University.


All paper used by Open Book Publishers is SFI (Sustainable Forestry Initiative), and PEFC (Programme for the Endorsement of Forest Certification Schemes) Certified.


Printed in the United Kingdom and United States by
Lightning Source for Open Book Publishers

*In Memory*
*of*
*George L. Mosse*

In its present form, this study is the outcome of a productive partnership of editor, author, and publisher. I would like to thank Alessandra Tosi, a director of Open Book Publishers, for the lively interest she took in it from the start and for her hard work, patience, and sound advice as it went through the editing process. I would also like to thank the Committee on Research in the Humanities and Social Sciences at Princeton University for contributing toward the cost of publication and thus lending its support to an exciting new publishing venture that ensures unlimited access to scholarly work.

# Contents

Introduction:
An Unusual Book and a Strange Collaboration     1

Part I: Seeking a New Religion: *Gott in Mir*
1. The Title     15
2. The Epigraph and the Envoy     43
3. The Poem     47
4. Appendix to Part I: The *Völkisch* Rejection of Christianity     57

Part II: Serving New Gods
5. Marie Adelheid, Prinzessin Reuß-zur Lippe: Society, Ideology, and Politics     65
6. *Nordische Frau und Nordischer Glaube*     89
7. *Die Overbroocks*     95
8. After 1945: Unrepentant Neo-Nazi     107
9. Concluding Reflections     127

Notes     131

Bibliography     179

Index     195

Online Appendices: http://www.openbookpublishers.com
  A. *Gott in mir.*
    1. Scan of the original book in the Department of Rare Books and Special Collections, Firestone Library, Princeton University. Also viewable on the Library site:
http://libweb5.princeton.edu/visual_materials/Misc/Bib_2934672.pdf
    2. English translation of the poem.
  B. Image portfolios
  Image portfolio 1: From *Jugendstil* to *Agitprop*. The Itinerary of Heinrich Vogeler.
  Image portfolio 2: A selection of works by artists of the period 1880-1933 – paintings, drawings, book illustrations – expressing a religiosity similar to that of *Gott in mir*.

# Illustrations

Cover: Fidus (i.e. Hugo Höppener), header (detail) in *Der Kunstwart*, October-December, 1914, vol. 28, p. 125; also in Prof. Hermann Reich, *Das Buch Michael* (Berlin: Weidmannsche Buchhandlung, 1916), p. 117.
*Princeton University Library.*
This figure, representing Germania, appeared, on the outbreak of war in 1914, in many other forms produced by Fidus, as a drawing, a lithograph, an inexpensive postcard, sometimes alone, sometimes as part of a more elaborate image. In a few it was explicitly named, as in "Germania aufbebend, zürnend" ("Germania quivering with rising anger"). A version of it was used by the artist again, on the eve of the stunning triumph of the National Socialists in the Reichstag elections of September 1930, for the cover design of the first number (January-February, 1930) of a right-wing women's magazine *Frigga: Blätter für deutsches Frauentum*.

1. (Frontispiece) Heinrich Vogeler. Frontispiece for Marie Adelheid Reuß, Prinzessin zur Lippe, *Gott in mir* (Bremen: Angelsachsen Verlag, 1921).
*Rare Books Division, Department of Rare Books and Special Collections, Princeton University Library. Photo: John Blazejewski.*

2. Heinrich Vogeler. "Ekstase." Title-page of Franz Pfempfert's progressive, pacifist weekly *Die Aktion*, vol. IV, no. 22, May 30, 1914.
*Princeton University Library. Photo: L. Gossman.*

3. Heinrich Vogeler. Cover design for *Deutsche Kunst und Dekoration* (April, 1902) dedicated to his work, with an article on him by R.M. Rilke.
*Marquand Library of Art and Archaeology, Princeton University.*

4. Heinrich Vogeler. Design and illustration for R.M. Rilke, "Die heiligen Drei Könige," in *Die Insel*, 1, no. 6, March 1900.
*Princeton University Library.*

5. Heinrich Vogeler. Title-page for *Frühlingskranz* by the Romantic poet Clemens Brentano (Königsberg: Paul Alderjahn's Verlag, 1907).
*Princeton University Library.*

6. Heinrich Vogeler. Cover illustration for his pamphlet *Das neue Leben* (Hanover: Paul Steegemann, 1919).
*Princeton University Library.*

7. Heinrich Vogeler. Cover design for his pamphlet *Expressionismus der Liebe* (Hanover: Paul Steegemann, 1919).
*Princeton University Library.*

8. Heinrich Vogeler. Cover design for pamphlet *Expressionismus: Eine Zeitstudie* (Hamburg: Henry Hoym Verlag, 1919).
*Princeton University Library.*

9. Heinrich Vogeler. Cover illustration for his pamphlet *Die Freiheit der Liebe in der kommunistischen Gesellschaft* (Hamburg: Konrad Hanf Verlag, 1919).
*Princeton University Library.*

10. Advertisement for Roselius's Kaffee HAG in Herwarth Walden's *Der Sturm*, III, no. 117/118, July 1912, p. 99.
*Marquand Library of Art and Archaeology, Princeton University.*

11. Bernhard Hoetger. "Lebensbaum" [Tree of Life] sculpture originally on façade of Atlantis House (1931).
*Photo: Archiv Böttcherstraße Bremen.*

12. Ludwig Fahrenkrog. Vignette in his *Baldur* (Stuttgart: Verlag von Greiner & Pfeiffer, 1908), p. 47.
*Princeton University Library.*

13. Ludwig Fahrenkrog. "Baldur, Sonne, Geist des Alls," in his *Baldur* (Stuttgart: Verlag von Greiner & Pfeiffer, 1908), p. 104.
*Princeton University Library.*

14. "Fidus" (Hugo Höppener). Header in Julius Hart, *Triumph des Lebens* (Florence: Diederichs, 1898), p. 51.
*Princeton University Library.*

15. Wolfgang Kirchbach. Cover of *Ziele und Aufgabe des Giordano Bruno-Bundes* (Schmargendorf bei Berlin: Verlag "Renaissance" – Otto Lehmann, 1905). *Flugschriften des Giordano Bruno-Bundes*, no. 6.
*Princeton University Library.*

16. Cover of Wilhelm Schwaner, *Germanen-Bibel*, 2nd. ed. enlarged (Berlin: Volkserzieher Verlag, 1905).
*Princeton Theological Seminary Library. Photograph by John Blazejewski.*

17. Cover of pamphlet extracted from Ludwig Fahrenkrog's *Das Deutsche Buch* to promote the *Germanische Glaubens-Gemeinschaft* (1921).
*Princeton University Library.*

18. Rear cover of pamphlet from Fahrenkrog's *Das Deutsche Buch* (1921). *Princeton University Library.*

19. Publicity announcement by Eugen Diederichs Verlag, Jena, of a forthcoming series devoted to Nordic sagas and literary texts as manifestations of the "essential, inherent strengths of German being," April 1933. *Princeton University Library.*

20. Copy of the Princess's letter to U.S. High Commissioner McCloy. *http://www.italiasociale.org/storia07/storia060307-1.html*

21. Cover of the Princess's collection of poems *Freundesgruß* in the extreme rightwing series *Kritik: Die Stimme des Volkes*, no. 46, 1978.

*"Die Quellen, aus denen heute eine neue religiöse Sehnsucht aufsteigt, sind meist unrein und verhängnisvoll. [...] Das Verhängnisvolle dieser Herkunft liegt darin, daß sie [...] jeder Verwirrung ausgesetzt, allen Surrogaten gegenüber unsicher [ist] und blind in das Schoß der falschen Propheten taumelt."*

                Gertrud Bäumer
                a leading figure in the German Women's Movement in the early 20th century, in *Die Frau*, vol. 27, no. 5, p. 129 (February 1920).

2. Heinrich Vogeler. "Ekstase." Title-page of *Die Aktion* (1914).

# Introduction: An Unusual Book and a Strange Collaboration

In the year 1921 a slim volume of verse entitled *Gott in mir* [God in Me] appeared in Bremen, Germany. (See online Appendix A). One of the first books to be published by the Angelsachsen Verlag [Anglo-Saxon Publishing Company], founded in 1921 by Ludwig Roselius, a wealthy Bremen merchant in the overseas trade,[1] it consisted of 41 printed pages, interspersed by eight blank pages, along with a title page, a page containing an epigraph, and another containing an envoy of four well-known lines from Goethe's *West-östlicher Divan*. A frontispiece illustration (fig. 1) – a somewhat altered version of a pen and ink drawing of 1914, entitled variously *Neugeburt* [New Birth], *Ekstase* [Ecstasy] and *Eine Vision*, that first appeared in Franz Pfemfert's dissident, anti-militarist and anti-chauvinist weekly *Die Aktion* [Action] (fig. 2) and clearly purports to evoke the dawning of a new day, the beginning of a *vita nuova* – was by the then still well-known, Bremen-born *Jugendstil* artist Heinrich Vogeler, in the expressionist manner with which he was experimenting at the time.[2] The spacious layout of the book, in no way cramped or economical, and the exceptionally high quality of the rag paper give no hint of the hard times Germany was going through when the book was produced. Everything points rather to a well-financed small edition for a select clientele. The book is in fact listed in only five library catalogues world-wide.[3] The author is given as Marie Adelheid Prinzessin Reuß-zur Lippe.

*Gott in mir* is of interest not so much because of its rarity as because it is an unusual testimonial to the situation in Germany at the time of its publication. The blue-blooded but rebellious God-seeking author (1895-1993) subsequently became an ardent National Socialist, was employed as an aide to the Nazi Minister of Food and Agriculture, R. Walther Darré, one of the main ideologists of *Blut und Boden* [Blood and Soil], and dedicated her writing talent to the promotion of National Socialist ideals, especially those of Darré, in prose and verse. Copies of her other writings prior to 1945, though rare, are to be found in the collections of several libraries in the United States and Europe. They include an essay on *Nordische Frau und Nordischer Glaube* [Nordic Woman and Nordic Religion], published in 1934 by the neo-pagan *Nordische Glaubens-Gemeinschaft* [Nordic Religious Community, founded in 1927], *Deutscher Hausrat* [Setting up the German Household] an advice leaflet for the new German woman (Leipzig: Strauch, 1936), two edited collections of writings by her mentor Darré,[4] and two novels, *Mutter Erde* [Mother Earth] (Berlin-Schöneberg: Verlag Neue Nation, 1935) and *Die Overbroocks* [The Overbroocks] (Berlin: Ährensen Verlag, 1942).

A convinced and impenitent Party member, the Princess continued her extreme right-wing political activities after the Second World War, both as a writer and translator and as an active member of various neo-Nazi organizations. The German translation of the notorious Holocaust-denying *Le Drame des Juifs européens* [The Drama of European Jews] (Paris, 1964) by the French Socialist *député* and sometime Communist, Paul Rassinier, is her work (*Das Drama der Juden Europas* [Hanover, 1965]). She also published two more volumes of poetry. In *Weltfrömmigkeit* [Earthly Piety] (Hamelin: Verlag Soltsien-Der Gute Gabe, n.d. [1960]), she took up again the neo-pagan religious themes of *Gott in mir*, even borrowing several long passages from the earlier work. Eighteen years later, *Freundesgruß: Rückblick auf sechs Jahrzehnte* [Greeting from a Friend: A Retrospective View of Six Decades], richly illustrated with woodcuts by the Nazi artist Georg Sluyterman von Langeweyde, celebrated the idealism, courage, and dedication of those in the National Socialist movement. It appeared in a special number of *Kritik: Die Stimme des Volkes* [Criticism: The Voice of the People] (no. 46, 1978), a neo-Nazi journal with which the Princess was closely associated.

In contrast, Heinrich Vogeler (1872-1942), the artist responsible for the frontispiece, had been elected in the revolutionary climate of November 1918 to the local Workers' and Soldiers' "Rat" or Council at Osterholz, the administrative center for the celebrated Worpswede artists' colony, of which he had been one of the leading lights until he was transformed by his experience of the war from a *Jugendstil* aesthete (figs. 3, 4, 5) into a radical left-wing political dissident. Even though he did not personally participate in the government of the short-lived *Räterepublik* [Workers' and Soldiers'

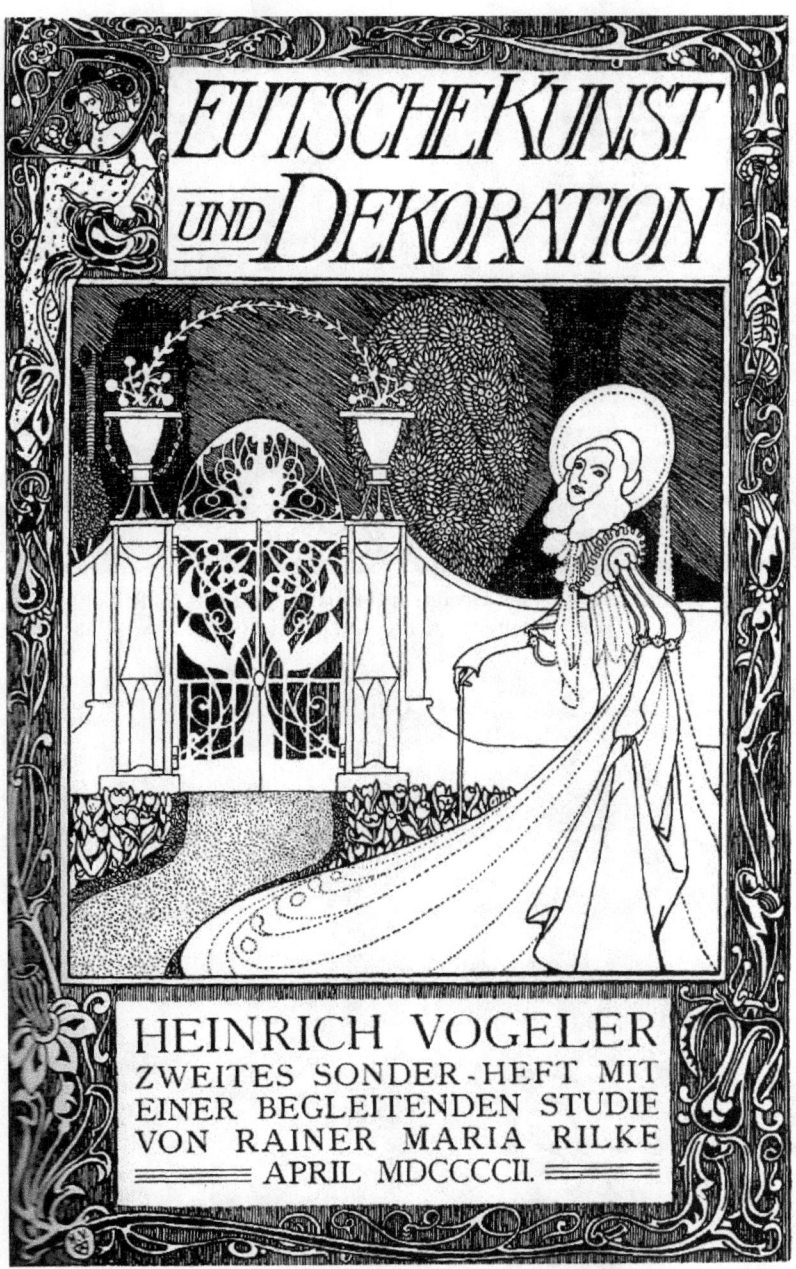

3. Heinrich Vogeler. Cover design for *Deutsche Kunst und Dekoration* (1902).

4. Heinrich Vogeler. Design and illustration for R.M. Rilke, *Die heiligen Drei Könige* in *Die Insel* (1900).

5. Heinrich Vogeler. Title-page for *Frühlingskranz* by Clemens Brentano (1907).

Council Republic, January-February, 1919] in nearby Bremen, where he was born and his mother still lived, he had been elected to the Bremen Workers' and Soldiers' Council. Moreover, he was so closely associated with many of the Republic's leaders that he had to go into hiding after it was overthrown by a right-wing militia (one of the notorious *Freikorps*, under the command of Colonel Wilhelm Gerstenberg) acting on behalf of the middle-of-the-road Majority Socialist central government that had come to power in Berlin in the wake of Germany's military defeat.[5] Shortly afterwards, Vogeler turned his elegant property in Worpswede, the Barkenhoff, into a commune, a place of asylum for left-wing agitators and deserters (or men simply making their way back from the front as their units broke up), a home for the children of persecuted Communists, and a progressive school, before finally handing it over in 1924 to the *Rote Hilfe*, the German section of an international Communist relief organization. He had designed the Barkenhoff himself and built it in the decade before the war as an island of art, beauty and fantasy, a refuge from the ugly everyday reality of modern industrial society. His visiting friends here had included the poet Rainer Maria Rilke, the writer Carl Hauptmann and his now better-known brother Gerhard, and several students of Ferruccio Busoni (then at the height of his fame), in particular the pianist Egon Petri, who was to become a celebrity in his own right, and the avant-garde Jewish-American composer Louis Gruenberg. Vogeler also joined the Communist Party in the early 1920s, and from the end of 1923 until June 1924, headed the Art Department of the Communist University for Western Minorities in Moscow. In 1931, after visiting the country four times (1923-24, 1925, 1926, 1927), he emigrated definitively to the Soviet Union. During those years Vogeler experimented with new forms of art in an earnest, if ultimately unsuccessful attempt to devise a style appropriate both to his new political and philosophical convictions and to what he saw as an emerging new reality.[6] After the National Socialists assumed power in Germany, he collaborated with the poet Johannes Becher, who had also left Germany for the USSR, on a collection of anti-Nazi poems, which he illustrated with cartoons, and when Nazi Germany invaded Russia in 1941, he broadcast from Moscow to the German troops on behalf of the Soviets. In late 1941, along with many other native Germans resident in the Soviet Union, Vogeler, already a sick man, was sent to Kazakhstan, where he died on 14 June 1942, destitute and lacking medical attention.

In the years just before and after the German Revolution, however, (i.e.

at the time he provided the illustration for the Princess's poem) Vogeler was not yet unequivocally a Communist. Like many other artists and intellectuals, he had been turned by the war into a pacifist and a socialist inspired by diffuse religious feelings of brotherhood, compassion and the unity of the entire cosmos.[7] When you visit the Barkenhoff, the poet and playwright Friedrich Wolf – who later emigrated, like Vogeler, to the Soviet Union – wrote to his fiancée in June 1921, you will find in Vogeler "einen wahren Christus-Mensch" [a genuine Christ-figure].[8] Like many on the Left at the time, Vogeler opposed what he saw as the authoritarian tendencies of the recently constituted German Communist Party. Power, he insisted, should be in the hands of the free workers' communities themselves, not vested in a centralized Party apparatus, and action should be spontaneous, not centrally planned. Equally, the Party, it appears, did not think much of him. Even the extreme non-Party Left (represented by anarchist newspapers like *Der Syndikalist* [The Syndicalist] or *Der Freie Arbeiter* [The Free Worker]) was not quite sure what to make of him.[9] His artwork at the time carried titles like *Werden* [Becoming] (1921) and *Die Geburt des neuen Menschen* [The Birth of the New Man] (1923), and he gave similar titles to the numerous pamphlets he published in those same years: *Das neue Leben* [New Life] (1919) or *Expressionismus der Liebe* [Expressionism of Love] (1919). (Figs. 6, 7, 8, 9) His leading ideas, in his own words, and the foundation stone of his socialism, were "Hingabe im Gesetz des Ganzen" [surrender of the individual self according to the law of the Whole], "innere Gesetzmäßigkeiten des Werdens" [inner laws of becoming], and "Frieden! Harmonie mit den Weltgesetzen des ewigen Werdens" [peace – harmony with the universal laws of eternal becoming].[10]

Vogeler appears to have owed more at this time to the then pervasive Nietzsche-influenced doctrines of *Lebensphilosophie*, with their emphasis on "Werden" [Becoming] instead of "Sein" [Being], than to the highly systematic dialectical materialism of Marx. Likewise his vision of a communist society owed less to Marx than to the anarchist ideas of Prince Kropotkin, the German translation of whose *Khlieb i volia* [Bread and Freedom, 1892], first published in 1906 as *Die Eroberung des Brotes: Wohlstand für alle* [The Conquest of Bread: Wellbeing for All], was republished by the Syndicalist Press in Berlin in 1919 in an edition designed and illustrated by Vogeler.[11] Typical of his position in those years was an oil painting of 1922, presently in the *Katherine Dreier-Société Anonyme* Collection at Yale University – one of a very small number of works by Vogeler in the United States, all of

Introduction    7

6. *Das neue Leben* (1919)

7. *Expressionismus der Liebe* (1919)

8. *Expressionismus: Eine Zeitstudie* (1919)

9. *Die Freiheit der Liebe in der kommunistischen Gesellschaft* (1919) [12]

Heinrich Vogeler. Cover illustrations for various pamphlets.

them acquired by Dreier in the 1920s. Entitled *Eine Vision* [A Vision], it combines a representation of the head of a sleeping Buddha, emerging from a background of plants, with a semi-abstract Soviet star motif.[13] In a study of the Worpswede artists put out in 1922 by the same Angelsachsen Verlag that published *Gott in mir*, the popular Bremen writer S. D. Gallwitz wrote that while Vogeler "enthusiastically called himself a Communist, his Communism was of a very individualist character. [...] Organized, politically oriented Communism had so little use for him that it considered him a spoiler. [...] The alpha and omega of all his demands was in the last instance religious in nature."[14] Vogeler's second wife, Zofia ("Sonja") Marchlewska – the daughter of a leading Polish Communist activist, art critic, and collaborator of Lenin – confirms that observation. Vogeler's publications in the early to mid-1920s, she notes in her memoirs, were all "composed in a mystical language that demonstrates how far the artist still was from understanding the ways and goals of Communism."[15] The future Communist who felt "ein gesetzmäßiges Werden in mir" [an orderly Becoming in me], who described the "God of our Germanic forefathers" with reverence as "Odin, der Odem, der Atem, das indische Atma, der große Wind und Atem der Natur" [Odin, Odem, Breath, the Indian Atma, the great wind and breath of Nature], and to whom "the two ravens on [Odin's] shoulders, Hugin and Munin," symbolized the reconciliation in God of all seeming dualisms – "inhalation and exhalation, high and low, day and night, summer and winter, sun and moon"[16] – was not yet perhaps too far removed in spirit from the future Nazi Princess who experienced "Gott in mir."[17]

As for the publisher of *Gott in mir*, Ludwig Roselius (1874-1943), besides being a highly successful businessman – the inventor of decaffeinated coffee, he founded and directed the internationally renowned firm of Kaffee HAG (fig. 10) – he was an active patron of the arts in Bremen and Lower Saxony and a champion of North German artists, especially those associated with Worpswede, such as the sculptor-architect-painter-designer Bernhard Hoetger and the pioneering woman painter Paula Modersohn-Becker. He also supported Vogeler and continued to do so for some time even after the artist had moved to the radical Left – in the hope, as the correspondence between the two suggests, of weaning him back.[18] For a while he even provided emergency subsidies to Vogeler's agricultural commune at Worpswede, which was never economically viable. In addition, his pointedly named Angelsachsen Verlag [Anglo-Saxon Publishing

10. Advertisement for Roselius's Kaffee HAG in Herwarth Walden's *Der Sturm* (1912). Roselius advertised his coffee regularly in this avant-garde art and literature periodical.

Company] published in 1925 a German translation of *Wilderness: A Journal of Quiet Adventure in Alaska* (1920) by the American artist Rockwell Kent, who was subsequently to become, like Vogeler, a man of the Left, close to the Communist Party.[19]

Roselius was at the same time an ardent advocate of the theory that the Arctic region, the home of the "Nordic race," was the cradle of human culture, and that the island continent of Atlantis, whose Nordic inhabitants were supposedly dispersed after it was submerged beneath the waves, had really existed. The celebrated Atlantis House in Bremen, designed by his protégé Hoetger and completed in 1931, with the great expressionist sculpture of Odin (or Wotan), the Nordic Christ (fig. 11) on its façade, bears witness to his commitment to the "Nordic Idea." (Damaged during World War II, it was rebuilt in 1965, but Hoetger's "Tree of Life" sculpture, "dedicated to Odin," was not replaced. Though it is now one of the tourist attractions of Bremen, it is unlikely that all visitors know how the Haus Atlantis came by its name).

Roselius also subsidized the scholarly investigations of the Dutch philologist and archaeologist Herman Wirth, who was later (1935) appointed

11. Bernhard Hoetger. "Lebensbaum" [Tree of Life] sculpture, "dedicated to Odin," originally on façade of Atlantis House (1931). Destroyed in World War II.

by Himmler to head his *Ahnenerbe* (full name: *Ahnenerbe Forschungs- und Lehrgemeinschaft* [Ancestral Heritage Society for Research and Teaching]) research foundation. The businessman subscribed to the scholar's fantastic theories of Nordic preeminence, which in one form or another were widely shared in Germany at the time. In addition, he supported efforts to find, collect, and preserve the ancient artifacts of the Nordic peoples and to protect their traditions and racial purity in the hope that the decadent culture of the modern world might be regenerated by a revived Nordic race. In the aftermath of the First World War, he advocated a concerted effort by the Nordic peoples or "Anglo-Saxons" to establish dominion over the entire universe. (Like Julius Langbehn, the author of the vastly influential *Rembrandt als Erzieher* [Rembrandt as Educator], first published in 1890 and constantly reprinted afterwards, Roselius included in this category the North Germans, the Dutch, the English, the Scandinavians, and the Americans – viewed as Anglo-Saxon colonizers).[20] A critic of liberalism in politics and economics – but not at all of capitalism as such – Roselius had helped in 1917, as popular discontent was on the rise and the socialists were gaining ground, to found a right-wing party that professed to stand above all classes and unite all true Germans. The leading figure in this *Deutsche Vaterlandspartei* [German Fatherland Party] was none other than Wolfgang Kapp, who three years later led a (failed) putsch against the Weimar Republic. Roselius sympathized with the goals of National Socialism from early in the movement's history. He met with Hitler in the early twenties and later joined the NSDAP or *Nationalsozialistische Deutsche Arbeiterpartei* [National Socialist German Workers' Party]. His relations with the Party were not always smooth, both because of his continued support of Hoetger and celebration of Modersohn-Becker, whom he saw as quintessentially "Nordic" in their art but whose work was denounced as "degenerate" by the Nazis, and because of his commitment to Wirth, who fell out of favor in the late 1930s after he began promoting the idea that the earliest Germanic societies were matriarchies and lent his authority to a supposedly ancient Frisian chronicle that even many National Socialist scholars dismissed as a nineteenth-century forgery.[21] (His learned *Was heißt deutsch?* [What Does Being German Mean?] [Jena: Eugen Diederichs Verlag, 1931] carried the dedication "Der deutschen Frau und Mutter" [To the German Wife and Mother]; for the dedication of his edition of the *Ura Linda Chronik* [Ura Linda Chronicle] [Leipzig: Koehler& Amelang, 1933] he cited what he claimed was a first-century inscription from Cologne – "Meinen

Germanischen Müttern" [To My Germanic Mothers]). In addition, some in the NSDAP, including at times Hitler himself, came to view excessive emphasis on theories of Nordic supremacy as divisive and not conducive to the aims of the Party.[22] Roselius and his family nevertheless remained committed to National Socialism and to Hitler personally.[23]

As a publishing venture, *Gott in mir* thus brought together three diversely talented individuals, who by 1921 were probably already evolving in different directions politically, but who might well still have felt that they shared similar ideals and aspirations. It stands as vivid testimony to the confused mix of anger, rebelliousness, and unorthodox political and religious fervor that characterized the immediate post-war period and was shared by many Germans – on both the Right and the Left. Though well rooted in the pre-war Wilhelminian period, these feelings were greatly aggravated by the disillusionment and disorientation of the last days of the First World War and the collapse of the Wilhelminian state. For some, especially in the officer class and the bureaucracy, it was the alleged betrayal of the army by Socialists and Jews in the rear (the so-called "dagger in the back") along with the prospect of "Bolshevik" revolution that stirred up feelings of outrage and revolt; for others, chiefly in the working class, it was the perception that they had been deceived by the former ruling elite and then betrayed by the Majority Socialist Party leadership's suppression of the grassroots revolution that had broken out in the wake of the military defeat and the abdication of the Kaiser; and for a few, chiefly younger members of the aristocracy, it was their own class's spineless response both to the military situation at the front and to the demand for the Kaiser's abdication.

My aim in this essay is not so much to conduct a detailed literary analysis of the Princess's poem as to provide an interpretative context for its main themes and invite reflection on what made the collaboration of three such diverse individuals possible. In Part I, I consider the title, the epigraph, the envoy, and the poem itself. In Part II, I outline the subsequent career of the Princess and offer an account of several of her later works. An Appendix contains a fasimile of the poem as originally published, a rough translation of it, and a portfolio of images. The aim of Part I, in short, is to use *Gott in mir* as an entry into the mental and cultural outlook that presided over its publication. The aim of Part II is to contribute, by way of an account of the Princess's career and writing, to our understanding of the attraction National Socialist ideology had for many Germans.

# Part I

## Seeking a New Religion: *Gott in Mir*

# 1. The Title

The Princess's poem is presented in three typologically distinct parts. In the first of these – twenty-one pages of loosely connected verse, printed on very high quality paper in large-font *Fraktur* or traditional German rather than Roman lettering[1] – the text is divided into sections of uneven length (anywhere from four to seventeen lines) each of which, even the shortest, has a page to itself and can be read either as an untitled individual poem in a collection or as an integral part of a loosely constructed but continuous poetic whole. These twenty-one pages are followed by twelve pages, where text – once again of varying length – appears only on the right-hand page and the left-hand page remains blank. These in turn are followed by another six consecutive pages of text, once again divided into sections or individual poems of uneven length, one on each page. In physical appearance, the book thus has a spacious, almost monumental character, despite its modest dimensions.

The most common verse form is iambic pentameter, occasionally rhyming, with some preference for feminine rhymes. As in Goethe's *Faust*, Part I, lines of four feet vary the pentameters, either interspersed among them or forming entire poems (or sections of the work). The form, which may have been designed to evoke memories of Goethe, Schiller, and Hölderlin in the reader, appears to have been intended, like the typeface, to generate an impression of faithfulness to national tradition, the implication being that the seemingly new and revolutionary content – the assertion of a religious faith distinct from the Christianity of the established churches and of an ethics at variance with Christian ethics as commonly understood – also belongs in fact to a long-established, authentic Germanic tradition. In this respect, the Princess's poem takes its place alongside other works of the time advocating a faith grounded in the native religious traditions of the

"Germanic race," such as the *Germanen-Bibel* [Germanic Peoples' Bible] – a Holy Book composed of texts by great German writers and philosophers – of Wilhelm Schwaner, editor of the *Volkserzieher* [People's Educator] and co-founder (with the artist and art teacher Ludwig Fahrenkrog) of various neo-pagan religious groups which came together in 1913 to form the *Germanische Glaubensgemeinschaft* [Germanic Religious Community]. Originally published in 1904, Schwaner's *Germanen-Bibel* had been reprinted in a popular edition in 1920 and again in yet another edition in 1921, the year of the appearance of *Gott in mir*.[2]

Likewise, the themes of the Princess's poem anticipate the later writings of the Tübingen Orientalist and sometime Christian missionary Jakob Wilhelm Hauer, who gradually moved in the course of the 1920s toward a conception of a German faith rooted in Nordic and Aryan traditions and radically opposed to all "Near-Eastern and Semitic" religions (Christianity as well as Judaism and Islam), and who in 1933 helped to bring most of the non-Christian, Germanic religious movements together under the single umbrella of the *Deutsche Glaubensbewegung* [German Religious Movement] and served as that movement's first leader.[3] The Princess's later writings show a marked affinity with Hauer's ideas, as we shall see in Part II of this study. In addition, both form and subject matter of *Gott in mir* are typical of a certain genre of poetic production in late nineteenth- and early twentieth-century Wilhelminian Germany.[4]

Thanks to the generosity of Princeton University Library's Department of Rare Books and Special Collections, a scanned copy of the original German text of the Princess's poem has been made available as an online appendix to the present study for the benefit of German-speaking readers. A rough translation into English has also been provided and, in addition, the poem has been quoted from liberally in translation.[5] While the language of the poem, in the original no less than in the translation, is not always entirely clear at the most basic level of meaning, the rhythms and syntax of the German are decidedly spacious, close to those of ceremonial speech or prophecy, rather than condensed and elliptic as in much modern poetry. They suggest a speaker or poetic voice who is an exceptional – aristocratic – individual and at the same time fully in tune with her language community, her *Volk*, and who may therefore be regarded by the reader both as a leader and model and as a mirror image of what is deepest in him or herself.

\*\*\*

The title of the Princess's volume, *Gott in mir*, would not have struck an educated reader of 1921 as particularly strange. Pantheistic, immanentist, and Gnostic religious currents had long been well represented in Germany and had gathered new strength in the late nineteenth and early twentieth centuries in a climate of growing disaffection from the traditional Christian teachings of the established Churches. In 1903 two translations into modern German of the writings, in Middle High German, of the medieval mystic Meister Eckhart (c. 1260-1328) appeared – one by the Jewish anarcho-socialist Gustav Landauer (who, as a member of the government of the *Räterepublik* of Bavaria during its brief existence, was murdered in 1919 by right-wing counter-revolutionaries) and one with the influential and innovative publisher Eugen Diederichs, whose sympathies tended to be with the *völkisch* Right rather than the socialist Left.[6] Diederichs also commissioned the Jewish philosopher and theologian Martin Buber to compile an anthology of writings by mystics of all times and all places (*Ekstatische Konfessionen* [Ecstatic Confessions], 1909).[7] The young Heidegger planned to write a book on Eckhart and to teach a course on mysticism, and a few years after the publication of the Princess's poem a smaller collection of mystical texts appeared in Munich under the title *Gott in uns: Die Mystik der Neuzeit* [God in Us: The Mysticism of the Modern Age].[8] Contemporaries of the Princess referred regularly to Meister Eckhart and to the great German mystics of the early modern period, Jacob Böhme (1575-1624) and Angelus Silesius (1624-1677). Goethe's nature-philosophy was sometimes integrated into this tradition and exercised an unmistakable influence on Rudolf Steiner, who devoted his earliest writings to the national poet and later named the temple of his anthroposophical faith after him. The theosophical movement, based on the writings of Helena Petrowna Blavatsky (1831-1891), had won a considerable following, as one historian reports, among "thinking people who felt intellectually and spiritually cut adrift, unwilling or unable to choose between the sterility of scientific positivism and the impotence of a diminished church."[9] Its harmonizing notion of "the One Life, the Soul of the World, the ultimate reality in which each living thing shares" and of which every thing that exists is a kind of emanation, appealed especially to those, chiefly in the non-commercial or pre-industrial middle and upper classes, who felt threatened by the growing power of big business and organized labor in late Wilhelminian Germany and rejected the utilitarianism and crass selfish or class interests – the "materialism," as they called it – that they saw displacing long established, communally respected traditions and values. Oppressed by what they perceived as the decadence of the age and the degeneration of the German people as a whole, these disaffected elements were drawn to a variety of movements promising regeneration of both the individual and the social fabric and commonly grouped under the umbrella concept of *Lebensreform* [Reform of (All Aspects of) Life].[10]

Instead of a unified and harmonious nation, it was felt in the circles of the disaffected that the long-desired and long-awaited breakthrough to a new, united Germany in 1871 had brought alienation, fragmentation, selfish and unrestrained pursuit of individual gain, and bitter class conflict. "Fragmentation and disunity" [Zersplitterung und Uneinigkeit] will be seen as the characteristic feature of our age, declared Julius Hart, one of a team of two brothers who were enormously influential in *Lebensreform* circles at the turn of the century. "All creative energies lose their unity and strike out in separate directions" [Alle Kräfte sondern sich und streben auseinander].[11] Whence, according to Max Weber, the many calls, among the more educated, for salvation from inner or spiritual distress – to which most *Lebensreform* programs were in one way or another a response, and which Weber contrasted with calls by the lower classes for salvation from outer or material distress. In Weber's words, what the disaffected middle and upper classes longed for was "'union' with oneself, with human beings, with the cosmos" ['Einheit' mit sich selbst, mit den Menschen, mit dem Kosmos].[12] This longing led some in the educated classes to situate themselves on an idealistic, anarchist or radical socialist "Left" that defined itself as "modern," and others to situate themselves politically on a "Right" that emphasized the community of the *Volk* or nation and was outspokenly critical of "modernity" (by which they understood modern capitalism and big business and the displacing of traditional values, folkways, and social structures by economic liberalism and political democracy). The longing for "Einheit" or wholeness was thus common to both a certain "Left" and a certain "Right," to so-called "Modernists" and "anti-Modernists" alike – a situation that helps to explain the difficulty of labeling complex figures like Eugen Diederichs or Ferdinand Avenarius – the editor and publisher of the lively, popular, literary and cultural magazine *Der Kunstwart* [The Art Custodian] – either "modern" or "anti-modern."[13]

"A searing pain runs through this age and the agony can no longer be borne," the essayist and critic Hermann Bahr wrote in 1890. "There is a common clamor for a savior, and the crucified are everywhere. [...] That

12. Ludwig Fahrenkrog. Vignette in his *Baldur* (1908)

salvation will come out of suffering and grace out of despair, that there will be daylight again after this horrific darkness... – the faith of modernity lies in such a glorious, blessed resurrection" [Es geht eine wilde Pein durch diese Zeit und der Schmerz ist nicht mehr erträglich. Der Schrei nach dem Heiland ist gemein und Gekreuzigte sind überall. [...] Daß aus dem Leide das Heil kommen wird und die Gnade aus der Verzweiflung, daß es tagen wird nach dieser entsetzlichen Finsternis... – an diese Auferstehung, glorreich und selig, das ist der Glaube der Moderne].[14] Throughout the play *Baldur* (1908) by Ludwig Fahrenkrog – artist, art professor, champion of everything Nordic and Germanic and co-founder with Wilhelm Schwaner of the neo-pagan *Germanische Glaubensgemeinschaft* (1913) – there is a repeated call for "Life! Light! Salvation!" [Leben! Licht! Erlösung!] (figs. 12, 13). The finale of *Baldur* consists of a *Song of the Youths and Maidens* in praise of the "Son of the Immortals" who "came to save us, bringing life and light."[15] (Baldur, the god of innocence, beauty, joy, purity, and peace, was the son of Odin or Wotan, the Norse or Germanic father-god, and is presented throughout the play as a native Germanic blend of Prometheus and Christ.[16]) Fahrenkrog's play was performed in the open-air "folk" theater at Thale in the foothills of the Harz Mountains, which had been founded and was being managed

13. Ludwig Fahrenkrog."Baldur, Sonne, Geist des Alls," in his *Baldur* (1908)

by the *völkisch* writer and publicist Ernst Wachler, another champion of "Germanic" and "Nordic" superiority. Despite his part-Jewish ancestry (which led in the end to his death at Theresienstadt) Wachler was one of the first members of Fahrenkrog's Germanic religious community and an early supporter of National Socialism. In fact, such "folk" theaters, designed to be places where the four elements of a cultural unity that modernity was accused of having torn apart – art, religion, nature, and *Volk* or nation – could come together, appealed chiefly to better-off, middle-class audiences, like the model of them all: Wagner's Bayreuth. So too, it can be reasonably surmised, did the *Germanische Glaubensgemeinschaft* itself, as well as the Princess's poem in its austerely luxurious presentation.[17]

Side-stepping the organized Left's demands for fundamental state-imposed social and economic change, the advocates of *Lebensreform* looked instead to remedy the alleged ills of modernity – which, for them, were above all feelings of spiritual emptiness and alienation from both the natural world and traditional communities – through freely chosen changes of lifestyle.[18] Vegetarianism, nudism, homeopathic medicine, sport and physical culture, free love, dance therapy, eugenics, education reform, *Wandervogel* youth groups, a return to life on the land, and the founding of new agricultural communities and garden cities, were some of the many programs proposed to effect those changes. *Lebensreform* was certainly in important respects a form of "bourgeois escapism,"[19] a revolt that avoided any real challenge to the established order, and a potentially dangerous retreat from the political arena, viewed as itself partly responsible for the social ills that had to be cured. Nevertheless, the changes in lifestyle it proposed, with their emphasis, in most cases, not only on community but on freedom from the restraints of convention and external authority, were themselves a "modern" rather than traditionally conservative response to the discontent and resentment produced in certain milieux by the rapid social and economic development of Germany in the second half of the nineteenth century and by the "materialist" and "Philistine" culture that those milieux felt had accompanied it. Exceptional in some respects (his Jewish origin and ultimate fate), the case of Gustav Landauer – who grew to manhood in the years of rapid expansion – is not untypical in others. It was his encounter with Ibsen, Landauer relates, that "transformed the dream of beauty in the lad I then was into a desire to create reality, that forced me [...] not to ignore the real basis of things – society and all its ugliness – but to criticize it and act against it through the rebellion and struggle of the individual. I understood nothing at that time of socialism and had not a clue about economic problems. What drove me into opposition to the ambient society [...] was neither belonging to a particular social class nor social compassion. It was my romantic longing constantly bumping up against fences established by a narrow Philistinism. And so it came about that I was an Anarchist, without acknowledging it, before I became a Socialist and that I am one of the few who did not come to Socialism by way of Social Democracy." The notion of "another" or "alterative Modernity" may better convey the complex and politically ambiguous character of the *Lebensreform* movement than the term "anti-modern."[20]

The poetry of the turn of the century is already permeated by *Lebensreform* notions and images, often in overt opposition to Christianity and bourgeois morality. Thus Max Bruns, a translator of Baudelaire and himself a publisher of works by many turn-of-the-century poets (Richard Dehmel, Max Dauthendey, Karl Henckell, Ludwig Jacobowksi), celebrates the body, the natural world, and their deep-seated inner harmony in a "Lied von der Jugend" [Song of Youth] from his 1897 collection *Aus meinem Blute* [From My Blood] (dedicated to Dehmel):

> O Kraft in mir, du göttliche, jauchzende Kraft! Kraft des jungen Leibes und der jungen Seele [...] O Sonne, Sonne! Allklare du in deiner rein strahlenden Nacktheit [...] Und o Erde, Urgebärende alles Lebens, mit dem keuschen, nie welkenden Schoße! Und du, weites Meer, noch im Wechsel beständig dir gleichend, Urbild alles Menschenseins...
>
> [O vital energy in me, divine, exulting energy! Energy of the young body and the young soul [...] O sun, sun! All bright in your pure luminous nudity [...] And o earth, original birth-mother of all Life, with your chaste, never withering womb! And you, vast sea, ever the same in the midst of change, primordial image of all human existence...] [21]

In Julius Hart's *Triumph des Lebens* [Triumph of Life] (1898), beneath a characteristic header design by the illustrator Hugo Höppener (fig. 14), better known as "Fidus" (like the Princess, both a rebel against convention and authority and an early supporter of National Socialism), the poet celebrates the arrival of spring in nature and in his own body. The poem opens on an erotic evocation of the marriage of Heaven – the Sun – and Earth, that is the union of seeming opposites, the overcoming of tenacious and life-destroying dualisms: light and darkness, spirit and matter, male and female, the divine and the human:

14. Fidus (Hugo Höppener). Header in Julius Hart, *Triumph des Lebens* (1898).

Der Frühling glüht durch alle Lüste,
die Wolke blitzt von weissem Licht,
herniederströmt ein Feuersamen,
der aus dem Leib der Sonne bricht.
Geöffnet ist der Schoß der Erde,
nackt liegt sie noch in welkem Struth,
und liebesschauernd dehnt sie zitternd
sich in der neuen jungen Glut.

 [Spring glows through all desire,
the clouds flash with white light,
fiery seed bursts forth
from the body of the sun and pours down.
The womb of the earth is open.
Naked she still lies in the withered swamp,
and shuddering with desire stretches out her trembling limbs
in new and youthful ardor][22]

A religious feeling for the unity of the universe underlay most *Lebensreform* projects and it was widely held among the advocates of *Lebensreform* that a new or renewed religion would be a significant component in the desired rejuvenation of both individuals and the community as a whole – that is, the German nation or *Volk* or, as more and more people were coming to think of it, the German race.

In the age of Darwin and Nietzsche, many deemed traditional Christianity not only incapable of providing that component, but itself part of the problem, rather than the solution. Christianity was accused of having adulterated and enfeebled the once energetic and creative

Germanic or Nordic race.[23] Far from being "anti-modern," the *völkisch* critics of Christianity were thoroughly in tune with "modern" values and ideas when, following Nietzsche, they rejected Christianity as a slave religion, a religion of subservience, like its Judaic parent, to a tyrannical God, and demanded in its place a "modern" religion compatible with the native, inborn love of personal freedom that, since Tacitus, had been ascribed to the Germanic and Nordic peoples. Some tried to reconnect with an indigenous German pantheistic and mystical tradition. Herman Büttner, whose modern German translation of Meister Eckhart's Middle High German writings and sermons was published by Diederichs in 1903, declared in his Introduction that the work of the medieval German monk represented "nothing less than a new religious creation, a fundamentally different religion from the mediator-based Christianity of the Church."[24] The considerable success of theosophy at the turn of the century reflected the same dissatisfaction with the Christianity represented by the established churches. Both Helena Petrowna Blavatsky's theosophy and Rudolf Steiner's breakaway movement of anthroposophy, it has been said, were "forms of pantheism and metaphysical monism," even if the theosophists themselves denied this.[25]

To the children of Darwin's generation the attraction of theosophy may have been that it appeared to offer a middle way – the possibility of reaching God not through a discredited faith that required the submission of the free, modern intelligence to an ancient and "alien" dogma, or through the action of an external mediator, but "scientifically," through a "higher" knowledge, such as Mme Blavatsky's "Secret Doctrine." It is not surprising that theosophists like Rudolf Steiner were among the founding members of the *Giordano Bruno-Bund* [Giordano Bruno Association] and the *Deutscher Monistenbund* [German Monist Association] – both of which were formed in response to popular ideas, derived from Darwin, about the nature of man and the universe and both of which rejected any separation of God and the world or man and nature. The *Giordano Bruno-Bund* was established in 1900 when Bruno Wille – a sometime theologian, mathematician, and philosopher, a founder of the avant-garde *Neue deutsche Volksbühne* [New German People's Theater] in Berlin, and a leading figure in the *Deutscher Freidenkerbund* [German Association of Freethinkers][26] – joined forces with Wilhelm Bölsche, a highly successful popularizer of Darwinist evolutionism, to mark the 300th anniversary of the burning at the stake of the great Renaissance nature philosopher Giordano Bruno, by creating

15. Wolfgang Kirchbach, cover of *Ziele und Aufgabe des Giordano Bruno-Bundes* (1905).

what the founders described as a "Hochburg aller reinen, starken und geistig-adeligen Bestrebungen, zugleich eine Kampfgenossenschaft gegen alles Dunkelmännertum"[27] [a citadel of all pure, strong and intellectually noble endeavors, at the same time a comradeship-in-arms against obscurantism of every kind]. The founding members included, besides Steiner, the *völkisch* artist Fidus, a member, like Wille and Bölsche, of the literary and cultural *Friedrichshagener Kreis* [Friedrichshagen Circle]; the liberally inclined poet and essayist Wolfgang Kirchbach, a close friend of Ferdinand Avenarius, editor of *Der Kunstwart*; the writer Carl Hauptmann, a frequent guest of the Vogelers and the Modersohns in Worpswede; Count

Paul von Hoensbroech, an aristocratic ex-Jesuit turned passionate critic of Roman Catholicism; Rudolf Penzig, an educational reformer, President of the Berlin *Humanistengemeinde* [Humanist Community], and editor of the magazine *Ethische Kultur* [Ethical Culture]; along with a fair sprinkling of academics.

In a pamphlet published by the *Bund* in 1905 (fig. 15), Kirchbach outlined its "Ziele und Aufgaben" [goals and tasks]. "First and foremost" among them was "the cultivation and development of a monist worldview, that is, a unified view of the universe, embracing all its known creative and driving forces, its physical and chemical nature, its ethical powers, its inner intellectual and spiritual movements, as well as its external material forms, [...] in all their variety and, at the same time, in the unity that is the core, ground, and meaning of their existence." From its foundation, it was the aim of the *Bund*, Kirchbach went on, "to analyze and expose the absurdity of the dualistic systems, with their oppositions of body and mind, spirit and nature [...], to which church dogma and the dogmas of philosophical and scientific schools reduce the infinite variety of phenomena – and to demonstrate through observation [...] the underlying unity of everything." The second task of the *Bund* was the cultivation of "Andacht" [reverence]. Monism as a modern philosophical and scientific position was thus to be complemented by monism as a modern form of religion. "From the outset it was expected that the *Bruno-Bund* would seek out those who were more or less repelled by the content of dogmatic religion, by religious sectarianism, and by the growing intolerance of the established churches, and who hoped to find in pure religious feeling both consolation and a way of developing their moral and logical convictions." For the founders were convinced that "in the massive modern process of criticizing and destroying obsolete ideas, it was not enough to substitute abstract philosophical ideas for the lost comforting beliefs of childhood, and that something of positive value for the moral life and for the imagination was needed to provide new nourishment for the soul and make up for the loss of the old." For this new nourishment Kirchbach looked to "the reverence inspired by poetry, art, and music." The *Bund* organized poetry-reading and musical evenings, botanical and geological study excursions, recitations and talks in the open air and in the woods around Berlin, and a celebration of the summer solstice near Lake Tegel in the northern outskirts complete with ritual dances and costumes.[28] Kirchbach's own understanding of the universe as revealed by Darwin and Haeckel appears to have had a religious dimension. "The totality of the force of nature is in us too" [die Totalität der Naturgewalt (ist) auch in uns], he wrote his brother in September 1882, anticipating the Princess's *Gott in mir*, "and every creature is a piece of the great All that also moves the planets around each other."[29]

The *Deutscher Monistenbund* was founded in January 1906, only a few years after the *Giordano-Bruno Bund*, by the Darwinist Ernst Haeckel with the twin aims of "promoting a unified view of the world and of life, based on modern natural science, and of bringing all the adherents of such a view together in a single organization." "The monist worldview," according to a modern account of it, "sought to resolve [...] apparent contradictions – between freedom and necessity, nature and spirit, body and soul, the individual self and the cosmos, God and the World." The *Bund* itself was to be more than an association of people with a shared "scientific" view of the world. It was to be "an agent for promoting a general cultural transformation. By presenting itself as an alternative to Christian religious communities, monism and the scientific view it represented were thus raised to the status of a substitute religion." The *Bund* aimed, moreover, to reach out to the popular masses and enlighten those kept hitherto in ignorance by the dogmas of the churches. This was to be accomplished through the action of convinced Monists professing their beliefs in newspapers and magazines, public lectures and evening discussion groups, and organizing monist festivals in celebration of the seasonal changes of spring, summer, and winter. The talks on Monism given by the 1909 Nobel prizewinner and pioneer of physical chemistry, Wilhelm Ostwald, were published under the title *Monistische Sonntagspredigten* [Monist Sunday Sermons] (Leipzig: Akademische Verlagsgesellschaft, 1911) and were intended to be read at Monist gatherings at the same hour as services in the Christian churches.[30]

The same years that saw the creation of the *Giordano Bruno-Bund*, the *Monisten-Bund* as well as several more directly literary, artistic, and cultural associations with reformist aims, such as *Die Kommenden* [The Coming Generations], established in 1900 by the poet Ludwig Jacobowski, the *Neue Gemeinschaft* [New Community] (1900) of the Hart brothers, the *Dürer-Bund* [Dürer Association] (1902), founded by Ferdinand Avenarius, and the *Verdhandi* or *Werdandi-Bund zur Förderung jungdeutscher Kunst* [Werdandi Association for the Promotion of Young German Art] (1907), whose chief promoters included Moeller van den Bruck and Houston Stewart Chamberlain, also saw the establishment of a large number of more explicitly nationalist societies with similar heterodox religious agendas.

Whereas the *Bruno Bund*, the *Monistenbund* and most of the literary societies did not have a single, clearly defined political orientation and included members from different backgrounds and of various political persuasions[31] – even if a majority of members of the *Dürer-Bund* and the *Werdandi-Bund* seem to have been associated with *völkisch* circles (i.e. nationalist circles in which national identity was usually based on race)[32] – the nationalist societies were more rabidly and uniformly xenophobic and anti-Semitic, and generally no less anti-Christian than the Monists. Among the earliest were the *Germanenbund* [Teuton Association], founded in Salzburg in 1886, the militarist and anti-democratic *Alldeutscher Verband* [All-German Association], founded in 1891 to promote German imperial ambitions and preserve the purity of the German race, and the *Deutschbund* [German Association], founded in 1894 by Friedrich Lange in order to cure "the ailing essence of our people" and save it from being delivered "into bondage to the Jews," made subservient to "English arrogance and cunning," and "ousted from its own land by waves of immigrant Slavs."[33] Lange, the author of *Reines Deutschtum: Grundzüge einer nationalen Weltanschauung* [Pure German-ness: Basic Principles of a National World View] (Berlin, 1894), deemed Christianity unsuited to the task of bringing about a rebirth of German "Volkstum" and advocated a return to pure German ways. The secret society of the *Ordo novi Templi* [Order of the New Templars], founded in 1900 by the racist Lanz von Liebenfels, aimed to "revive the ancient ario-heroic idea of a *Männerbund* or male fraternity based on racial identity," develop settlements or "racial reservations" for the breeding of a racially pure population, promote a more natural lifestyle (vegetarianism and "Sonnen-, Licht- und Luftkultur" [regular exposure to sun, light, and air]), and establish columbaria [Urnenfriedhöfe] as part of a revival of the forgotten ario-heroic cult of the dead.[34] Similar ambitions inspired the establishment of the *Guido von List Society*, with its select inner core of devotees, the so-called *Armanen-Orden* [Order of Armans]. ("Armanen," meaning inheritors of the sun-god, was the name given by List to the most pure-blooded Germans). List himself was a prolific writer of essays, novels, and festive plays celebrating the so-called "Ariogermanen." The goal of the *Germanen-Orden*, founded in 1912 by Hermann Pohl, was the rebirth of a racially pure German nation, from which the "parasitic and revolutionary rabble-races" (Jews, anarchist crossbreeds, and gypsies) would be deported, the promotion of an "Aryan-Germanic religious revival", and the creation of a pan-German "Armanist Empire" [Armanenreich]. The *Hammerbund*

[Hammer Association], formed in 1910 around the rabidly anti-Semitic Theodor Fritsch's monthly magazine *Der Hammer* (1902-1940; the reference is to the hammer of the Nordic God Thor), the program of which, carried on the back cover of every issue, was "die Ausscheidung des Judentums aus dem Volksleben" [the extirpation of the Jews and their culture from the life of the people], proclaimed as its goals "Schulreform, Rechtsreform, Bodensitz-Reform, Schutz der rechtschaffenden Stände gegen die Unterdrückung durch das Grosskapital wie auch die blöde Massen-Herrschaft, Vertretung einer gesunden Mittelstandpolitik, religiöse Erneuerung im modernen Geiste" [school reform, legal reform, land-property reform, defense of the honest middle classes against oppression by Big Business as well as by the stupid rule of the Masses, support for healthy centrist policies and for religious renewal in a modern spirit].[35]

The most famous of these nationalist groups was doubtless the mysteriously funded *Thule-Gesellschaft* [Thule Society], which was founded in Munich in August 1918 and played a major role in the overthrow of the Bavarian *Räterepublik* in 1919. The name referred to the mythical island in the far north, which had supposedly been the home of a great Nordic culture, like the Atlantis evoked by Hermann Wirth and his patron Ludwig Roselius. The goal of the *Thule Society* was to restore the grandeur and power of that culture and the purity of the race that had created it. Consistent with this goal, proof of Aryan blood was required for membership of the society – as indeed it was for many of the other nationalist societies referred to. "We recognize no international brotherhood of man, only the interests of a particular people, we know of no brotherhood of man, only the brotherhood of blood. [...] We hate the slogan of equality. Struggle is the father of all things, equality is death. [...] We are not democrats, we reject democracy absolutely. Democracy is Jewish, all democratic revolution is Jewish. [...] We are aristocrats." ["Wir kennen keine internationale Brüderschaft der Menschen," its founder, the enigmatic Rudolf von Sebottendorf, declared, "sondern nur völkische Belange, wir kennen nicht die Brüdershaft der Menschen, sondern nur die Blutbrüderschaft. [...] Wir hassen das Schlagwort von der Gleichheit. Der Kampf ist der Vater aller Dinge, Gleichheit ist der Tod. [...] Wir sind keine Demokraten, wir lehnen Demokratie durchaus ab. Demokratie ist jüdisch, alle Revolution der Demokratie ist jüdisch. [...] Wir sind Aristokraten."] When the Republic was proclaimed in Munich in November 1918 and Prince Max of Baden announced the resignation of the Kaiser, Sebottendorf's fury knew no bounds: "Yesterday we experienced the collapse of everything that was familiar, dear, and precious to us," he cried at a meeting of the *Society* in the Four Seasons Hotel in Munich. "In place of our blood-related Prince there now reigns our deadly enemy: Juda. [...] A time of struggle, of bitter affliction, a time of danger is coming. [...] As long as I hold the iron hammer, it will be my goal to engage the *Thule Society* in this struggle. Our Order is a Germanic Order. Fidelity is Germanic. Our God is Walvater. His rune is the aarune. [...] Aarune means Aryan, the original Fire, the Sun, and the Eagle. And the Eagle is the symbol of the Aryans. The eagle was made red to convey its capacity for self-immolation [...]. From today onwards, the eagle is our symbol. It should remind us that we must pass through death in order to live."[36] The *Thule Society* is generally held to have been one of the main instigators of the NSDAP.[37]

Virtually all the nationalist and racist movements – of which only a few have been mentioned here – had a religious dimension. Even the more open and more liberally inclined *Neue Gemeinschaft* of the Hart brothers set itself the goal of solving the problem of social alienation through a "new religion." Drawing on a pantheistic-monistic notion of the unity of the All, invoking Spinoza and Giordano Bruno, and following in the footsteps of Zarathustra and Heraclitus, the writers and artists who came together in the *Neue Gemeinschaft* felt that they were "people of the future" who, by remaking themselves, would remake the world. They hoped to lead the way "to the New Man, who will be the God and artist of the world." "We say, exactly as did Christ and Buddha, that we do not intend to abolish the old religions but to lead them forward. In destroying them, we restore them to life, fulfill them and complete them. [...] Through all religions there runs a deep and hidden doctrine: that of eternal rebirth."[38]

In fervently *völkisch* circles the emphasis on religion, which in those circles meant a so-called "German" religion, a religion related to German blood and race (an "Aryan" Christianity, cleansed of all Old Testament and Jewish components, or an overtly neo-pagan, purely Germanic and Nordic religion), was even greater than in the eclectic and largely literary milieu of the *Neue Gemeinschaft*. According to Uwe Puschner, who has studied the *völkisch* movement extensively, "religion is at the very center of the *völkisch* world-view;" as one writer put it in 1926, it was "the true soul of the movement."[39] For it was a fundamental *völkisch* conviction that the main goal of the movement – "the spiritual and moral renewal and rebirth of the German people" and the construction of a *völkisch* polity – was attainable only through "the inclusion of religion" and specifically through a "Germanic religious reformation."[40] "Every nation needs its own national religion," Paul de Lagarde, one of the most influential German writers on religious topics of the late nineteenth century, had maintained only a few years after the founding of the Empire under Wilhelm I. Only religion, he explained, binds the members of a people together in such a way that, while each individual retains complete freedom, there is no danger to the unity of the nation, since each individual is an inseparable member or limb of the whole and thus cannot will anything contrary to the will of the whole. A nation can indeed be held together by pure power, but the response to power is revolution. Acknowledging that a new religion cannot be artificially created, Lagarde argued that the task for those who seek a new and great Germany "is to do everything appropriate to prepare the way for a national religion and to prepare the nation to accept that religion, which – essentially un-Protestant – cannot, if Germany is to become a new country, be simply an improved version of the old religion, [and] which – essentially un-Catholic – must be a religion for Germany alone, if it is to be the soul of Germany."[41] A 1902 pamphlet entitled "The Religion and Philosophy of the Future" called for a "German-national religion," on the grounds that the traditional Protestant and Catholic churches do not offer a religion that "corresponds to the living feelings of the German *Volksseele* [soul of the people]."[42] Germany needed a new religion that would embrace and reunite all the aspects of the people's life, Wilhelm Schwaner declared in similar vein: "Our families, our schools, our houses of worship, our temples of art, our dwellings – everything, absolutely everything should be sanctified by religion, but by a native, not a borrowed, alien religion. The Holy and Blessed Land, for us, is Germany. The Rhine, the Elbe, the Oder, and the Danube are our Holy Stream. The Brocken, the Hermannstein, the Riesenkoppe and the Wartburg are our Holy Mount. The *Edda*, *Faust*, and the *Ring* are our Holy Books."[43]

A "German religion" was the "condition of German rebirth" after the catastrophe of 1918, in the words of the very title of a work by Joachim Kurd Niedlich, a prolific writer of books and essays advocating a German Christianity purged of all Judaic elements and a leader of the movement in favor of a "German people's church" and a German people's religion. Religion, Niedlich and other *völkisch* spokesmen held, was especially important to Aryans and Germans inasmuch as it binds individuals into a community. It was "a fundamental feature of their being and of their culture."⁴⁴ For that reason, for the German people to abandon religion would be tantamount to its abandoning the very source of its greatest strength.⁴⁵ A year before the National Socialists seized power, Artur Dinter reiterated that the work of creating a united German nation was still – for lack of a national religion – incomplete. "We are still not a nation for one reason and one reason only: because nothing in the depths of our being unites us. The things that give us cause to call ourselves German – the same blood, the same language, the same homeland – all these remain on the surface unless they are given depth in religion and custom. [...] Not until we recognize that our religion and our eternal obligation on this earth is to serve the people and the fatherland by sacrificing ourselves and dedicating our entire lives to them, can the growth and development of our people take deep root."⁴⁶ Alfred Rosenberg, who saw himself as the "philosopher" of National Socialism, likewise considered that "it will be the chief task of the awakening Germany [...] to create a church for the German *Volk*. We will work until a second Meister Eckhart one day [...] embodies, enacts and shapes this German community of souls. [...] To give the Nordic race-soul its form as a German church under the sign of the mythos of the *Volk*, that is for me the greatest task of our century."⁴⁷

In *völkisch* circles, Mme Blavatsky's theosophy and Rudolf Steiner's anthroposophy may well have seemed less in tune with the general shift of emphasis from intellectual knowledge and understanding to biology and "life" than some newer religious movements, which took as their point of departure not an occult doctrine but an immediate inner experience of the divine. Thus Wilhelm Hauer, the future founder of the German Faith Movement, writing in Diederich's periodical *Die Tat* [The Action], noted with obvious regret that "anthroposophy is strongly marked by rationality." "Dr. Steiner," he added, "combats purposefully and energetically the modern predilection for the subconscious and the irrational," which he views as a regression to primitive stages of human development.⁴⁸ In addition, both theosophy and anthroposophy were internationalist and universalist, rather than nationalist. The charter of the *Theosophical Society* (1875) announced that the "principal aim and object of the *Society* is to form the nucleus of a Universal Brotherhood of Humanity," while Steiner insisted that his teaching was "an affair of humanity, like mathematics" and in no way "an affair of one particular nation."⁴⁹ The new emphasis on life and biology, in contrast, favored a "concrete" notion of the larger whole (itself a part of the even larger Totality or Cosmos) as a distinct "Volk" or race, a community united by blood rather than an allegedly abstract, purely conceptual "humanity." It also encouraged a view of religion as an integral part of both individual life and national life (or the life of the racial community), organically related to and uniting both. Religion, in short, was inseparable from biology. For each race, many believed, there was a form of religion that was "natural" to it, part of its very being.[50] "Religion is race, race religion," as one *völkisch* ideologist put it.[51]

Those who held this view of religion and sought to lay the foundations of a "German" religion could nevertheless claim to be tolerant of other races' religions, which allowed them to rail against the "intolerance" of Christianity (and especially of the Roman Catholic Church) with its claim to be the only "true" religion, while at the same time excluding from their own ranks all those who were not of pure German blood or descent.

Houston Stewart Chamberlain, for instance, presented tolerance as a characteristic feature of Aryan peoples, in contrast to the intolerance he declared characteristic of the Semites and taken over from them by Church Christianity.[52] According to Wilhelm Schwaner in the Afterword of his *Germanen-Bibel* of 1904, while every people must create its own bible and the Germans therefore must have one appropriate to their national spirit, not to that of the Jews, later generations may compile from the "Bibles of the Jews, the Christians, the Germans, the Latins, and the Slavs that which one day will inspire and unite them all: the Bible of Humanity."[53] In the early 1930s Wilhelm Hauer insisted that the attitude of the *Deutsche Glaubensbewegung* to other religions was one of respect for all authentic men and women of faith, but with the clear understanding that every people has its own native religious form and that the religion of one people is not right for another and cannot ever be successfully imposed on another.[54] A similar note was struck in the revised guidelines (16 May 1933) of the *Deutsche Christen* [German Christians], a nationwide religious association that sought to retain Christianity as the national religion by eliminating its Judaic elements and was here trying to reach out to a broad audience: "Recognizing the difference between peoples and races as a God-given order for this world, we urge that the cultural heritage of other peoples should not be destroyed by the mission to the heathen."[55]

In practice, needless to say, toleration was less in evidence than anti-Semitism and racism, and the real reason for rejecting missionary activity is found in the first, unrevised Manifesto of the *Deutsche Christen* (26 May 1932): "We regard the mission to the Jews as a grave danger to our culture.

Through its doors alien blood is imported into the body of our nation."[56] In a sensational address to an audience of 20,000 in the Berlin Sportpalast on 13 November 1933, Reinhold Krause, the leader of the Berlin *Deutsche Christen*, proclaimed that "it will not do for German Christian pastors to explain: 'We stand where we have always stood, on the basis of the Old Testament,' although, on the other hand, the guiding principles speak of 'racially attuned Christianity.' In practice the one excludes the other." Krause demanded that the New Testament be purged of "all obviously distorted and superstitious reports" and that "the whole scapegoat and inferiority theology of the Rabbi Paul" be eliminated. In May 1939, the *Deutsche Christen* opened a research institute, the avowed aim of which was the "dejudaizing of the Church and of Christianity."[57]

The particular form taken by religion among native Germans – Germans by race – was widely held to be an immediate inner experience of the divine. This was allegedly demonstrated by the long tradition exemplified among German churchmen by Meister Eckhart, Jacob Böhme, and Angelus Silesius, and continued by countless German artists and writers in whose music, poetry, and painting the native religious impulse took refuge, according to Alfred Rosenberg, in the face of persistent efforts by the orthodox established Church to suppress it.[58] The Judeo-Christian emphasis on external influences and authorities – Scripture, doctrine, the action of a mediator, and the institution of the Church itself – like the Judeo-Christian view of God as transcendent and radically other, was considered "artfremd," that is, alien to the race or breed of the Germans.

In the search for the truly German religion, the religion biologically proper to the German race, there was much disagreement. Countless sects arose – and competed with each other for adherents. Among those who wished to remain Christian many followed Houston Stuart Chamberlain in asserting that Christ himself, whatever his debt to Judaism, was racially not Jewish but Aryan[59] and in doing everything possible to divest Christianity of its Jewish roots and thus develop it into an Aryan religion, a truly and fully German Christianity.[60] In late nineteenth- and early twentieth-century Germany Gnosticism had a field day.[61] Others asserted that Christianity was ineradicably "Semitic" at its very core, with an oppressive Roman-style ecclesiastical superstructure tacked on to it, and was therefore incompatible with and destructive of the "freedom-loving" German spirit. A truly German religion, they held, would draw on the ancient religious traditions of the Germanic peoples, which, they claimed, Christianity had either appropriated to its own ends or destroyed. "Only where Christianity has ceased to be," the so-called National Bolshevist Ernst Niekisch declared in 1930, "can the true religious feeling of the German begin." A return to paganism [Verheidung] was the condition of a Germanic-*völkisch* feeling for the divine, through which "das Germanisch-Heroische" would be revived.[62] Notwithstanding the differences among them, however, almost all these new sects and groupings subscribed to a view of God as not outside the individual but dwelling within him and substantively identical with him. "Gott in uns," in one form or another, was the essential conviction of all the new religions. Thus Wilhelm Schwaner in *Der Volkserzieher* [The People's Educator] (1905): "We educators of the people call ourselves Godseekers: we recognize a divine being that, as the creative, sustaining, and regulating principle, is all-pervasive, but we do not seek that being beyond the clouds; we seek it in ourselves."[63]

As part of the Introduction to the first volume of his *Germanen-Bibel* (1904-5) (fig. 16) Schwaner printed a text entitled *Die Religion des Geistes* [The Religion of the Spirit] by Eugen Heinrich Schmitt (1851-1916), a prolific writer of works – several published by Diederichs – promoting anarchism (1897, 1904) and Gnosticism (1903), as well as of books on Nietzsche (1898), Tolstoy (1901), with whom he entertained a correspondence (published in 1926), and Ibsen (1908). Schmitt's claim, clearly endorsed by Schwaner, was that he was "annunciating a new Man and a new World, the God-Man [Gottmensch]" – not, Schmitt insisted, "the God-Man seated on a throne, far from all earthly misery, at the right hand of the Heavenly Ruler," but "the living, present God-Man […] who awaits his awakening, his emergence in the soul of each one of the least among you." "We have come," Schmitt went on, "to reveal the great mystery of the God-Man within you […] to bring about the raising of Man to Divinity." This implies no dogma and no written law. "We have not come simply to repudiate the teachings or the dogma of any church or sect; our teaching is simple, like no other, a bringer of blessedness [beseligend] and liberation to the world [weltbefreiend], like no other. It has slumbered in the depths of all the religions and philosophies of Mankind; it was the hidden goal seen glimmering, like the sun behind the clouds, by all the great visionaries and poets." The new religion unites man "with the Ground of all beings, the Original Unity, the Father of all beings" [mit dem Urwesen der Wesen, der Ureinheit, dem Vater der Wesen] as well as with everything human, in blessed community, through love." "Seek not the resurrected one in the grave, seek him not in

16. Cover of Wilhelm Schwaner, *Germanen-Bibel* (1905) The oak tree, standing alone in the center of the landscape and solidly rooted in the earth, serves here as a symbol of the strength of Germanic faith and its rootedness in the native soil. (The oak was the tree preferred by the God Thor.) Readers might have been reminded of Caspar David Friedrich's iconic "Einsamer Baum" (Lonely Tree) of 1822, now in the Alte Nationalgalerie, Berlin. Friedrich's tree, though blasted, stands firm in the center of his painting, an emblem of German tenacity and resilience.

imaginary heavens," readers of the *Germanen-Bibel* are told. "For lo, the resurrected one is here. You yourselves are the resurrected ones! [...] You have been taught a God filled with insatiable thirst for revenge, a God who brandishes the threat of eternal punishment in Hell. Our Divinity is the awakening, all-binding love and reason in each one of us. [...] Seek God in the spirit of Man. Whoever does not find him there will never find him."[64] According to another contributor to the Introduction to the *Germanen-Bibel* (Ernst Eberhardt-Humanus), "the fundamental principle of our national myth is self-redemption [Selbsterlösung – i.e. salvation that requires no mediator]. Its call to us is: 'Break through, break through! Through Night to the Light!'" [Hindurch, hindurch! Durch Nacht zum Licht]

In the first of two articles entitled "Germanen-Tempel," published in 1907-08 in Schwaner's *Volkserzieher*, Ludwig Fahrenkrog offered yet another version of the "God in us" theme as the basis of a new Germanic religion. "Are you, German soul, not rich enough to build your sanctuary out of your own primal native heritage?" he asked rhetorically, and lamented the subservience of fervent, young Germans in matters of faith to the "suggestive pomp of Orientals, always zealous for absolutes." By Orientals, he explained, he meant "Moses with his 'Thou shalt not,' Jesus's 'Love thine enemy,'" and Paul's inflexible claim that there is only one road to salvation. "Remember too," he added, for good measure, "the Pope's infallibility in matters concerning the human soul." In sum, in Christianity "the Germanic is in subjection to the Oriental" and the free spirit of the German has been overwhelmed by the slavish obedience of the Oriental to a tyrannical and intolerant external authority. But Jesus himself, Fahrenkrog noted, "spoke of a divine truth, according to which 'The kingdom of heaven is within you!'"

Fahrenkrog had in fact answered his own question a year earlier, in his *Geschichte meines Glaubens* [History of my Faith], a narrative of his spiritual journey.[65] His basic article of faith, he had written then, was "Gott in uns": "If God is in everything, hence not only in me, then I am also the Other. If, however, God is in me, then his law is also in me and I have no need either of written law or of a Mediator. Likewise I cannot expect to achieve salvation otherwise than in and through myself." His "new-won view of the world" could be summarized, Fahrenkrog explained, in three short phrases: "God in us – the Law in us – self-redemption."[66] Later, in 1912, Fahrenkrog incorporated the essence of his religious ideas in a proposed profession of faith for the *Germanisch-deutsche Religionsgemeinschaft* (the immediate predecessor of the *Germanische Glaubensgemeinschaft*), of which the first two articles were: "I am physically and spiritually a part of the World–All" [i.e. the divine]; and: "As Self, I am also the Other (this follows from article 1)." Later still, he proposed a somewhat differently worded profession of faith, article 3 of which stated mystically: "It is. The All is in me and I am in the All. [...] All things spring from the same original source. There is no difference between God-All and human soul. Man is part of the Totality, a particular being. And yet he is also God." According to Fahrenkrog, the immediate, incontrovertible experience of the indwelling of God in the human soul is the essence of all true religion: "Whoever does not find these propositions self-evident is not truly religious. They refer to fundamentals. Neither faith nor dogma plays any role here."[67]

The final, formal profession of faith of the *Germanische Glaubensgemeinschaft* was printed in Fahrenkrog's *Das Deutsche Buch* [The German Book], published in the very year that the Princess's poem *Gott in mir* appeared (1921), as well as separately in a small booklet drawn from it[68] (figs. 17, 18). The principles of the new faith were stated more systematically here, but "Gott in uns" remained for Fahrenkrog the essence of religion. (It still appears on the cover-page of every issue of *Germanen-Glaube*, the journal of the revived post-World War II *Germanische Glaubensgemeinschaft*.) Other aspects of the faith of the *Germanische Glaubensgemeinschaft*, as formulated in the movement's 1921 *Bekenntnis* or Profession of Faith – self-fulfillment as each individual's obligation to the All; reverence for nature in all its manifestations; "purity" (which, it was underlined, is not the same as "innocence"); love of beauty, wisdom, strength, and action; the values of family and heritage (marriage, children, respect for one's parents); honor and loyalty to other members of the community; and "Rasse und Reich, Heimat und Land" [race and country, homeland and native soil] – are so much part of the Princess's outlook in *Gott in mir,* as well as in all her later work, that it is hard to imagine she was not familiar with the *Bekenntnis* or even perhaps a member of the *Germanische Glaubensgemeinschaft*.

"Gott in mir," "Gott in uns," the indwelling of God in Man, and the underlying identity of substance of God and Man remained in effect the fundamental religious experience and the basic principle of virtually all the advocates of a German national faith throughout the twentieth century. It was the conviction both of the publisher Diederichs himself and of many of his authors – such as the prolific Arthur Bonus, author of a widely acclaimed plea for the "Germanization of Christianity" (1911-12) [Zur

Germanisierung des Christentums, volume 2 of his Zur religiösen Krisis (On the Religious Crisis)], and Herman Büttner, the translator of Meister Eckhart, who asserted in his *Büchlein vom vollkommenen Leben. Eine deutsche Theologie* [The Book of the Perfect Life: A German Theology] of 1907 that since God is in us, a perfect life can be lived without abnegation of the self or total surrender of the self to God. It was the conviction of the poet Dietrich Eckart, who befriended and groomed Hitler in the latter's early Munich days. It was the conviction of the passionately anti-Judaic and anti-Christian Mathilde von Ludendorff, the founder, with her second husband, the famous First World War general Erich von Ludendorff, of the *Verein Deutschvolk* [German People's Union] and the author of innumerable books and pamphlets in the 1920s and 1930s (and right on into the post-World War II period), propagating her idea of "Deutsche Gotterkenntnis" [The German Way to Knowledge of God]; as it was the conviction of her rival as a religious leader, Jakob Wilhelm Hauer, who in the early 1930s founded and for a time headed the *Deutsche Glaubensbewegung*, and for whom God is present "in allem, was erscheint, so auch in uns" [in every phenomenon, hence also in us]. It was the conviction of the political theorist and sociologist Paul Krannhals, who declared in 1933 that "Gott ist in uns und wir sind in Gott" [God is in us and we are in God]; while in Nazi leadership circles a similar immanentist view of the relation of the divine and the human was put forward by Alfred Rosenberg in *The Myth of the Twentieth Century* (1930).[69] Even some of the *Deutsche Christen* (who tried to retain a Christianity purged of Judaic elements) rejected "theology's attempts to separate God and Man and to justify its own existence by proving that man is fallen, weighed down by original sin, and therefore in need of the salvation the Church can offer." "We recognize no God/Man division," Reinhold Krause told the 20,000 people gathered in the Berlin Sportpalast in November 1933.[70]

17. Cover of pamphlet extracted from Ludwig Fahrenkrog's *Das Deutsche Buch* to promote the *Germanische Glaubensgemeinschaft* (1921).

> **Edda-Künstlerpostkarten.**
> Lebenskluge, kraftvolle Sprüche der Edda aus dem Hâmavâl, dem „Lied des Hohen", in eigener, den Runen angepaßter Schrift mit reichem, phantastischen Ornamentenschmuck v. Walther Schulte vom Brühl. Eine Folge, d. i. 10 verschiedene Karten Mk. 1.20.
>
> **Zeitkarten**
> von demselben Künstler mit Bild und sinnvollem Spruch. 5 Karten Mk. 1.—
> Geschäftstelle „Kraft u. Schönheit" Berlin-Steglitz.

> **Das hochheilige Hakenkreuz**
> ist das uralte Stammeswappen und Heilszeichen aller Arier und Germanen besonders. Jeder Blutsdeutsche sollte es als Ehrenzeichen auf Schreibbogen, Postkarten usw. führen.
> Gummistempel Mk. 1.—
> Farbkissen dazu  „ 1.—
> Geschäftstelle Kraft und Schönheit, Berlin-Steglitz.

> **Wenn einer Ihrer Freunde wissen will,**
> was Körperkultur und Lebensreform ist, so empfehlen Sie ihm unsere Probebände von „Kraft und Schönheit", drei ältere Hefte enthaltend, zum Preise von 1.— Mk., die ihm alles das in Wort und Bild vor Augen führen, was heute jeder Gebildete darüber wissen muß. — Die Probebände sind durch jede Buchhandlung, oder von uns zu beziehen.
> Verlag „Kraft und Schönheit" Berlin-Steglitz.
>
> Druck von Karl Hoffmann, Pulsnitz i. Sa.

18. Rear cover of pamphlet from Fahrenkrog's *Das Deutsche Buch* (1921), with advertisements for illustrated postcards of wise sayings from the *Edda*, for rubber stamps of the swastika, "the ancient sign of the Aryans and particularly the Germans," which "every German by blood should have imprinted on writing paper, postcards, etc.," and for the journal *Kraft und Schönheit*, in case the reader and friends are interested in learning about body culture and *Lebensreform*.

# 2. The Epigraph and the Envoy

Like the title itself, the epigraph and the envoy of the Princess's poem are intended to announce and sum up the essential message of the poem or collection of poems as a whole (as, indeed, of all her subsequent work): that there is no absolute barrier between the community and the individual who is joined to it by blood, or between the All and its particular manifestations, or between God and Man, or Life and Death – only constant change and becoming. The epigraph, from the *Tales of Rabbi Nachman von Bratslow* (1772-1811), a Chasidic text, published in 1906 in a German adaptation by Martin Buber, reads: "Wer das wahre Wissen erlangt, das Gottwissen, dem ist keine Scheidung über Leben und Tod, denn er hängt an Gott und umfaßt ihn und lebt das ewige Leben wie Gott allein" [Whoever attains to true knowledge, God-knowledge, knows no separation of life and death, for he clings to God and embraces Him and lives the eternal life, like God alone]. The envoy consists of some famous lines from Goethe's *West-östlicher Divan* [West-Eastern Divan] "Und so lang du das nicht hast/ Dieses Stirb und Werde,/ Bist du nur ein trüber Gast/ Auf der dunklen Erde" [Until you possess this maxim: 'Die and Become,' you are but a gloomy guest on the somber earth].

It might seem curious, in view of the Princess's Nordic racialism and anti-Semitism – more explicitly proclaimed later but in all likelihood already embraced by the time of the poem's composition – that she chose an epigraph for her poem in a Jewish text. In fact, the *Tales of Rabbi Nachman von Bratslow* – along with other writings by Buber, such as the collection of mystical texts from ancient India to seventeenth-century France (*Ekstatische Konfessionen*) published in 1906 by Diederichs, who, as we have seen, also published many outspokenly anti-Semitic writers, like Adolf Bartels, Arthur Bonus, and Herman Wirth[1] – had become popular in some *völkisch* circles, largely no doubt because Chasidism seemed to bear witness to the unity of Man and God and to the intimate relation between a people, its God, and its religion.[2] Buber, moreover, had written his doctoral thesis on

Böhme, had been strongly influenced by Nietzsche, and in his early years at least shared many of the ideas about the relation of race and culture of the *völkisch* movement.³ He had significant contacts with some of its most prominent representatives and maintained these ties until fairly late. He was in correspondence, for instance, with Wilhelm Schwaner as well as with Wilhelm Hauer.⁴ As late as the winter of 1932-33, Hauer invited Buber, in the warmest terms, to give a talk at a public colloquium which he had organized in Kassel on the topic "Die geistigen und religiösen Grundlagen der völkischen Bewegung" [The intellectual and religious foundations of the *völkisch* movement] and at which Ernst Krieck, already a prominent National Socialist scholar and intellectual, had also agreed to speak.

While Hauer never questions that there is a "Judenfrage" [Jewish Question] and came to define history as "the multi-millennial struggle between the Near-Eastern-Semitic world and the Indo-Germanic world,"⁵ he appears – prior to 1933, when he sought to ingratiate himself and his movement with the National Socialists – to have imagined that a peaceful solution acceptable to all parties should be sought and, with the help of scholars like Buber, could be found. Many years later, one of his most devoted followers remembered him as a man able and eager to bring together "Communists and National Socialists, Jews and anti-Semites," and to "build bridges and foster exchange without hostility and hatefulness." Hauer, on his side, reminded his young disciple of the value of liberalism. Even though he himself had never been a "liberal," he declared (November 1930), "it should not be forgotten that the struggle against the enslavement of the conscience and the spirit to orthodoxy and bureaucratism was led by liberalism." The young "ought not to forget that in the end they stand on the shoulders of the men of 1848, who were liberals in the proper sense of the word."⁶ In the spirit no doubt of the love of freedom attributed to the Germanic peoples since Tacitus, Hauer held that, while "it goes without saying that no Jew can be a member of the *Deutsche Glaubensbewegung*" – since a Jew is not a German – and that "there can be no compromise on that point, taking that position in no way affects my conviction that every genuinely religious person, of whatever race or *volk*, is ultimately [in letzter Wirklichkeit] a brother to me."⁷ Given that to Hauer the core of religion was a *feeling* for the divine, a universal "religiöser Urwille," [inborn religious impulse] rather than any specific theological doctrine,⁸ it was possible for a *fundamental* fellow-feeling with Buber to co-exist in him with actual estrangement and even hostility: "The innermost core of Martin Buber is

*The Epigraph and the Envoy*  45

oriented to essentials and is of the same nature as mine," he wrote in a private letter dated 21 January 1931. "That is: an intense feeling for God. The empirical covering of that [core] is Jewish and is in many respects repulsive to me or in any case alien." In the same vein, on 2 June 1933: "I have a relation of complete candor with Buber. When he conveys what is innermost in him, I feel a close bond with him. When he moves away from that and especially when it comes to his notion of the Jews' being chosen, I stand, as a German, in sharp opposition to him. And he knows that."[9] Buber, in sum, was viewed by some in *völkisch* circles as a kindred spirit, albeit of an alien race.

As for the envoy, *Stirb und Werde*, it had become a commonplace of *Lebensphilosophie* – a philosophical outlook in which life, both in fact and normatively, had precedence over thought, the intuitive over the analytical and conceptual, the biological over the mechanical, change or becoming over being and permanence. A reaction against both Kantian and Hegelian rationalism, *Lebensphilosophie* had become pervasive in Germany by the end of the nineteenth century, thanks in considerable measure to the enormous (posthumous) popularity of Nietzsche (*Zarathustra*, it has been said, was the single most influential work of the Wilhelminian age[10]), as well as to popular interpretations of Darwin. Paradoxically, the social and economic condition of the success of *Lebensphilosophie* was probably the very hectic pace of commercial and industrial development in Germany in the decades following the Prussian victory over France and the founding of the Empire that was denounced by many of the adherents of *Lebensphilosophie*. As one historian of the Wilhelminian age has put it, "it was change that supplied the Wilhelmine era's strongest continuity."[11]

*Stirb und Werde! Naturwissenschaftliche und kulturelle Plaudereien* [Die and Become! Scientific and Cultural Conversations] was the title chosen by Wilhelm Bölsche, co-founder of the *Giordano Bruno-Bund* and author of the hugely successful *Das Liebesleben in der Natur* (1898) [Love Life in Nature], for one of his many popularizations of Darwinian ideas, this one published by Diederichs in 1913 and again in 1921, the year of publication of the Princess's poem. *Stirb und Werde!* remained a formula to which many educated Germans resorted in trying times. In the last months of the Great War, for instance, in face of the devastating numbers of the dead and the maimed, 'Stirb und Werde!' was the title given by Avenarius to the lead article he wrote for the October 1918 issue of his influential magazine *Der Kunstwart*. The inevitability of defeat and national humiliation having become obvious to everyone in Germany, Avenarius asked rhetorically, how many more sons, husbands, and fathers would still have to be killed, how many more civilians would still have to perish from the effects of malnutrition before the reality of the situation was acknowledged. The enthusiastic support of the entire population for the war four years earlier meant that no one was without responsibility; the task, therefore, he claimed, was not to attribute blame but to save the German people and its culture from total destruction, not to look back in anger but to accept the judgment of Fate with fortitude and prepare for new action. Fate, he wrote, requires that Germans kill in themselves that which they adored, that they move on from where they were in 1914, in order to survive – and indeed triumph – as an active, creative, and influential force in the world. "For all who seek what is most important in the condition of being human – i.e. the strength and joy in action of a well integrated personality – the powerful expression *Stirb und werde!* now has special meaning." Germans, Avenarius urged, should look to the future, to the "countenance of the Superman of tomorrow. [...] One moment of history has ended. When the next arises, let it find in us a generation ready to shape it...*Stirb und werde!* If we truly are the people richest in creative energies, now is the time for us to demonstrate it. Come into being, oh you new manifestation of German-ness, come into being!" [Werde, du neues Deutschtum, werde!][12] Avenarius's reflections on the theme of *Stirb und werde* in 1918 are clearly close to the spirit of the Princess's work of three years later and presage her response later still to the even more catastrophic defeat of 1945.

*Stirb und werde* also figured prominently in the worldview of Herman Wirth, the maverick Dutch scholar who placed his research and erudition in the service of arguments for the superiority of the "Nordic" race and of the theory that human culture originated in the Arctic North. Supported financially at times by both the publisher of *Gott in mir*, Ludwig Roselius, and the author, the Princess herself,[13] Wirth was selected by Himmler in the mid-1930s to head his *Ancestral Heritage* research institute [*Ahnenerbe*]. Summing up the 64-page findings, supposedly based on archaeological and linguistic evidence, of an inquiry into the question *Was heißt deutsch?* [What does being German mean?], Wirth concluded in 1931 that "being 'German' means being 'derived from God,' being the 'life of God.' – Life comes from God, from the Time of God, the 'Year' of God; 'Die and become' [Stirb und werde], the law of eternal recurrence [die ewige Wiederkehr], is the Revelation of God in space and time, the moral order of the world [...]."[14]

# 3. The Poem

Within the body of the Princess's poem, several prominent themes can be identified, many of them recognizably inspired by *Lebensreform*, especially in its more *völkisch* manifestations:

– creation of a New Man and a New World, liberation from "unnatural," life-denying beliefs and social conventions;

– rejection of modern liberal, capitalist, urban civilization, regarded as responsible for encouraging egoism, undermining community ties, and destroying the nobler human qualities and values;

– recovery of an authentic native German culture still close to the natural world and uncontaminated by modern rationalism and alienation;

– repudiation of established religious faiths, especially in the form of an allegedly un-natural and alien transcendentalist and "legalistic" Christianity rooted in Judaism, in favor of a quasi-pantheist or Gnostic faith, according to which man and nature are infused with divinity and are thus good, not sinful, and which is often presented as grounded in the original ancestral beliefs of the "Nordic race" and at the same time – though this is not spelled out by the Princess – closely connected with Buddhism and Hinduism (usually assumed to be the belief systems of Aryan peoples related to the Germans[1]);

– cult of the energetic, active, heroic, independent-minded individual, freed from the constraints of a false or alien morality, standing above the crowd, and called on to lead it forward into New Life;

– emphasis, at the same time, on the larger community or *volk* and ultimately on the All or Cosmos or Life-Force or God, from which every individual emerges, whether as leader or as led, which lives and acts within every individual, to which every individual ultimately returns, and to which the authentic individual dedicates his entire being freely, unreservedly, and spontaneously – the divine law being not external to the individual, but located within him, not imposed on him from without, but inscribed in his very being, so that his will is identical with the will of the cosmos.

The poem or series of poems is in effect a conversion narrative, told in the first person. As in earlier Pietist and Puritan conversion narratives, the narrator's intention was doubtless to present herself as a model to the reader and to lead the latter also toward conversion. The religion to which the speaker in the poem was converted – or rather which the speaker discovers in herself, as the reader is likewise encouraged to do – bears a strong similarity to that outlined in the profession of faith devised by Fahrenkrog for the *Germanische Glaubensgemeinschaft* and published in the same year as the poem.

*Gott in mir* opens on the speaker's experience of alienation, isolation, and imprisonment in a soul-less modern world. "Wherever I look, nothing but chains – chains and gigantic, unscalable walls. Unrelenting darkness, heavy silence. Not a single ray of sunshine from the high heavens." This bleak experience contrasts with the vision of "a land where love and friendship dwell and where joy reigns in spring-like warmth over everyday life,"[2] a vision that fades from view as the speaker, responding to the "threats and entreaties" of family and friends, temporarily allows "weakness [to] become the mistress of his/her strength, weariness [to] overwhelm his/her mind, and baseness [to] triumph yet again." The first section of the poem ends on an act of revolt – anticipating both that which the Princess herself appears to have carried out as a young woman when (as we shall see in Part II of this essay) she renounced her class in favor of marriage to a commoner and association with a mass political movement, and that of the heroine of her 1942 novel *Die Overbroocks*, who agrees, though she is the daughter of a distinguished upper-class military family, to marry a poor student and become the mother of his child, in order to save his peasant farmer's blood line from extinction and restore it to its ancient heritage in the soil of Northern Germany. The speaker in *Gott in mir* asserts her freedom and refuses to "allow [her] guiding star to be taken from [her]." "You were endowed with your own free soul!" she reminds herself. "You were made to be your own judge of yourself." The claim is identical to that of Fahrenkrog in his 1907 *Volkserzieher* article: If God is in us, then the Law is in us, and we have no need of external written laws to prescribe behavior; we are our own judge and our will is God's will. "Go, you child of royal birth," the speaker finally tells herself. Break with family and convention.

"It is nobler to die than to live as a prisoner." (pp. 9-10) The temptation to backslide must be resisted: "Oh, tempt me not! Get thee behind me, Satan! I feel as though the eyes of a world that awaits redemption are on me. If I lay down my arms and go faintheartedly from hence, thinking only of my own comfort, it will be a betrayal. From every bush, from every twig and every leaf I hear the anxious whispering of Nature: 'Is this soul strong enough [...] to become a victorious conqueror?'" (Once again the question seems to echo, perhaps consciously, Fahrenkrog's question in the 1907 *Volkserzieher* article: "Are you, German soul, not rich enough to build your sanctuary out of your own primal heritage?") The speaker's soul proves strong and rich enough and does not yield. But she appeals to the World-Spirit for added strength: "No, I must keep faith and bear the burden. I may not think of my own peace and quiet. Great Spirit that floats through the entire Universe, send down new strength to your child, so that she may find the path of thorns that leads to the goal!" (p. 11)

In the next poem or section, the speaker looks back on her childhood and describes her early spiritual development. An allusion to Parsifal reinforces the "Germanic" character of her itinerary. "I was a child, lonely and ignorant, like Parsifal, who set out in search of God." The child's untutored mind grasps that "God is love," but balks at accepting that he is "severe and harsh and can be reconciled only through the blood of his son," through an external mediator; that "beauty is sin and unnaturalness morality;" and that "there are clear boundaries between Right and Wrong," so that the "guiding star and Law" of behavior becomes "the command 'Thou shalt.'" (p. 12) This lesson "entered [her] ear but never [her] heart," small as she was. Instead, she continued her own search for God and "after a long and fervent struggle" found him – within herself. As a result, the law of God is no longer external to her. There is no difference between divine law and the law of her own heart: "The compelling command 'Thou shalt' has become 'I will.' And this I know today: God is good." (p. 13)

The following poems or sections recount the "long and fervent struggle" to find God and the blinding moment of insight or discovery.

> I lived a dream-life, not knowing in which direction to turn my wavering steps. [...] Everything I did was trivial, without significance. Often my arms, raised to God in ardent prayer for strength, sank wearily and despairingly to my side. I was a plaything on the ocean of Time. Every wind blew me toward a different shore. Nevertheless, a prescient spirit drove me to continue seeking: 'Your hour must come, must come!' It came. And as a flash of lightning from heaven illuminates a fearfully

dark nocturnal landscape, so that the smallest blade of grass can be distinguished, an understanding flashed through my heart: a Titanic belief in the God within Man, the God that is unfolded by the human spirit itself.

In that moment, "I threw off all weakness and timidity and felt gigantic powers growing within me." (pp. 14-15) The speaker now realizes that "every soul is a fragment of the World Soul, broken off and lovingly formed in God's hands until, in their gentle warmth, it dreamily opens its eyes." (Perhaps this moment of birth in the warming hands of the Divine was what Vogeler's frontispiece was intended to evoke). It is then "sent down from the eternal solar heights," after receiving "the hot glow of a flaming kiss" that makes it "sink into sleep, so that it does not feel the pain of separation from its luminous star-filled home." Its mission on earth is not prescribed in advance but freely chosen. There is no scriptural law, in other words, no role for a Moses. Nor is there any need of a mediator; salvation is the work of each individual soul. "God tells it in a soft whisper of the mission of redemption that waits to be carried out on earth, and says: 'How you carry it out, child, let that be left to you. I can only fix the hour when I shall recall the life I gave you, when, delivered from your earthly shell, you will be permitted to return, blissful and free, to your origin, to your father's heart." (pp. 16-17)

The text now moves toward more general reflections on the difficulty of finding one's true way in a world that fears the light of Truth and jealously guards the habits and conventions that protect it from Truth. The section ends, in the spirit of those advocates of a "Germanic" religion for whom Jesus and Wotan were indistinguishable, on the evocation of a heroic, rather than a suffering Christ-figure. Many, we are told, wander the earth as strangers, uneasy and discontented throughout their entire lives. They "heard the call and detected the sprit of God within them," but they were "too slothful to bestir themselves and too weak to move toward the goal." (pp. 18-19) Others, "scarcely born, had already lost the proud strength needed for struggle and turned only on their own axis. They saunter apathetically and aimlessly through life," having "forgotten their divine mission." (p. 20) Others still "sallied forth and engaged in the struggle for existence with glowing pride. They bore life's hardships playfully because they were open to every form of beauty. And at every new bend in their road, they thought they were about to enter the last stretch. [...] But the rocks piled ever higher, the climb became steeper and steeper. A deathly silence fell on them." In this predicament, they hear voices calling them back – those entreating calls of friends and family that the speaker had told of resisting earlier in the poem "'Come back, you poor, weary soul. We forgive you your youthful errors! Blessed is he who can sleep away all pain in his own home. You cannot change the world or lift it off its hinges. Take the advice of age and wisdom! Renounce the follies of your arrogant youth and we will welcome you home." (p. 22) The speaker then describes these "men and women, wending their way homeward because the drive toward higher things has abandoned them." They are loved by others, but they "hate themselves because they failed to fend off temptation." (p. 24)

The following few sections focus on a particular case, a Christ-figure that could conceivably also refer to some historical individual or individuals from the Princess's own time. The age did not lack heroic martyrs in one cause or another. Up to a point the narrative might even be applicable to the poet herself as well as to the artist who provided the frontispiece for her book – although Heinrich Vogeler's search was to take him, politically, in the opposite direction from the Princess. As a successful *Jugendstil* artist, Vogeler had indeed seen and painted Utopian "gardens of paradise where others saw barren steppes;" he was an inveterate "Gottsucher" [seeker after God], especially after he returned from the Eastern front; and his ardent seeking, as noted earlier, had met with hostility and misunderstanding. "I know of one," the speaker begins,

> whose magical eyes had strange and mysterious depths. He looked with wonder on the bustle of the world; he put his ear with wonder to his own soul; he did not complain that he was not like others…for he saw gardens of paradise where others saw barren steppes. One thing alone tormented him and gave him no respite: incessant seeking and the never-ending question – 'To what end am I on this earth? What was God's wish when he sent me here?' And people called him distracted and scolded him as a person of perpetually shifting moods. He took all this without complaint and struggled silently within himself. One belief kept him going: that a certain recollection would be restored to him. And behold, it was restored. He heard the voice whisper once again the words it spoke at his creation: 'Struggle for the divine empire of Love.' Speechless, shattered, he fell to his knees. 'God, my God, where shall I find the strength?' Whereupon he heard the divine voice admonish him gently: 'Dear child, the world must otherwise perish!' – Then warm currents coursed through his veins and his spirit turned to fire, his whole soul swelled up in compassion and with humility he proudly took up the burden.
>
> But when the stupid people saw that he had suddenly become different,

that he knew for sure whither the road led and that this road led away from them, they raged and threatened, pleaded and beseeched him by all that is dear to turn back from his devious path. But he only shook his locks mildly: 'Let me be, I must follow the divine voice, for I am a part taken from it! My soul has been endowed with power over the highest things in heaven and on earth. Oh, you men and women, may you come to understand that you too are parts of God's heart – not servants, but children of royal birth – and that you too must travel the same road!' But they upbraided him for being an arrogant fool and wrung their hands in anguish. He in turn suffered with them, for he felt that they could never understand him. Most painful to him was that even those who loved him and called him 'Master' often tried to make him waver, because they did not understand his sacred duty and feared for his beloved life. The day finally came when the henchmen took him, and his dearest friend basely betrayed him. And they beat him and scorned him and they hung him on the sinners' wooden cross and did not know how they could inflict enough torture on the hated brother. Calmly and in silence he bore all the suffering. This hour, which his earthly body had feared so strongly, found him invincible. Thus the blind crowd killed Christ himself, the shining messenger of Truth, because they could not bear his love. And he had no anger. He had long known that he would have to suffer such pain in order to bear witness in the world to the splendor of God's glory, before which earthly suffering and joy fade into insignificance. And his dying was joyful and proud, for he did not pass over like a poor sinner, but royally and victoriously, with words of holy love on his lips and in the knowledge that it was his own strength and purity that had enabled him to follow the road right to the end. (pp. 24-29)

After a blank page, the speaker comments on the destiny just described, emphasizing that it was that of a victorious and free hero, not of a humble and obedient sufferer: "When the Lord calls such a human soul home to the solar heights, his heart swells in joyful pride that his creature was splendid, […] free, […] and victorious over a world of hate and temptation." (p. 31)

The focus now shifts to the meaning of death. Once again the position adopted in the poem corresponds to that of most *völkisch* religions, including the *Germanische Glaubensgemeinschaft*. To the taunts of the grim reaper, the speaker responds with the confident assertion that death will be "a glorious offering to the Spirit, to which I have given my entire life and dedicated all my strength and love" and that dying means simply returning "to the world soul, from which a creator's hand once took me." (pp. 31-35)

The final sections of the poem take up the themes of sacrifice, morality and the individual's relation to others, the need to replace a way of life directed toward individual happiness and consumption with one directed toward struggle and creative action, and finally the fundamental obligation to develop oneself to the fullest extent possible, not for egotistical reasons, but in order to contribute to the maximum, even if it involves pain, to the All of which one is a part.

The value of "the red flame of sacrifice" is that "it scorches everything petty, timid, and wavering." The individual "in whose heart it has been lighted" becomes capable of acts of selfless heroism and, like all heroes, has to renounce the comforts of easy companionship and "become lonely as in death." (p. 37) But through willingness to "offer the whole heart and every drop of blood in sacrifice" to a meaningful life, the individual becomes "a bearer of eternal glory." For "you no longer live for yourself. Your being, with its little pains and little joys, is woven into the fabric of the new Earth." Words and actions must now be taken seriously for they affect the entire universe. "Gentle, blissful dreaming" – such as marked the *fin-de-siècle*, *Jugendstil* fantasies of a Vogeler – "has come to an end. Let every word be spoken in full consciousness of its gravity, let every deed be enacted." (p. 39) The speaker then calls on all to build and join in a new life, to sweep away the old. "Away with your weak, moody dreams, your dull, sick symphonies of color, away with feelings unconscious of their endless vacillating! Away with them! Let a fresh storm wind blow. Let your mind's ideas be clear and sharply drawn. [...] Let a bold and virile spirit enter you! You were born for struggle, not for dreaming." (p. 41)

Whoever participates in this "joyful faith" is "upright and firm in unbending love toward others, [...] strength to strength." Friends are those of similar faith, who "march in step." But this joyful, Nietzschean band, this "new nobility" – to quote the title of a book by the Princess's friend and mentor in later years, the high-ranking National Socialist government minister R. Walther Darré – should be strong, not presumptuous. The task is not to despise or mock, but to lead and assist the weak. "Let us spread our hands tenderly and gently under the weary feet of our weak brothers. The laughter on our lips should not be arrogant. Let our entire life radiate goodness." (p. 43) That goodness must manifest itself, moreover, not so much in feelings and words as in actions. (p. 45)

If the members of the "joyful faith" act with goodness, it is "not because a lord on high commanded that we love even our enemies and promised us eternal bliss if we believed his word with childlike faith. [...] Nor is it because one will be met with a tearful look of gratitude. [...] Woe to them who are so poor and petty that they must be bought by promises of earthly and heavenly reward. No! Act with goodness only out of Titanic inner strength and inexhaustible, world-consuming love, out of creative will and joyful strength," out of a spontaneous generosity that pays no heed to past or future, and expects no reward. Once a deed has been done, moreover, it should be consigned to oblivion, as though it had never happened. It should not be an object of reflection or calculation, or a cause of either satisfaction or guilt. (p. 44) We should not be prisoners of the past, but creators of the future. At each moment of our lives we should be free and undetermined: "*stirb und werde!*"

Human beings can perfect themselves only "through [their] own strength and not through another's." We are responsible for our own salvation. No mediator, no obedience to external laws can win it for us. "You stand alone!" the poem's speaker tells her readers. "That word is like a thunderclap! Learn to understand it and you will grow ever taller." (p. 46) Although "as a human, you are a pitiful drop in the vast Universal stream" and will be washed away and lose all consciousness of your individuality "when all the drops are fused into one," that does not constitute a license to "throw ourselves away." Here the speaker evokes the example of a heroic Christ-figure who "sanctified from on high, and glow[ing] from within, nevertheless sojourned among us – alone, and yet bound in love to the world." Therein lies the mystery of the new faith proposed by the speaker: "Be you alone in the midst of the community!" That is to say, do not lean on the crutch of a law, a church, or a mediator; be aware that there is no law, no church, no mediator, only the "law within us" (as Fahrenkrog had put it), the law of each individual's being as a fragment of the world-soul. "If you learn to understand this," the speaker insists, repeating her earlier words, "you will grow ever taller. If you learn to understand this, you will fall humbly to your knees." (p. 46) The poem closes on an un-Christian, Nietzschean reflection on death and, above all, on life as continuous destruction and creation.

> Dying is nothing, transitoriness is nothing, it is only a moment, like birthing. Existence is nothing and life is a game, a tiny grain of sand in the divine hourglass of the universe. He alone may lay claim to Being who each day experiences anew 'dying' and 'coming into being' – who each day experiences anew the great miracle of having been ordained to bear the sacred torch in pure sacrificial hands before the people and to view the eternal goal in its rosy radiance, while the crowd crawls dully in the dust.

At times, especially toward the end, the Princess's poem is too mystical to be intelligible at virtually any level. Most of the time, it propagates values that were to be embraced by many National Socialists before, during, and even after World War II – as well as by later devotees of so-called "New Age" ideas. A fair number of passages, including several recently quoted, anticipate existentialist ideas popular in the 1950s and 60s. As poetry, it now seems overblown and bombastic. What the fair-minded reader must concede, however, is that, confused as it sometimes is, *Gott in mir* does convey the impression of having been sincerely felt – as indeed do even the author's later, blatantly ideological novels, *Mutter Erde* and *Die Overbroocks*. Moreover, the rebelliousness of Marie Adelheid Prinzessin Reuß-zur Lippe, her longing for a better, nobler world, her existentialist ethics, and her vision of heroic loneliness and sacrifice were by no means unique to her; nor did they lead necessarily, as they did in fact in her case, to membership in the National Socialist Party. In the aftermath of World War I thoughts and feelings similar to those expressed in *Gott in mir* were shared by men and women of many political persuasions, including artists, musicians, poets, and even theologians. It is by no means impossible that the future Communist Heinrich Vogeler responded to them and contributed his frontispiece in the belief that he and the author who later earned for herself the sobriquet of the "Brownshirt Princess" had much in common.

# 4. Appendix to Part I: The *Völkisch* Rejection of Christianity

Christianity – and especially its Jewish origin – was the target of many rebellious, avant-garde spirits, most of them inspired by Nietzsche, around the turn of the nineteenth and twentieth centuries. The case of the Polish writer Stanislaw Przybysczewski can be taken as fairly typical. A well-known figure in Bohemian circles in Berlin, a friend of the painter Edvard Munch and the playwright August Strindberg, widely read in Germany and Scandinavia as well as in his native Poland, Przybysczewski led a wildly adventurous erotic life, dabbled in anthroposophy and occultism, flirted with socialism, and was a champion of both estheticism and sexual liberation. In number 32 (6 October 1910) of the avant-garde Berlin literary and artistic weekly *Der Sturm* [The Storm] – the organ of Herwarth Walden (a.k.a. Georg Lewin), the Russian-born Jewish art dealer, critic, and advocate of modern art, who was briefly married to the Jewish expressionist poetess Else Lasker-Schüler and who promoted the careers of many modern artists and writers (Kokoschka, Hermann-Neisse, René Schickele, Richard Dehmel) – Przybysczewski mounted a violent attack on Judaism. "Judaism," he declared in the lead article on the front page, appropriately entitled "Das Geschlecht" [Sex],

> "has debased sex and trampled it in the mire; it has castrated love. […] It has turned the sexual drive in itself into a crime and a disgusting sin, nakedness into something scandalous and shameful, and the sexual act itself into a filthy puddle teeming with horrifying vermin. Judaism has injected the beautiful human soul with a poison that continues to degrade humanity to this day; it is responsible for making beauty repulsive and vile. […] But from afar the rumbling of the turning tide can be heard; it is

already beating here and there on the shore, and the day is drawing nigh when the soul will begin to cleanse itself from the garbage of Judaism and will celebrate its resurrection in beauty and in renewed glory of the senses. [...] The highest ethics is that of the individual who knows how to transform everything into beauty, for only beauty, and beauty alone, can be ethical."

Born and raised as a Catholic, Przybyszewski probably found it easier to attack the repressive influence of Christianity by naming Judaism as the culprit, but there can be no doubt that the object of his wrath and scorn was Christianity, no less than Judaism. A year later in the pages of Franz Pfemfert's radical, left-leaning, internationalist, and anti-militarist *Die Aktion*, Ludwig Gurlitt, a leader in the school reform movement of the time, published an article entitled "Der Fluch der toten Religion" [The Curse of the Dead Religion], in which he lamented that an alien religion had been imposed on "die Germanen" [Germanic men and women] and had sapped the innermost core of their nature.[1] Roselius, the friend and publisher of the author of *Gott in mir* and the onetime patron of the future Communist Heinrich Vogeler, defended his creation, the Böttcherstraße in Bremen, and Hoetger's expressionist Odin sculpture on the façade of the Haus Atlantis from Nazi criticism of them as "degenerate," by asserting a deep inner connection between the Germanic-Aryan Christ-figure and the modern Führer. "I am not a religious leader," he wrote to the National Socialist Mayor of Bremen, "but I am a man who has deep roots in the homeland that bore him. [...] I have never believed in a Jewish Christ, but only in an anti-Jewish Christ, who at that time did the same for the world [...] as Hitler today. I hold therefore that the Old Testament has no place in the education of the German people. But if we no longer have the Old Testament as the basis for the Christian religion, then we need a German basis. Christ thus becomes again the man that he was in reality, a German who in a foreign land, through his German purity, brought order into a world that was then as deranged as the world of Bolshevism is today."[2]

The *völkisch* ideologues who denounced Christianity as "oriental," alien to the Germanic peoples, and a prime cause of their alleged degeneration and enfeeblement were thus participating in their way in a "modernist" revolt against traditional religion. They differed from Nietzsche or Strindberg or Przybyszewski in that the struggle they wanted to lead was not between "humanity" and a doctrine allegedly destructive of it, but – as was more in evidence in the case of Gurlitt and all too clear in the case of Roselius – between men and women of Germanic race and culture and what they charged was the corrupting influence of the religion of a foreign, utterly alien people on them. The *völkisch* concept of race was itself also "modern," moreover. Conceiving of race and culture in biological terms would have been impossible in a "pre-scientific" age.

The *völkisch* attack on Christianity began early. In a booklet published in 1900 (republished in 1930), which one scholar has described as "the protoype of all subsequent 'neo-pagan' prophetic writings," Ernst Wachler, the director of the *völkisch Harzer Bergtheater*, denounced Judaism and its offspring Christianity for having "imposed a long night of ignorance and narrow-mindedness on the ancient world that lasted until the new dawn of the Renaissance" and for having had a no less ruinous influence on the Germanic world. "To subject [that world], Christianity had to make it meek and sick. This task was accomplished over five centuries by the use of every instrument of force and persuasion. The foundations of the Germanic world were shattered. [...] The normal course of development of our people was brought to a halt. [...] Native belief and myth, poetry and morality, custom and law were destroyed or distorted and robbed of their creative energy. The natural feelings and views of youthful [Germanic] peoples were fettered by a distant power, the remnant of a late, alien culture. [...] The world view of the medieval Catholic Church repressed nature and culture alike: the body was neglected, starved, and mistreated, bathing and swimming were despised; the perfect soul was sought in the anaemic, emaciated corpse." Wachler's account of the role of Christianity was confirmed by the influential Viennese poet, journalist and master of the occult, Guido von List. According to von List, the arrival of Christianity marked the end of a great Aryan high culture and brought in its train immigrants who adulterated the purity of the Germanic race.[3]

Otto Sigfrid Reuter, founder of the *Deutsch-religiöse Gesellschaft* (subsequently renamed *Deutsch-gläubige Gesellschaft*) in 1911 – and half-brother of the famous Social Democratic Berlin mayor Ernst Reuter, who described him in letters to an English friend in 1934 and 1937 as "an old and faithful adherent of the Wotan-religion [...] but always very kindly to me" (English in original) and as "ein persönlich sehr anständiger Mann, aber ein ganz großer Wotan-Anbeter"[4] [a very decent man personally, but a great Wotan worshipper] – held Christ responsible for undermining the Germans' energy and capacity to act. "The Nazarene wanted us to win victory through suffering and endurance," he wrote. "But our religion is that of the champion of light, who finds joy in action and fights his way to peace through victory. That is the language of Sigfrid."⁵ A contributor to Wilhelm Schwaner's *Volkserzieher* in 1910 warned that Christianity was a threat to the German national state: "The neighborly love developed in the bosom of the Church has produced a truly poisonous effect on German nationhood. The Church taught that every human being is our neighbor and every neighbor our brother. [...] It deliberately abolished the political demarcations between the nations. Its ideal is an international, undifferentiated, soft porridge of the faithful – an unhappy goal, murderous for every state."⁶ In vol. 1 of Schwaner's *Germanen-Bibel* (1904) the author of an introductory article argued that Christianity had brought Germany no good. On the contrary, with its otherworldliness, its doctrine of grace, and its emphasis on spirit and contempt for the flesh, it had encouraged irresponsibility and provoked the crassest sensuality as an inevitable reaction of the body to the denial of its physical nature.⁷

In similar vein, Schwaner's associate in the founding of the *Germanische Glaubensgemeinschaft*, Ludwig Fahrenkrog, denounced the submissiveness, passivity, and repression of natural impulses required, according to him, by the Christian religion: "We raise from the start the proud cry of our forefathers: 'Right, not Grace' [...] That is Nordic! The right of the will to live. The right of the body: sun, air, strength, beauty, promptness to leap forward – openness of all the senses, work and rest and purity of blood! The right of the mind: to learn and to teach, to find and to seek, to invent and to recognize the highest and best! The right of the spirit: to speak with God in its own way, to follow the moral sense and the good in ourselves."⁸ In the 1920s, the rabidly anti-Christian Mathilde von Ludendorff, wife of the famous World War I military commander accused "the Jew Jesus" of having uprooted people from their race, their nation, and their customs and traditions through his pernicious universalist teachings.⁹ Another champion of the "Germanic race" asserted that its degeneration began when Roman civilization and Christianity crossed the Alps, "uprooted German-ness and bound it in a chain that led via Rome to Palestine."¹⁰ Reflecting a popular reading of Nietzsche and Darwin, Ernst Ludwig Freiherr von Wolzogen branded Christianity in 1919 as "the religion of the physically and mentally inferior."¹¹

The advocates of a "German" Christianity were no less critical of the Christianity represented by the churches, especially the Church of Rome, than the neo-pagans. To Arthur Bonus, writing in 1911, both the Christian virtue of humility and the doctrine of original sin were incompatible with the desired renewal of the German people.¹² In rightwing student circles in Munich in the early 1920s, Hubertus, Prince zu Loewenstein, reports in his autobiography, it was held that "the Church [...] had always been in league with the Jew" and would have destroyed the wisdom of "our ancestors" had not "a means of expression been discovered that remained incomprehensible to the Church" – *viz*, the traditional German fairy tale, in which the ancient heritage was preserved in disguised form.¹³ In the early 1930s, Arthur Dinter, another passionate advocate of a Christianity purged of everything Jewish, charged that traditional "Judeo-Christianity [had] poisoned us from the cradle on" and would have to be completely "rooted out" if Germany was to be saved.¹⁴ In a text from the early 1930s Ernst Bergmann summed up the conflicted view of Christianity of the so-called *Deutsche Christen*. Christianity in Germany, he declared, is at the same time profoundly German, a product of the German spirit which has infused it with its own character, and a pernicious foreign influence responsible for Germany's woes: "The spirit of Germany is like a woman who was raped and made pregnant by a foreign plunderer. The mother bore the child amid tears. But she clasps it to her heart, despite its utterly alien features, for it is her child and Mother Germania shimmers somewhere in the depths of its blue eyes."¹⁵

Even this slight concession to a "German" Christianity was unacceptable, however, to convinced champions of a return to native Germanic ways and values. According to Alfred Conn, Christianity was simply incompatible not only with the native culture of the German *volk*, but with the entire doctrine, more and more widely accepted in *völkisch* circles, of the racial foundation of culture, the inseparable connection between a particular race or blood-group and its culture: "Xristianity is foreign to our whole being. Its roots are in a completely different nature from ours. Xristianity does not accept that there are different human races. It denies the indissoluble bond linking the individual human being to his blood-determined group. It knows only the absolute equality of everything that wears a human countenance. Hence its impact has been to undermine the purity of the races. The assertion that there is one truth and one salvation for all humans presupposes the denial of blood-determined differences. [...] In other words, whoever is a Xristian cannot desire a *völkisch* State based on blood and race, and whoever is *völkisch* cannot desire a Xristian state. Or: whoever is *völkisch* is not Xristian and whoever is Xristian is not *völkisch*."¹⁶

# Part II

## Serving New Gods

# 5. Marie Adelheid, Prinzessin Reuß-zur Lippe: Society, Ideology, and Politics.[1]

Marie Adelheid Mathilde Karoline Elise Alexe Auguste Albertine, Prinzessin zur Lippe-Biesterfeld (1895-1993), was born into a noble family whose roots can be traced to the twelfth century. On 19 May 1920 she was married to a descendant of a no less distinguished noble house, Heinrich XXXII (known as "Heino"), Prinz Reuß zu Köstritz, seventeen years her senior. Both the Reuß and the zur Lippe dynasties were connected with various royal houses in Europe, including those of Great Britain and the Netherlands. The marriage lasted less than a year, for the couple divorced on 18 February 1921. Not quite two months later, on 12 April 1921, the Princess was remarried in Bremen – to her former husband's youngest brother, Heinrich XXXV[2] (known as "Enrico"), Prinz Reuß zu Köstritz. In order for this second marriage to go forward Enrico had had, in turn, on 4 March 1921, to divorce his wife of ten years. A son Heinrich V (1921-1980), also named Heinrich like all the Reuß male children, was born to the newly wed couple six weeks later and named and numbered according to family tradition. The genealogies do not specify which of the brothers was the father. Within two years the Princess and her second husband had also divorced, and in 1927, in a clear act of defiance signaling her break with traditional aristocratic norms and, as we shall see, her embrace of the Revolutionary Right's idea of a "new nobility," the Princess took as her third husband a commoner named Hanno Konopath (originally Konopacki), a government official, who was a friend of R. Walther Darré – the future National Socialist Agriculture Minister and the advocate of a "Neuer Adel" or new nobility recruited from the *volk* – and who was soon to be a close associate of Goebbels in the running of the Nazi propaganda machine.[3] That marriage, during which the Princess signed herself simply Marie Adelheid Konopath, again ended in divorce, in 1936. The Princess remained active in extreme right-wing politics and literature, however, until her death in 1993, two years short of her hundredth birthday.

By the year 1921, when her long poem or collection of poems entitled *Gott in mir* was published, the threat of revolution in Germany had subsided, the main centers of insurrection – Berlin, Munich, and the Ruhr – having been brought to heel and the short-lived revolutionary regimes in the first two definitively crushed. Though all the German princes had abdicated along with the Kaiser in 1918 and some had even fled their residences, many princely houses appear to have successfully secured their fortunes. Even so, it was still, in 1921, a tumultuous time in Germany, marked by mass strikes and continued worker unrest. In addition, 1921 was the year of the Princess's divorce, her remarriage to her erstwhile brother-in-law, and the birth of her child. There is thus good reason to suppose that the real historical experience of the author is echoed in the poetic voice of *Gott in mir*: that of a headstrong, fiercely independent woman, scornful of convention and of the class-determined concerns of most of the people in her milieu; inspired by nebulous but distinctly unorthodox religious ideas; filled with an ardent desire for change and heroic self-sacrifice in the name of vaguely defined high ideals, yet not without a degree of condescending, aristocratic compassion for the weak; not insensitive to the alternating pleas and threats of her family, but determined to live her life according to her own lights. Twenty years later, as we shall see, in the midst of the Second World War, the Princess created in the novel *Die Overbroocks* (1942) a heroine whose values and outlook are strikingly consistent with those of the speaker in the long poem of 1921. The chief difference between the earlier work and the later one lies in the fact that in 1942, after two tumultuous decades of political engagement and historical action, it was possible to recast the values and worldview, which in 1921 could only be expressed in vague, pseudo-philosophical and religious outpourings, in the form of a narrative with unmistakable historical references. Lyrical and rhapsodic language and form gave way to the language and form of the novel – even though, as will be seen later, the novel itself is still more poetic than strictly realist. After 1945, in the face of the historical collapse of the political project with which she had been wholeheartedly associated, the Princess reverted to the poetic mode of her first published work.

In hindsight, as was argued in Part I, the characteristic features of an extreme right-wing ideology are easily detectable in *Gott in mir*, and it seems likely that the Princess was either already moving in right-wing circles at the time of its composition or on the verge of doing so. She was by no means the only aristocratic figure to be found in such circles. Dismayed by the failure of their class to respond with conviction and courage to the turmoil that precipitated and followed the end of the Wilhelminian Empire and lacking confidence in the ability of traditional conservative forces to intervene effectively in the political arena, many younger members of the old princely families were drawn – along with the ruined and impoverished petty aristocracy – to radical right-wing ideologies and populist political movements in the 1920s and 1930s.[4] Among the socially prominent early supporters of the NSDAP (the National Socialist German Workers' Party) were two sons of ex-Kaiser Wilhelm II – Crown Prince Friedrich Wilhelm[5] and his younger brother, the Kaiser's fourth son, August Wilhelm. "Auwi," as the latter was known familiarly, was later honored for his services to the Nazi cause by being made a *Standartenführer* (colonel) in the SA (*Sturmabteilung* [stormtroopers section], or paramilitary wing of the Party).[6] Carl Eduard, Duke of Saxe-Coburg and Gotha, born in England and educated at Eton, a grandson of Queen Victoria and first cousin of King George V, rose to the rank of *Obergruppenführer* (general) in the SA, conspicuously attending George V's funeral in 1936 in his stormtrooper uniform. Prince Bernhard zur Lippe-Biesterfeld, later Prince Bernhard of the Netherlands, whose grandfather was a brother of Marie Adelheid's grandfather, joined the NSDAP in the early 1930s and became a member of the SA and the *Reiter-SS*.

Closer to home, two members of the Princess's immediate family were also active on the extreme Right, one on the Reuß and one on the zur Lippe side. Her older brother, Friedrich Wilhelm, Prinz zur Lippe-Biesterfeld (1890-1938), made a reputation for himself in radical right-wing circles as the author of *Vom Rassenstil zur Staatsgestalt: Rasse und Politik* [From Racial Style to State Structure: Race and Politics] (1928).[7] He was also a friend of Ludwig Ferdinand Clauß, a well-known specialist in questions of race and so-called "Völkerpsychologie," whose *Die nordische Seele* [The Nordic Soul] (1923; eight editions by 1940) and *Rasse und Seele* [Race and Soul] (1926; 18 editions by 1943) were among the most influential literary products of the so-called *Nordic Movement*, in which the Princess was also soon involved.[8] An exact contemporary of the Princess on the Reuß side, from the zu

Schleiz branch of the family, Erbprinz (Hereditary Prince) Heinrich XLV (1895-1945), was "won over completely" to the National Socialist cause by Goebbels, after the latter met him at a dinner party hosted by another friend of the Princess's, Freifrau (Baroness) Viktoria von Dirksen, an important intermediary between the old nobility and the National Socialists, in May 1930. "He immediately understood us," Goebbels reported of his encounter with Reuß. Later Goebbels seems to have put him in charge of programs for the theater.[9] At any rate, he was sufficiently prominent in Nazi circles to have been arrested by the Russians in 1945, after which he was never heard from again.

Somewhat more distantly connected to the Princess, but very close to her in underlying motivation, in his unwavering adherence, until his death in 1983, to National Socialist and racist doctrines, and in his use of his literary talents for the propagation of these doctrines well into the post-World War II period,[10] was Friedrich Christian, Prinz zu Schaumburg-Lippe (a rival branch of the House of Lippe[11]). The prince was drawn to the Nazis in the mid-twenties, served as an aide to Goebbels from 1932 until 1935, campaigned vigorously to enlist the nobility behind Hitler, was sent on a mission to Sweden to drum up support for the regime in 1938, and, as both the text and the photographs in his published diaries testify, stood high in Hitler's favor as well as in that of his chief at the Ministry of Propaganda. Like the heroine of the Princess's later novel *Die Overbroocks*, he had been disillusioned and disgusted by the unheroic abdication and flight of the Kaiser, by the – in his view – even more cowardly abdications of the German princes and their spineless surrender to the revolutionaries of 1918, and finally by the ease with which, according to him, some sections of the old nobility abandoned ancient principles of honor and fidelity and accommodated themselves to the egoistical, materialist values of the despised Weimar Republic. Raised by tutors who combined traditional views of the prerogatives and obligations of the nobility with Frederician Enlightenment ideas about the education of princes and Nietzschean notions of heroic aristocracy, he had come to believe, as had the Princess, that neither the old conservatism nor the elitism of rightwing radicals like Moeller van den Bruck was adequate to the times. If there were ever to be a monarchy in Germany again, he held, it could not bear any resemblance to the old one. "Hitler," he noted optimistically in his diaries, "was in principle for the Monarchy." "But not," he added, "for the continuation of that which, in his opinion, had failed totally."[12] By the mid-1920s the Prince was convinced that those who still held to the values of the nobility had to break down the old barriers separating them from the common people, reach out to the masses, and "für die Straße entscheiden" [decide in favor of the street], that is, side with the National Socialists and accept their demagogic methods. Like a substantial fraction of the nobility, he liked to think of his own class as a kind of avant-garde of National Socialism and of the National Socialists as the true heirs of the old nobility.[13]

I have not been able to ascertain whether the Princess attended the Thursday evening meetings of the *National Club* hosted in the 1920s by the wealthy Baroness Viktoria von Dirksen at the old Hotel Kaiserhof (Hitler's headquarters in Berlin as of 1932) and patronized by eminent conservatives. She was, however, a regular, in the late 1920s, at meetings of the *Nordic Ring*, for which the Baroness provided space in the imposing Palais Dirksen on the Margaretenstraße, after the death in 1928 of her more traditionally conservative husband, Willibald Dirksen.[14] These meetings were a forum for the discussion of issues of race and eugenics and for promoting the "Nordic idea" [Der Nordische Gedanke], the proponents of which held that Occidental culture in general and Germanic culture in particular were a creation of the "Nordic race," that this long dominant racial strain in the population had been losing ground rapidly in the new industrial age through an influx of inferior races drawn by employment opportunities in the rapidly expanding cities, and that this trend would have to be reversed or at least arrested if Germany and the Northern countries, and along with them the entire culture of the West, were not to follow France, Spain, and Italy (where the Nordic element of the population had already shrunk catastrophically) into decline.[15]

The Nordic idea – essentially a special version of the obsession of the age with "decadence" – was widespread in the German middle and upper middle classes in the early decades of the twentieth century. As early as December 1907, for instance, Walther Rathenau – the son of the director of the AEG (*Allgemeine Elektrische Gesellschaft*), one of the most progressive industrial enterprises in Germany, the future Foreign Minister of the Weimar Republic, and a Jew (he was assassinated in 1922 by nationalist, anti-Semitic fanatics, who were memorialized after Hitler came to power) – announced in the magazine *Zukunft* [Future], the editor of which, Maximilian Harden, was also Jewish,[16] that if it was not to suffer drastic decline, Germany would have to reinforce the Nordic element in its population culturally and biologically. Six years later, on the eve of the First World War, Rathenau, himself a competent scientist and gifted business manager, repeated his call for such a "Vernördlichung" [northernizing] or "Nordifikation" of the nation in his *Zur Mechanik des Geistes* [On the Mechanics of the Spirit] (1913), a long meditation on the decline of culture in an age of increasing rationalization and utilitarianism.[17] The high value Rathenau placed on the "Nordic" involved an implicit, often explicit antithesis, in his pre-war writings, of "Nordic" or "Western" and "Oriental," of "Aryan" and "non-Aryan," of "blond" and "dark" races, of "men motivated by courage" [Mutmenschen] and "men motivated by fear" [Furchtmenschen], of "soul" and "intellect." These antithetical pairs in Rathenau's work correspond to others that were popular at the time, such as "culture" and "civilization" or Werner Sombart's "heroes" [Helden] and "tradesmen" [Händler]. Given this style of thinking in antitheses, it was virtually inevitable that anti-Semitism would become an inseparable component of the Nordic idea. The "Oriental," urban, "wandering" Jew, subservient to his tyrannical God and pursuing only his own selfish gain was the obvious foil for the true-hearted, free-spirited, courageous Nordic peasant or farmer rooted in his soil and his community. Even the somewhat less despised and hated Jew of the Old Testament, leading a nomadic existence in boundless, featureless deserts was seen as the polar opposite of the sedentary man of the North in his rolling green pasturelands and fertile, well-tilled fields.[18]

The anti-Semitic potential of the Nordic idea was reinforced by the claim of most of its adherents, that it also had a religious component and that religion was crucial to a people's life and culture. Germany – and with it the culture of the Occident as a whole – would be saved, it was argued, not only by revitalizing the Nordic racial strain in the nation but by renewing the original religion of the Nordic peoples and eliminating "oriental" faiths foreign to the Nordic race and Nordic "blood." To some, as noted in Part I, this meant building on supposed racially inherited, pre-Christian beliefs, to others, considerably more numerous, removing the "foreign" (i.e. Judaic) element from Christianity and retaining only that part of it that was held to be the natural religion of Aryan Germans, indeed – on the basis of Houston Stewart Chamberlain's assertion that the people of Galilee were Aryans and that Jesus was therefore not of Jewish stock – an Aryan creation. The new-old Savior of some champions of the Nordic idea was Wodan (or Wotan or Odin) or Wodan's son Baldur, of others a heroic, virile, Aryan warrior-Christ.[19] Needless to say, salvation was envisaged as this-worldly – the flourishing of the living *volk* and the self-empowerment of the living individual; not as otherworldly, the redemption of the sinner.

A previous version of the *Nordic Ring* had been founded as a secret society, the *Ring der Norda*, as early as 1907 by the eugenicist Alfred Ploetz (1860-1940), who claimed to be a socialist but also believed in the superiority of the Nordic or Germanic race. In the 1880s he had organized a society called *Pacifica*, the aim of which was to establish a community of men and women of pure Germanic descent on socialist principles in the American West, and to that end, in 1891, he and his wife had tried out life in a commune in Iowa based on the ideas of the mid-nineteenth-century French utopian socialist Etienne Cabet (*Voyage en Icarie*, 1842). The object of this early *Nordic Ring* – refounded in 1910 as *Nordischer Ring* – was to save the Nordic or Germanic race (the two terms were still interchangeable for Ploetz at this time) from the depredations of modern urban and industrial society and to promote what in Germany is usually referred to as "Racial Hygiene" – that is, population policies favorable to maintaining the strength of the race.[20] In a 1911 pamphlet entitled *Unser Weg* [Our Road], Ploetz defined his and his associates' goal as the implementation of a "nordisch-germanische Rassenhygiene."[21] When the *Nordic Ring* was expanded the following year into an athletic club and renamed *Bogenklub München* [Munich Archery Club], Ploetz made clear to his friend, the well-known and highly successful writer Gerhart Hauptmann, that the goals of the organization had not changed. The archery club was "more than a sports club," he told Hauptmann. It was "a shoot from which a true program of eugenics [rassenhygienische Betätigung] would grow."[22] In the revolutionary aftermath of the 1918 defeat, the *Archery Club* was in turn reconstituted as *Deutscher Widar-Bund* [German Widar Association], the aim of which was still "die Pflege deutschen Menschentums" [the fostering of the German human type]. The basic racialist orientation of the old *Nordischer Ring* was thus retained, with a more explicit but still relatively contained anti-Semitic strain, in the *Widar-Bund*.[23] By the early 1920s, however, these earlier formations appear to have broken up so that the *Nordischer Ring* established in 1926 and supported financially by Viktoria von Dirksen (and probably by the Princess also) represented a new association rather than a direct continuation of Ploetz's earlier one.

Along with Hanno Konopath, the government official with radical right-wing sympathies whom she married the following year, the Princess appears to have been one of the founding members of the new *Nordischer Ring*.[24] (Others included Professor Hans F. K. Günther, known as "race-

Günther," and the architect Paul Schultze-Naumburg, an early critic of the pompous historicism of the late Wilhelminian period and champion of a simpler vernacular building style, who had become a fierce opponent of Bauhaus modernism and internationalism). The author of a pamphlet entitled *Ist Rasse Schicksal? Grundgedanken der völkischen Bewegung* [Is Race Destiny? Fundamental Principles of the *Völkisch* Movement], which was published in 1926 by the Munich-based Lehmann-Verlag, a notorious breeding-ground of right-wing writers and ideologies,[25] Konopath was fully committed to the Nordic idea and its goal of *Aufnordung* or reinforcing the component of Nordic blood in the general German population. Thus in 1928 – again probably in collaboration with the Princess[26] – he set up a so-called *Nordische Vermittlungsstelle* [Nordic Exchange] with the aim of bringing together pure-blooded Nordic youths and maidens. Notices were placed in right-wing periodicals such as *Die Sonne, Volk und Rasse,* and *Deutschlands Erneuerung* offering assistance to Nordic men and women who had not succeeded in finding a biologically appropriate mate. In the same year, acting on behalf of the *Werkbund für deutsches Volkstum und Rassenforschung* [Working Association for German Popular Culture and Race Research] and the *Jungnordischer Bund* [Young Nordic Alliance], Konopath encouraged a racially motivated interest in family genealogical tables by instituting a public competition for the best *Ahnentafel* or family tree. The drawing up of such genealogies had been strongly urged on his readers and followers by Jörg Lanz von Liebenfels, one of Hitler's Viennese mentors and a major voice in German racist circles. In the aristocratic camp, the new racial stringency had found expression in the so-called *Edda* (*Eisernes Buch des deutschen Adels deutscher Art*), a new registry of noble families from which any family having admitted more than one Semite or non-European person since the year 1800 was explicitly excluded.[27]

In 1931 Lehmann issued a second edition of Konopath's *Ist Rasse Schicksal?*, which doubtless led to his being recognized by the Social Democratic *Münchner Post* as "the well known 'Rassenforscher' [race researcher], Chief Councilor R. Hanns [sic] Konopath" in a satirical article entitled "Neue Scherze des Rassenclowns" [The Latest Jokes and Tricks of the Race Clown].[28] His racist credentials can only have been further enhanced when, through the *Nordischer Ring*, he organized a celebration to mark the hundredth anniversary of the death of Arthur de Gobineau, usually considered the founder of modern racism, in Berlin on 13 October, 1932. Major National Socialist Party figures like Wilhelm Frick and

R.Walther Darré took part in this event.

Meanwhile, as a NSDAP official, Konopath turned out numerous articles for the weekly *Nationalsozialistische Partei-Korrespondenz* with titles like "Wir haben die jüdische Kunst satt" [We Have had Enough of Jewish Art].[29] He also contributed regularly to the extreme rightwing monthly *Die Sonne* [The Sun], the subtitle of which was *Monatsschrift für nordische Weltanschauung und Lebensgestaltung* [Monthly Magazine for Promoting the Nordic Worldview and Way of Life].

An article in this journal gives an account of one of the more picturesque activities of the *Nordischer Ring*. It describes a Wagnerian celebration of the summer solstice at the Bismarckwarte on the Müggelberg in the south-eastern suburbs of Berlin on 21-22 June 1930, on the occasion of the Nordic *Thing* (Assembly or Thing) there, in which 600-700 people took part. At a signal from an old Nordic luder horn the doors of the tower swung slowly open, we are told, and eight handsome Nordic maidens, led by Frau Konopath – i.e. the Princess – emerged, their blond tresses untied, carrying fiery torches. With measured steps, to the accompaniment of music, they descended the stairs and circled the high woodpile, before setting it alight. As the flames leaped high into the night sky, the peace of the *Thing* was proclaimed. Pathfinders lit their torches from the burning woodpile and placed themselves around the tower. After a brief blessing of the fire and another sounding of the horn, the principal speaker came out of the tower and delivered the poetic address in praise of Fire to great effect. The summer solstice song, "Rising Flame," was then sung in unison. The "beautifully orchestrated" celebration ended, according to the article in *Die Sonne* with the intoning of the old-Nordic Brunnhilde ballad by a choir and soloist, by praise of fire and leaping over it, and by singing in which all present participated.[30]

Like his friend R. Walther Darré, Konopath may have hesitated for a time to join the NSDAP, despite strong sympathy with much of its agenda, because of what he perceived as its predominantly urban focus and the mainly urban character of its support base. A conversation with Goebbels in April 1930 seems to have overcome whatever residual reservations he may have had, however,[31] for by the end of that year he had been appointed to a leading position in the branch of the Party organization that was charged, under Constantin Hierl, with building up the cadres of the future state. (Another branch, under Gregor Strasser, was charged with the work of undermining the existing state). While Darré was chosen to head the section on Agriculture and Hans Frank, the future Governor-General of Poland, the section on Legal Matters, Konopath was made head of a new section on Race and Culture[32] – apparently on instructions from Hitler himself, who thereby passed over the more obvious candidacy of Alfred Rosenberg in favor of a relatively unknown newcomer.[33]

In 1931 Konopath was listed as the Party's *Reichsleiter für Kulturfragen* and in that capacity, along with Göring and Goebbels, preceded Hitler as a speaker at the NSDAP *Gauparteitag* in Chemnitz on June 7, 1931. In June 1932, once again along with Goebbels, he addressed a meeting of NSDAP Gauleiters in Munich, this time as head of the Party's *Abteilung Film und Rundfunk* [Department of Film and Radio]. In the National Socialist Yearbook for 1932 he was still listed as "Chief of the Department of Race and Culture," but in June of that year he was removed from his post "wegen einer Privatangelegenheit" [because of an affair in his personal life] – possibly a sexual indiscretion that may also have led to the Princess's divorcing him in 1936. He was then appointed Director of the Reichslotterie, a position he still held in 1938.

Evidently, after joining the Party, Konopath fulfilled multiple functions in its operations, even if he never attained the notoriety of a Goebbels or a Rosenberg. As head of the Film and Radio Section, for instance, he was given responsibility for imposing the National Socialist Party agenda on a pressure-group, the *Reichsverband deutscher Rundfunkteilnehmer*, that had been set up in 1930 by the Stahlhelm veterans' association and other right-wing conservatives for the purpose of influencing the character and selection of radio programs.[34] Probably his most important Party assignment was to mediate, as head of the Department of Race and Culture, among a number of rival and quarrelsome Protestant Christian groups strongly sympathetic to National Socialism and bring them into a single umbrella organization, through which the NSDAP could better exploit their support, while at the same time maintaining its proclaimed "neutrality" in confessional matters and not becoming embroiled in the disputes (mostly revolving around degrees of racism and anti-Semitism) that divided them. Thus in 1931-32 he was instrumental in bringing into being the *Glaubensbewegung deutscher Christen* [German Christians Movement], the aim of which was to purge Christianity of its Judaic elements and the members of which were permitted by the Party to present themselves at the Prussian Church elections in 1932 as *Evangelische Nationalsozialisten* – i.e. as implicitly sanctioned by the Party notwithstanding the latter's frequently announced policy of religious neutrality. Though Konopath's own sympathies lay with the neo-pagan movements grouped together in 1933 in Wilhelm Hauer's non-Christian *Arbeitsgemeinschaft der deutschen Glaubensbewegung* [Working Community of the German Faith Movement], he served briefly, from February to May 1932, as President of the new *Glaubensbewegung deutscher Christen*.[35]

The inspirer of the Konopaths' *Nordischer Ring* and the couple's intellectual mentor was the specialist in race studies, Professor Hans F. K. Günther. Günther's earliest major work, *Ritter, Tod und Teufel: Der Heldische Gedanke* [The Knight, Death, and the Devil: The Heroic Idea], published in Munich the year before the Princess's 1921 poem, combined the *völkisch* tradition of nationalist neopaganism with biological racism in a mix that appears to have proved popular, for there were new editions of this work in 1924, 1928, 1935 and 1937. Günther's masterwork, however, was his *Rassenkunde des deutschen Volkes* [Ethnogeny of the German People] which went through no fewer than sixteen editions between 1922 and the Nazi take-over in 1933 and of which 124,000 copies had been printed by 1943. (A shorter popular version, published in 1929, had been printed in 272,000 copies by 1943, bringing the total to 396,000.[36]) In this work, as in others, such as *Rassenkunde Europas* (1925; Engl. translation: *The Racial Elements of European History,* London, 1927), *Adel und Rasse* [Aristocracy and Race] (1926), *Der nordische Gedanke unter den Deutschen* [The Nordic Idea among the Germans] (1925), *Führeradel durch Sippenpflege* [An Aristocracy of Leaders through the Cultivation of Good Stock] (1936) Günther developed the idea that of the various European races he had identified – the "Nordic," "Falic," "Eastern," "Western," "Dinaric," and "East Baltic," each of which had its particular qualities and defects – the Nordic, still predominant only in the area of Lower Saxony (which surrounds the "free Hanseatic city of Bremen" and on the edge of which the Principality of Lippe is located), was the most dynamic, enterprising, and adventurous, "characterized by outstanding will-power, judgment, cool realism, truthfulness on a man-to-man basis, chivalry, and justice."[37] A race of conquerors, it had pushed South and West at the time of the great migrations, extending its influence over the whole of Germany, Austria, Northern Italy, and large parts of France and Spain. From it emerged the Aechean Greeks of the heroic age and the still surviving ruling castes of many European countries. Inevitably, however, it had been overwhelmed by the sheer numbers of the races it had conquered and with which it ultimately intermarried. Even in most regions of Germany it had become only part of the racial stock of the population;

people of pure Nordic race were a small minority. In the modern world it was under mortal threat from a series of new developments – urbanization and industrialization, the flight from the land, a burgeoning industrial proletariat made up of immigrants of other races whose fertility was favored by the social welfare policies of the modern state. And yet everyone agreed that even though the Nordic element had become a drastically reduced part of the German population, it was still the most "authentically German" [echt deutsch] part of it.[38] Günther conceded that mixtures were not always to be avoided. The Nordic (predominantly North German) component, characterized by adventurousness and risk-taking, could usefully be balanced by the Falic (predominantly Rhenish) component, for instance, the chief characteristics of which were perseverance, defiant firmness, and reliability. He also noted that certain types of creativity might be fostered by the inner tension that arose when the admixture in a mostly Nordic individual of another racial element caused the (light) Nordic strain in that individual to struggle against the other (darker) strain.[39]

Nevertheless, the greatest danger facing the German people, in Günther's view (and in the view, as we saw, of many of his contemporaries), was still the diminution of the Nordic element in its racial composition: "Entnordung" [denordification]. To Günther this was synonymous with the adulteration and deterioration of the race as a whole. The goal of all concerned with the revival of Germany must therefore be *Aufnordung* [renordification] – preserving and reinvigorating the Nordic strain in the population. In the words of another writer, who claimed to have demonstrated "scientifically" that the Nordic strain had once been much stronger in South Germany than it was currently, "the greatest reserve capital of natural strength seems today to have been stored up in the Lower Saxon stock and so the last hopes of a regeneration of our people out of the true German spirit are firmly attached [...] to that stock."[40]

Günther distinguished his goal of *Aufnordung* from the general goal of *Aufartung* embraced by one of the pioneers of race policies, Alfred Grotjahn (*Soziale Pathologie*, Berlin, 1912). Grotjahn, Günther recalled, had enjoined the supporters of the Nordic movement to give up their specifically Nordic project in favor of a broader movement to improve the general racial quality of the German population as a whole. In so doing, Günther objected, Grotjahn showed that, however much he may have been interested in promoting the racial health [Erbgesundheit] of the population, he had not given much thought to the spiritual and psychological aspects of race [rassenseelische Richtung]. General racial health is a goal that any population may pursue, whatever its race. What distinguishes the *Nordic movement*, however, is that it is concerned precisely with the "rassenseelische Richtung des Deutschtums" [the spiritual and psychological aspects of racial development in the Germanic peoples and cultures], i.e. with preserving and reinforcing the specifically Nordic element – and its accompanying spiritual and psychological qualities – in the German people and its culture. This cannot be State policy, Günther conceded, since engaging in an effort to promote a particular race would violate the State's necessary neutrality with respect to the races represented in the population.[41] Consequently *Aufnordung* has to be a voluntary project, undertaken by the Nordic people themselves and by Germans convinced of the special qualities of the Nordic race. As a private initiative, the *Nordischer Ring* was thus fully justified by the acknowledged scholarly leader of the Nordic movement, along with the other activities, such as the *Nordic Exchange*, through which the Konopaths hoped to influence people and to reinvigorate the Nordic strain in the German population. Günther, moreover, traveled around the country giving talks in support of both the *Nordischer Ring* and the related *Nordische Gesellschaft*.[42]

In the Germany of the 1920s and 1930s Günther was by no means the only champion of the Nordic idea with scholarly credentials.[43] Others included, to mention only a few, Gustav Kossinna, an internationally admired professor of archaeology at Berlin University, as well as his students and followers – Otto Höfler, Gustav Neckel, Bernhard Kummer – all of whom occupied university chairs and sympathized with or were co-opted by the National Socialist movement; Rudolf John Gorsleben, translator of the *Edda* (1922), founder of the *Edda Gesellschaft* (1925), and editor-publisher of the periodical *Deutsche Freiheit* (subtitled *Monatsschrift für arische Gottes- und Welterkenntnis* [Monthly Journal for Aryan Understanding of God and the World], later renamed *Arische Freiheit* [Aryan Freedom]); the Berlin University Professor Ludwig Ferdinand Clauß, already mentioned as a friend of the Princess's brother; the political philosopher Carl Schmitt; and the Dutch-born scholar of ancient history, archaeology and linguistics, Herman Wirth – the friend, mentor, and protégé of both the Princess and her publisher Roselius – who had settled in Germany in 1924 and joined the NSDAP in 1925.

In 1921 the publisher Diederichs, another faithful patron of Wirth, launched a series of old "Nordic" texts, under the general title *Thule:*

19. Publicity announcement by Eugen Diederichs Verlag, Jena, of a forthcoming series devoted to Nordic sagas and literary texts as manifestations of the "essential, inherent strengths of German being," April, 1933.

*Altnordische Dichtung und Prosa*, that comprised 24 volumes by the time it was completed in 1938[44] (fig. 19). A number of women scholars also lent their support to the new ideas, writing – like the Princess herself – on themes such as the "Nordic woman," "Nordic philosophy," and "Nordic religion."[45] In the Party leadership Heinrich Himmler and Alfred Rosenberg were especially haunted by the threat of "downfall and destruction" that, as the historian Joachim Fest put it, hung over "Germanness, the priceless sediment in the bowl of Nordic blood."[46] The development of the powerful anti-Christian, neo-pagan element in the Nordic movement, already perceptible in the Princess's poem of 1921, owed much to the *Nordische Glaubensbewegung* [Nordic Faith Movement],[47] established shortly after the *Ring*, in 1927, and subsequently absorbed, along with Ludwig Fahrenkrog's *Germanische Glaubensgemeinschaft* (founded 1913) into the *Arbeitsgemeinschaft deutscher Glaubensbewegung* [Working Community of the German Faith Movement], an alliance of organizations with similar aims, led by the scholar of linguistics and former student of the celebrated Basler Mission, Jakob Wilhelm Hauer.[48] The Princess's brother, Friedrich Wilhelm, Prinz zur Lippe, was especially well known as a strong supporter of "Nordic" religion and an opponent of Christianity. At a July 1933 meeting of various *völkisch* religious organizations, convoked by Hauer in the hope of persuading them to agree on a common platform and join in a common organization, the Prince was identified as one of the "Nordics" – along with the artist Ludwig Fahrenkrog of the *Germanische Glaubensgemeinschaft*, Wilhelm Kusserow of the *Nordisch-religiöse Arbeitsgemeinschaft*, Otto Sigfrid Reuter of the *Deutschgläubige Gemeinschaft*, and the Princess's husband Konopath – who objected strongly to a proposal to divide the new organization into two branches, a Christian and a Germanic. There should be no place, according to Friedrich Wilhelm, in the new organization for Christianity in any form. "Wir wollen uns freimachen von der inneren Bindung zur Kirche."[49] No doubt the Prince subscribed to the views laid out in a 1933 position paper of the *Nordisch-religiöse Arbeitsgemeinschaft*, to wit:

> Christianity in any form is a dangerous gate through which we are invaded by Asiatic influences, the Jews, and Marxism. National Socialism sows the seed of a healthy racial feeling in the hearts of the German people, but it does not engage in struggle against Asiatic, Judeo-Marxist Christianity. If we do not succeed in rooting out this poisonous weed, down to the last fiber, National Socialism itself will succumb to it. All struggle and sacrifice would be in vain, and perhaps the last chance of a breakthrough for the German people lost, unless our movement takes up and carries forward the struggle at the point where National Socialism these days abandons it.[50]

The attempt to make a place for a *völkisch* form of Christianity in the organization did not succeed and the Prince later lectured on "Rasse und Glaube" [Race and Faith] at a 1934 meeting of Hauer's *Deutsche Glaubensbewegung*, at which he shared the platform with Fahrenkrog. His talk was such a success that he gave it at other gatherings designed to drum up support for Hauer's movement.[51]

Among the promoters of the "Nordic idea," the Princess appears to have been particularly close to R. Walther Darré (1895-1953), also a member of the *Nordic Ring*. A specialist in animal breeding by training and profession, the Argentinian-born Darré is now remembered chiefly as the leading exponent of the ideology of "Blood and Soil" in the NSDAP. Like his longtime friend Heinrich Himmler (until they quarreled over policy issues in the late 1930s), Darré had been a member, as a young man, of the *Artamans*, an anti-urban, anti-Slavic, and anti-Semitic youth group, founded in 1924. Influenced by standard *Lebensreform* ideas, such as physical culture, the cult of fellowship, the need for *Bodenreform* [land reform], and a return to nature, the *Artamans* had a two-pronged program: 1) to bring about a return to the land, the root and foundation of the German people, as the essential means of regenerating the nation and curing it of corrupt cosmopolitan capitalism and greedy, self-centered individualism, and 2) to bring about the triumph of the "Nordic instinct" in the relentless struggle – as they saw it – between "Nordisches Blut und unnordisches" [Nordic and un-Nordic blood]. (The group had a special section devoted to race studies and a program for promoting and encouraging marriages among the best representatives of the Nordic race).[52] A small-circulation magazine put out by the movement for a few years conveyed these two related goals in its title: *Blut und Boden: Monatsschrift für wurzelhaftes Bauerntum, für deutsche Wesensart und die nationale Freiheit* [Blood and Soil: a Monthly Magazine for the Promotion of a Peasantry rooted in its own Land, of native Germanness, and of National Freedom]. Most of the *Artamans*, including Darré and Himmler in their early years, offered their services as workers on the land, especially in Eastern Germany, where they aimed to protect German soil and German stock from foreign, in particular Slavic encroachments in the form of Polish summer workers hired by the landowners of Silesia and Mecklenburg.[53] (The movement is evoked admiringly, as will be seen shortly, in the Princess's 1942 novel, in the shape of two young male characters who come unexpectedly to the aid of the heroine after she has recovered her dead husband's family farm in Lower Saxony and who become role models for her twin sons). Darré did not join the NSDAP until 1930, his hesitation being probably due to what he may have perceived as a misfit between the Party's heavily urban base and his own radically anti-urban ideology.[54] But in March of that year he succeeded in having his agrarian program – aimed at promoting a return to the land and preserving traditional family holdings – adopted by the Party leadership. He then conducted a vigorous political campaign in rural areas and won the support of the German farmers for the NSDAP. For this he was rewarded in 1933 with the post of Reichsminister for Food and Agriculture, a post he held until 1942, when he was forced to step down, his inflexible commitment to restoring individual peasants' or small farmers' holdings in the German lands having been found not only to have failed to produce the desired results but to be incompatible, grounded as it was in the idea of the peasant's rootedness in his native soil, with the "Drang nach Osten" and the plans of his sometime friend Himmler to repopulate the conquered territories in the East with sturdy German farmer-warriors.[55]

As could be expected, Darré was a strong advocate of strict racial policies. Along with Himmler, he was one of the editors of the magazine *Volk und Rasse*. The return of the people to the land was inseparable, for him, from the preservation of the Nordic race. *Das Bauerntum als Lebensquelle der Nordischen Rasse* [The Peasantry as the Life Source of the Nordic Race] was the title he gave to one of his earliest books (1929).[56] "The community of our people [Volksgemeinschaft] is a community of blood," he declared in a later work; "the institutions of our national life are nothing; the blood of our people is everything." Race and blood are the basis of community. Humanitarian ideas only estrange people from "Life": "Against the ideas of 1789, the ideas of liberty, equality, and fraternity, [...] and the life-destroying deification of Reason, [...] we set the Law of our Blood. We envisage the future of our people as built on the foundation of the blood inherited from our forefathers."[57] This did not entail support of the old nobility. Darré advocated using the breeding techniques he had learned as a student of agriculture to build a new German aristocracy from native peasant stock, since the existing aristocracy, tainted by elements of alien blood, lacked real legitimacy, in his view, and had demonstrated its moral bankruptcy in 1918.[58] The race question was also relevant, he claimed, to the resettling of the population on the land. Thus he did not advocate indiscriminate resettling to resolve the problem of "an uprooted, urban German population" [eines entwurzelten, städtischen Deutschtums]. That, he warned, would result in a disastrous "total denordification of the German people" [eine totale Entnordung des deutschen Volkes].[59] Consistently with his membership in the *Nordic Ring* and his earlier association with the *Artamanen*, he took the title of the monthly journal he launched in 1932 – *Odal: Monatsschrift für Blut und Boden* [Odal: Monthly Magazine for Blood and Soil] – from the Odal rune, the sign of an old Norse and Northern German legal bond between family or tribe and land.[60] The Princess – his "little sister," as he called her[61] – was Darré's chief editorial assistant in running this journal. She also contributed articles to it in which she expressed no less vehemently than he her contempt for the "hoffnungslose Allerwelts-Gleichmacherei" [hopeless making everybody everywhere equal] that had "resulted from a centuries-old false doctrine" and her conviction that "blood, not books," determines character and level of culture. "We are what we are," she proclaimed, "thanks to our fathers and mothers."[62]

Holding the position of "Arbeitsleiterin für Frauenkultur" [Director of Women's Education and Culture] under Darré as "Reichsbauernführer" [Leader of the Reich Farmers],[63] the Princess was one of the *Blut und Boden* theorist's earliest and most loyal devotees. Rebellious and independent-minded as she was, she could not but respond favorably both to his high regard for the Nordic woman, whom he represented, following Günther, as an equal partner of her husband, in contrast to the subordinate role allegedly assigned to women by "Oriental" or Semitic peoples, and to his idea of a "new nobility." In fact, her association with Darré may well have encouraged the Princess to complete the revolt against her caste that she had begun a decade earlier – for Darré's plan for a new peasant or farmers' aristocracy to replace a nobility he considered corrupt and besmirched by alien blood, was understandably not well received in most noble families, including those that had rallied to National Socialism.[64] In general, Darré's influence may well have played an important role in turning the vague longings and aspirations, still couched in *Gott in mir* in mystical and religious terms, into adherence to a particular political program. Both the Princess and her husband Konopath joined the NSDAP in the late Spring of 1930, around the time that Darré joined.[65] Thereafter the Princess appears to have chosen to define herself as a loyal Party member. At some point this must have entailed some downplaying of her earlier association with the *völkisch* religious movements and sects that had in all likelihood inspired *Gott in mir*. For once the National Socialists had attained power, these quarrelsome and competing movements, which had helped in some measure to prepare the way for the Party's success, quickly came to be viewed as eccentric, divisive, disorderly, and inconvenient, equally incompatible with the image of a dynamic, forward-looking, united nation that the Nazis were trying to promote and with the hegemonic ambitions of the National Socialist Party and its ideology. In contrast, establishing solid relations with the long-standing national Churches – which were understandably extremely hostile to the sects, in particular to the openly anti-Christian ones – was seen as tactically indispensable to promoting the ends of the regime. The sects were therefore deliberately marginalized or in some cases banned altogether as the Party sought to rid itself of its more unruly elements and get itself seen as a Party of order, national tradition, and national unity.[66] After the collapse of the Nazi regime in 1945, however, the Princess reverted to her early enthusiasm for *völkisch* politics and religion.

In the 1930s and early 1940s, the Princess did her utmost to propagate Darré's views about the fundamental role of blood and soil. The key to the Nordic idea, she wrote in the foreword to a volume of Darré's essays and articles that she collected and edited in 1940 – most of them taken from the extreme right-wing journals *Deutschlands Erneuerung* and *Die Sonne*, the organ of the *Artaman* movement – lies in recognizing "the issue of race and breeding, on the one hand, and the significance of the peasantry, on the other, as the dual basis of everything that happens in the areas of politics, economics, and culture."[67] Above all, as we shall see, her novel *Die Overbroocks* was a grand celebration of Darré's ideas.

\*\*\*

After joining the Party in May 1930, the Princess and her husband appear to have been quickly caught up in the social activities of the Nazi leadership. They continued to frequent the salon of Viktoria von Dirksen, one of a number of wealthy women who had become infatuated with Hitler in the 1920s and had supported him financially.[68] The stepmother of Herbert von Dirksen – who later served as Ambassador to Tokyo, Moscow, and London – Dirksen was known to have contributed handsomely to the NSDAP, and to have served, as one source put it, "as an intermediary between the National Socialists and the old courtiers," thereby earning for herself the sobriquet "Mother of the Movement." According to the same source, "Hitler, Goebbels, Helldorff, and the other accomplices held their weekly meetings at her home," while her brother, the science-fiction writer Karl August von Laffert, attended her receptions "in the full splendor of his SS uniform." Even after President von Hindenburg banned the SA, the men "used to arrive [at Frau von Dirksen's] in full uniform under long capes." It seems that both she and her youngest daughter wore a large diamond swastika "pinned conspicuously on their bosoms."[69] It may even have been at the Baroness's that the Princess first met Konopath, just as in 1930 it was through the Baroness and her royal guest, Prince Auwi, that Magda Quandt, the recently divorced wife of one of the richest men in Germany, is said to have met her future second husband Goebbels.[70] At all events, "the two Konopaths" were named among the guests at a late evening reception ("from 11 until 2 in the morning") at Freifrau von Dirksen's in November 1930, at which the other guests were Göring and a couple of his relatives, Goebbels, Baroness Marie von Tiele-Winckler, Prince Auwi and his son Prince Alexander, the banker von der Heyd, the head of the Mannesmann steel tubing works Erich Niemann with his wife, and Admiral Magnus von Levetzov, later appointed chief of police in Berlin after the Nazis came to power.[71]

Goebbels for his part tells in his diaries of a dinner party at the Görings' a few months earlier (June 1930), at which the guests included, besides himself, "Frau Schultze, Frick, the Konopaths, Epp, and a director of the UFA [the powerful German film company *Universum Film AG*]."[72] In Nazi terms, this was top rank company indeed. Wilhelm Frick had just been named Education Minister in the coalition government, which included National Socialists, of the state of Thuringia, and had immediately appointed Hans F. K. Günther to a professorship at Jena (over the objections of the faculty), issued an "Ordinance against Negro Culture" (1 April 1930) which purported to rid Thuringia of all "immoral and foreign racial elements in the arts," dissolved the state school of architecture in Weimar, headed at the time by the moderate Otto Bartning – the Bauhaus having already been forced by pressure from petty-bourgeois artisans to relocate in Dessau – and appointed the architect Paul Schultze-Naumburg, a close friend of R. Wilhelm Darré, whose *Blood and Soil* ideology he shared, to head a new "united school" combining painting and architecture with the applied arts. Frick went on, after 1933, to become Hitler's Minister of the Interior, one of the drafters of the Nuremberg Laws, and the controller of concentration camps. He was sentenced to death at the Nuremberg trials and hanged two weeks later.

Frick's protégé, Schultze-Naumburg, whose wife was at the dinner (subsequently she separated from her husband and married Frick), had long been an advocate of a return both to the land and to a traditional building style appropriate to the German countryside, and had become a vehement critic of the "rootless," "urban," international style in modern architecture. He was the author of a book entitled *Kunst und Rasse* [Art and Race] (Munich 1928) and of numerous articles asserting the racial basis of art, including a pamphlet entitled *Kunst aus Blut und Boden* (1934), in which he maintained that Blood and Soil are the two sources from which the creative powers of man emerge. While the blood of the German people is a mixture of "nordisch, "dinarisch, "ostisch," and "westisch," he declared, referring to the races identified by his friend Günther, the most precious of these is the Nordic strain, to which, according to Schultze-Naumburg (once again following Günther), the art of Greek antiquity also owes its strength and purity. The first act of the new head of Frick's *Vereinigte Weimarer Kunstlehranstalten* was to fire 29 teachers from the schools, mostly because they were associated with Bauhaus style. He then proceeded to have 70 works of art, including paintings by Dix, Feininger, Kandinsky, Klee, Kokoschka, Franz Marc, and Nolde removed from the Weimar Schlossmuseum as representative of "eastern or otherwise racially inferior subhumanity" and to have Oskar Schlemmer's murals in the old Van de Velde building that had housed Gropius's school painted over.[73] Goebbels had already glowingly recounted a visit in June 1930 to Schultze-Naumburg's famous country estate at Saaleck, where he met Hans Günther, "der Rassenforscher," and was "shown around the entire house by Frau Konopath." Darré and Günther were regular members of Schultze-Naumburg's *Saaleck-Kreis* and her role as cicerone makes it seem likely that the Princess was also.[74] Only a month before the visit described by Goebbels, Hitler himself, accompanied by Rudolf Heß, had met at Burg Saaleck with the Princess's mentor, Darré, no doubt to discuss the latter's agrarian program for the Party.

The Epp at the Göring's dinner party was Franz Xaver, Ritter von Epp, a veteran of the genocidal war against the Herero people in South-West Africa in 1904-1906, as well as of the First World War, and the founder of the *Freikorps*-Epp in 1919, which the Majority Socialist government of Ebert used to put down the Bavarian Workers' Councils Republic or *Räterepublik* in Munich in 1919 and to eradicate Left-Wing Socialist and Communist resistance in the Ruhr in 1920. Both operations were carried out with unparalleled ferocity. In Munich, it has been said, "a 'white terror' ensued such as no German city, not even Berlin, had yet experienced. For a whole week the conquerors were at liberty to shoot at will, and everyone 'suspected of Spartacism' [i.e. left socialism, anarchism, or communism] – in effect Munich's entire working-class population – was outlawed." One conservative eye-witness described how "'Spartacists' were dragged out of wine-bars or railway trains and shot on the spot." Gustav Landauer, the well-known anarchist intellectual, friend of the Hart brothers, and translator of the medieval mystic Meister Eckhart, who had been appointed Minister of Education in the first Bavarian Workers' Councils government, was brutally murdered. During the suppression of the Communists in the Ruhr the following year, one member of the *Freikorps*-Epp wrote in a letter: "If I were to write you everything, you would say these are lies. No mercy is shown. We shoot even the wounded. The enthusiasm is marvelous. [...] Anyone who falls into our hands gets first the gun butt and then the bullet...We also shot dead instantly ten Red Cross nurses each of whom was carrying a pistol. We shot at these abominations with joy. [...] We were much more humane toward the French on the battlefield."[75] Epp joined the NSDAP in 1928, raised enough money, with the help of Röhm, to turn the *Völkischer Beobachter* into a National Socialist newspaper, was soon elected as a National Socialist member of the Reichstag, and after the National Socialists took power was appointed Governor (Reichskommissar) of Bavaria by Frick.

This, then, was the distinguished company the Princess kept during the 1930s.[76] Goebbels himself seems to have been on easy terms with the Konopaths. In one diary entry he tells of "going to the Konopaths for coffee" and from there, with the Görings and Dirksens to see "The Merry Widow."[77]

Everything did not go smoothly, of course. Besides the usual rivalries among the leading members of the Party – Goebbels confides to his diary at one point that Konopath is trying to wrest control of film propaganda from him – there was a more significant disagreement over what Goebbels who, as Propaganda Minister, had to be concerned about ideological inflexibility and potential divisiveness, termed Konopath's "Rassenmaterialismus" [racial materialism]. From the beginning, Goebbels had judged Konopath "intellektuell zu sehr vorbelastet" [intellectually too full of preconceived ideas], that is, not sufficiently attuned to tactics.[78] By the end of 1930, the two had had a heated discussion about the racial issue, at which, according to Goebbels, Konopath "had to give in." "We can't allow him too much room for his obsession with race," Goebbels noted in his diary.[79] But the disagreement clearly persisted, reflecting a divergence of views on the subject of race, within the Party, between tacticians like Goebbels and strict ideologues, and among Nazi sympathizers between those, such as the psychologist Carl Jung, for whom National Socialism was above all an awakening of the German nation, and those for whom it was above all a matter of physically eliminating foreign (i.e. Jewish, Slavic and other "inferior") elements and creating a physically perfect Nordic type. In his insistence on biology and animal-like breeding, Konopath probably had the support of a faction that included his wife, the Princess, along with her brother Friedrich Wilhelm Prinz zur Lippe-Biesterfeld, his own friend Darré, and Himmler, who had been a student of animal breeding like Darré.[80] A full year later Goebbels describes a scene at which he "polemisierte heftig gegen diesen Rassenmaterialismus" [argued heatedly against this racial materialism], and hints that Konopath's *Nordischer Ring* might have to be disbanded.[81] Barely a month afterwards a meeting took place in Goebbels' office at which, Konopath having again defended his "blond race materialism, [...] we flew at each other." The matter will have to be pursued further, Goebbels notes in his diary: "Konopath's arrogance has to be broken. He needs to rethink things. But I doubt that he is capable of that."[82] This disagreement between Goebbels and Konopath about the way to conduct "race propaganda," as Goebbels called it, probably reflects unease in Nazi leadership circles about the program of *Aufnordung*, which was resented by Germans, especially those from the southern areas of the country – to say nothing of the Propaganda Minister himself – whose physical appearance did not match the blond ideal.[83]

It may also be connected with Goebbels's effort, which often enough led to conflict with other high Party officials, notably Rosenberg and his *Kampfbund für deutsche Kultur*, to present an image of National Socialist culture that was modern, dynamic, turned toward the future, rather than nostalgic for a lost past. Hence his attacks on what he termed "National Kitsch," his efforts to preserve a place for twentieth-century German artists in the Nazi Pantheon, and his opposition to doctrines that might provoke division or challenge the ideological hegemony of the Party.[84] Thus Schultze-Naumburg ultimately fell out of favor, along with other *völkisch* ideologues and religious leaders whose views and organizations came to be considered not only damaging to national unity and the authority of the Party (which was more effectively upheld by good relations with the established Churches), but backward-looking and out of tune with the "new" Germany of autobahns, airships, and the "People's Car."

Throughout the thirties and during the War years the Princess served the National Socialist regime and the National Socialist ideology in every way she could – as a minor player in the National Socialist administration and above all as a writer, through her advice books for young "Nordic" women, her editions of the essays and aphorisms of her friend and mentor Darré, and not least her fictional writing, which was clearly intended to educate her readers and inspire them to serve the regime as devotedly as she.

The 1934 tract, *Nordische Frau und Nordischer Glaube* (new editions in 1935 and 1938), and the novel, *Die Overbroocks*, published in Berlin in 1942, offer an epitome of the Princess's mature thought along with a remarkable insight into the mentality and values of a dedicated National Socialist, who also appears to have been an unusually independent-minded woman – into the "Nazi Conscience," to borrow the title of Claudia Koonz's recent book.[85] For that reason they will receive special consideration here. Whereas in 1921, the Princess's ideas and feelings could be presented only in the abstract, philosophico-religious terms of the poem *Gott in mir*, by 1935 they could be articulated in more developed and practical political terms, thanks to her association with ideologists like Darré, Günther, and her husband Konopath and to her own involvement with the NSDAP. By 1942, after two decades of political action and nine momentous years of National Socialist government, it had become possible for her to represent these same ideas through the characters, actions, and concrete historical conditions required by the literary genre of the realist novel. The fundamental themes of *Gott in mir*, *Nordische Frau und Nordischer Glaube,* and *Die Overbroocks* remain, however, recognizably the same, as the following summary accounts of the tract and the novel should demonstrate.

# 6. *Nordische Frau und Nordischer Glaube*

In *Nordische Frau und Nordischer Glaube*, the second in a series of *Flugschriften der Nordischen Glaubensbewegung* [Pamphlets of the Nordic Faith Movement], the Princess articulated a feminist position – at once heroic and motherly – that was widely shared in "Nordic" circles and that she believed compatible with National Socialism.[1] With their characteristic loyalty, their faithfulness, their habit of internalizing and holding fast to their convictions, and their natural commitment to bringing up children and thus maintaining the continuity of family and race, women, she asserts in the opening section of the pamphlet, are the bedrock of any religious or political movement or institution. Thus Communism, she claims, was prevented from achieving political success in Germany because women, concerned about its materialist values and lack of respect for the family, withheld their full support. National Socialism, in contrast, attracted numberless women, despite its reputation for being hostile to women and its unwillingness to grant them certain rights that Communism did in fact propose to institute.

National Socialism appealed to women for a variety of reasons, she argues, as was only to be expected – in her view – from a people as racially heterogeneous as the German people had become. Some women wanted a new social order; others counted on the Party's ability to bring about a revival of the nation; others still sought to defend and shore up positive Christianity; finally, yet another group, albeit a minority, hoped to advance the cause of a new faith based on race. Along with those inspired by socialist ideals (the first group), these last were the most fervent supporters of the Party (pp. 3-5).[2] As varied as their motives might be, however, the important thing to note is that it was women who brought National

Socialism to power. This might seem surprising, the Princess concedes, in view of the fact that a loss of faith among many women had contributed to defeat in 1918. But that had been a different situation, she explains: the old order offered no vision of the future; the women could see only that their children had to go without food and clothing, without fathers, since these were at the front or had been killed, and often without mothers as well, since they had been enlisted to work in the munitions factories. What is clear, this section of the pamphlet concludes, is that if National Socialism is to make further advances, it must win the full support of German women, many of whom are still loyal to Christ and Christianity.

Part of the task of winning them over to National Socialism must therefore be to wean them from Christianity, to get them to see not only that Christianity is harmful to them, their children, their families, and their communities but that it is essentially alien to them as German women. This is the Princess's aim in the central section of her pamphlet.

She makes it clear from the start that her critique is directed against the New Testament no less than the Old. The values and world-view she deplores in the Old Testament and finds incompatible with the native values and world-view of the Nordic peoples – pessimism, passivity, fear and distrust of the world, a morality based not on freedom, generosity, and heroism but on strict observance of precept and the expectation of appropriate rewards, the idea that natural activities such as cultivating the soil and bearing children are a divine punishment and that natural pleasures are sinful – are all retained, she holds, in the New Testament. Above all, a low and demeaning view of women, as of the entire natural world, "runs like a red thread through the entire Bible" – Old Testament and New Testament alike. (p. 11) This should be no cause for surprise, according to the Princess, since both Old and New Testaments reflect the outlook, values, and mentality of an alien, "oriental" race. Christianity cannot be salvaged, she emphasizes, alluding implicitly to the popular thesis of H. Stuart Chamberlain, by asserting that Jesus was racially an Aryan and not a Semite. Real Christians, she maintains – in implicit opposition to the attempt by the so-called *Deutsche Christen* to rescue Christianity by cutting it off from its Jewish roots – know that the New Testament is inseparable from the Old. (pp. 7-8) At the same time, in a move reminiscent of the disclaimers of Günther and Clauß in the matter of the alleged superiority of the Nordic race, or of Fahrenkrog or Hauer in the matter of religion, she denies that her aim is to condemn Christianity as such. "We wish to refrain from all

## Nordische Frau und Nordischer Glaube

value judgments. We desire only to point out how alien the worldview of the oriental people that presented us with the Bible is from our own." (p. 6) Christianity, in other words, might well be suitable for the "Orientals" and "Southerners" [Südländer] among whom it emerged and still flourishes. But it is utterly foreign to the Nordic race and temperament. (The Princess's use of the terms "Oriental" and "Southerner" as virtually equivalent must have provoked serious misgivings in Nazi leadership circles, inasmuch as it appeared not only to create a division within the German *volk* but to imply an intimate and unbreakable connection between the alien, "oriental" religion of the Jews and Roman Catholicism, which was especially strong in Southern Germany and with which most top Nazi strategists sought not a quarrel but an accommodation.)

Christianity, the Princess warns the women of Germany, "cripples the spirit." (p. 10) The Biblical account of Adam's eating of the fruit of the tree of knowledge demonstrates that when the "Southerner" pulls aside the veil and is confronted with the knowledge of reality, he goes completely to pieces and loses every ounce of courage and confidence in himself. (p. 9) Hence the Catholic Church's discouragement or outright prohibition of independent inquiry and thinking. It is true that the Reformation instigated a revolt against the stifling of free and fearless inquiry, but "in the Evangelical Church we have just about returned to the point at which 'knowledge' and its utilization are once again forbidden."[3] (p. 9) Similarly, the deep hostility to women the Princess considers evident everywhere in the Bible was translated in the Middle Ages into the imposition of the rule of celibacy for priests, despite fierce popular opposition, especially in Northern countries, and into the persecution of talented, resourceful, and independent-minded women as "witches" – again chiefly in the lands of the North. The case of the Countess of Thuringia, known as "St. Elisabeth," provides a vivid and – according to the Princess – admonitory view of the ideal woman as Christianity envisages her. By birth she was Hungarian – that is, we are told, "a girl of alien [non-Nordic] race," of whom it was said that "her skin was so brown and her hair so black that her appearance stunned the entire Thuringian Court." Christianity appealed strongly, as was to be expected, to her southern and foreign nature and she soon began to act, out of piety, in ways that seem "to our sensibility totally out of line. She neglected her own children and, instead of caring for them, went among the lepers, even taking them into her bed. She prayed continuously and had herself flagellated by her own servants. [...] A prime example of religious hysteria, she was completely under the criminal influence of her father confessor, Conrad of Marburg, whose sole aim was to secure the victory of the Church over a noble princely house, and she blindly carried out all his commands. When she died at the age of 24, she was declared a saint and the German Emperor joined with the other princes of the Empire in carrying her bier, on which he had placed his crown." (p. 18) The "religious hysteria" and unnatural, world-denying behavior of the "fremdrassiges Ungarmädchen" [Hungarian girl of alien race] is contrasted by the Princess with the independence of spirit, loyalty, physical and moral courage, sense of self-worth and honor, capacity for love, and readiness to fight, at the cost of their own lives if necessary, for their children, family, and tribe or clan of the heroines of the Nordic sagas. In them, she claims, are to be found the natural instincts and temper of the woman of Nordic race.

To the Nordic woman, according to the Princess, the inheritance of race and blood trumps everything: "Die Art ist uns alles." (p. 21 [Kinship by blood is everything to us]) The Princess then articulates her conception of the faith of the Nordic woman, as opposed to that of the Christian. "We believe in rebirth in our descendants – not, to be sure, in the form of a 'transmigration of souls,' which would take us right back to individualism. We believe in the *Artseele* [the soul of the bloodline, breed or stock], in the holiness and indestructibility of our *Erbmasse* [inherited substance or nature], which can expect to celebrate its resurrection even in our remotest descendants. The individual, in the end, is only the bearer and protector of the *Artseele*." (p. 22) Consequently, "it does not matter whether we live or die, as long as the *Art* or bloodline is maintained. If the *Art* is eternal, we are eternal. If the *Art* dies out, we die also. That is true for everything in the world and in this respect we feel connected to the plants and the animals as to fellow-creatures." (p. 21) Death thus holds no terrors for the Nordic woman. "We carry the Hagal rune as the holy sign of 'Stirb und Werde' [Die and Become], the life-cycle into which we are born and which we affirm with complete and deepest love and joyfulness as the eternal, divine law of the universe." (p. 21)

The pamphlet closes on an appeal to German women. "We who are living now must pave the way for a coming time" when our "grandchildren will recover the natural, unreflected way of living that our ancestors once knew and that is accessible only to those of pure race," when "there will be no original sin and no despairing sense of powerlessness […] [but] an entirely new morality, the roots of which are nevertheless in ancient history," and when individuals will have value only to the extent that they are integrated into the racial community [Artgemeinschaft]. At the same time they will be sustained more firmly and valued more highly than ever before, because every man and every woman will be honored as the bearer of the eternal life of the entire *Volk*. [...] All the pettiness and contemptible triviality that has marked the existence of women and to some extent given men a right to despise the female sex will then fall away by itself." (p. 23)

It is true, the Princess concedes, that "countless women do not yet have, or no longer have, the strength to bear the spiritual loneliness and responsibility for their own decisions that are the source of a woman's inner happiness and dignity. They should not be scolded or scorned on that account. Every one has to tread the path he must without falsehood or deceit. That is the only thing we can demand absolutely and without exception of our fellow-humans. It is not for us to judge the path itself." (p. 23) But it is possible to lead by example. We can refuse to allow our children to be taught a conception of God in their schools that is alien to their race. "You may say: That will make it difficult for our children. They will experience unpleasantness as a result. But it is better for the children to experience some unpleasantness and to know why than to have their souls warped and deformed. That which triumphed only through so much blood and tears will not be overcome without 'unpleasantness.'" If, on the other hand "we take our convictions so lightly that we will not make any sacrifices for them, then we should stick with the old ways, for in that case we are truly not yet worthy of freedom [...]. We German women who have chosen to openly profess our heathen faith look upon German women of all classes with the deepest longing and concern. Will you have the strength, sisters, to resume your old role as priestesses? Will you once again bring a victorious joyfulness into the world after all the tears and anxieties that a foreign faith has brought us? Will you once again raise your families and develop their conscience in freedom and with a sense of grandeur. Will you once again make honor and responsibility to oneself the core principles in the education of your children? Will you learn once again to place the *breed* above the individual, to love the tree more than the blossom? The triumph of the Nordic-heathen faith in the world stands or falls with you. We stand on the brink of a great new age. Let not all of us be found weak and unworthy." (p. 24)

# 7. Die Overbroocks

Eight years after *Nordische Frau und Nordischer Glaube* and nine years into the Nazi regime, a woman is again at the center of the novel *Die Overbroocks*, which the Princess dedicated to her son Heike. An incarnation of "Mother Earth," as the reader quickly learns, and at the same time an evident projection of the author herself, Irene von Werth is the daughter of an upstanding general in the Kaiser's army. Her life is set to be spent in rounds of receptions and parties attended by the members of other "good families." Though she is restive in this decorative and, in her own eyes, meaningless role, her parents – especially her mother – believe, as does virtually everybody in their social milieu, that the practice of a useful profession is inappropriate for a person of their daughter's station in society. (pp. 8, 17)[1] For such a young woman to take art lessons does not contravene social convention, however, and it is at art school that Irene meets the man who will help her to discover her true destiny and to break with the codes of behavior adhered to by her family and class.

Unlike Irene, who has been permitted to study art because it is regarded in her world as decorative, not a serious activity, Christian Overbroock is a dedicated artist. His art, he tells Irene in the exchange of letters between the two fellow-students on which the novel opens, is the alpha and omega of his existence, the one thing that gives it meaning. Nor is Christian a member of a privileged social class; he is the descendant of generations of "rough, rugged, faithful, and loyal […] peasants" who had tilled "the sacred earth," borne children, and "fought for their land" for six centuries on the same farm in Lower Saxony – until a time came when they succumbed to the lure of the city, lost their roots, and no longer had the strength "to let the fruit ripen slowly on the tree." (pp. 5, 23) Christian's father, a pastor, had inherited the farm from his older, childless brother, but had sold it, we learn, because – in his son's reproachful words – "he loved his profession more than the ancestral soil." (p. 23) (Christian, we are evidently to understand, is what his name implies by tradition and upbringing, but in his deepest being he is a son of the "holy" North German earth). Thus "the land plowed by generations became a memory in the family's blood-heritage."

Christian, however, feels the call of his blood intensely and is possessed by the desire and duty, as the last surviving male member of his family's "stock," to rescue and restore it by returning it to its ancestral roots in the harsh Northern land of Lower Saxony. In addition, following another inner call, "from which there is no escape – the call of blood," Christian has volunteered for military service in the imminent European war. It was not all the heroic talk about sacrifice, he writes Irene in August 1914, that moved him to enlist, but something much more real and serious: "a longing for authenticity," (p. 14) for "the overthrow and destruction of our well-mannered, deeply immoral civilization, the construction of a new and nobler social order, [and] the elimination of class distinctions and snobbery" in favor of a society in which people will be "valued for their character and their contributions." (p. 8) An alien, artificial, liberal-capitalist civilization, still clad in the tatters of an obsolete aristocratic order, will be replaced, in other words, by an authentic, communal, organic culture. Therein lies the true reason for the war, he asserts. It will be fought "so that truth can finally find a home again in the world." (p. 14) Having participated in the oath-swearing at the great meeting of German youth on the Hoher Meißner in 1913, he has no doubt that the goal must be "to liberate the German people from the spirit of the foreigner, from fawning and flattering and bowing and scraping, and from the riff-raff of foreign blood that is destroying everything we hold sacred." (p. 9) He often reflects, he tells Irene, on the *Edda*, the Old Norse saga he – like the author of *Nordische Frau und Nordischer Glaube* – considers "the noble remnant of the Bible of Germanic heathendom." "Out of destruction," he explains, "a new, more beautiful world is born, for which Modi (Courage) and Magni (Strength) rescue the life-giving hammer of Thor. That is what must come and what will come, if only we truly and earnestly will it." (p. 15) For this, Christian is prepared, indeed fully expects, to die. He also does not believe, as so many people seem to do, that the war will be over in a month. "What kind of frivolous Jingoism is that! If the goals are great, it will take years to realize them." (p. 11) When Irene complains that he dwells too much on his own death, he replies that he does so because he has a deep intuition about it, not because he desires to die. No one loves life more than he, he protests, the more so as he believes in no world beyond this one, no Heaven and no Hell. "To me the visible and the invisible world constitute a single, great All, in which my own life is like a drop of blood in the incomprehensibly sublime divine pulse-beat. The meaning of my existence, my creative participation in the course of events lies in giving rich content and conquering strength to this pulse-beat of the Divine." (p. 16)

Christian finally persuades Irene that "the law by which [she is] governed – that is, [her] blood – is an extraordinarily exacting and unconventional one" and that she should take part in the "All" by bearing him a son, who will one day restore the Overbroocks to their ancestral soil. "I have followed the path my blood prescribed, Christian," she tells him as she yields to his appeal. He falls into her lap murmuring "Mutter Erde! Mutter Erde!" [Mother Earth! Mother Earth!] (pp. 28-29)[2] At that moment he realizes that a sculpture of "Mutter Erde" on which he has been working has the features of Irene.

Almost immediately afterwards, Christian departs for the front. His letters to Irene express his admiration for her and a sense of partnership with her in a common cause. She is a true soldier's daughter, he tells her. "You followed the path you recognized was the right one for you deliberately, with a clear head, and a sense of purpose." (p. 34) He will always carry the memory of her at the moment of their parting – pale, but without tears, and even a smile on her lips. On 8 November 1914 she writes to him that she is pregnant with his child. "Now I can fulfill the deepest wish of your heart, Christian. The Overbroocks will not wither away like autumn leaves. No, they will bloom with the freshness of spring." (p. 41) She signs herself "Mutter Erde." A week later she receives news of Christian's heroic death – at which point the epistolary form adopted hitherto by the author is replaced by a third-person narrative.

Irene gives birth to twin sons, whom she names "Kraft" and "Hartmut" [Strength and Valor or Resoluteness] – no doubt with Modi and Magni, the sons of Thor in Christian's beloved *Edda* in mind. The narrator now communicates Irene's thoughts as she reflects on what she sees as the task that has fallen to her. "It was essential that this race of Overbroocks, to which Irene was to give new life, become better, more noble, more free, and more bold than the mass that the German Volk had been rolled into." (p. 57) Unwillingly, to placate her parents, she agrees to have the twins baptized, but "handing them over to [this ritual], the moral basis of which repelled her, felt like a crime against truthfulness. For it was impossible to burden these two beautiful creatures with the weight of original sin." (p. 79)

Meanwhile, the war is grinding on. Writing in 1942, by which time the "dagger in the back" theory of the 1918 defeat had become official history, the Princess presents her heroine as outraged by the "defeatist" talk she hears around her from "mass-men and profiteers," people with "no sense of purpose, no higher goals." (p. 61) By 1917 Irene has identified these as Jews and possibly – though this is not spelled out – capitalists and socialists. The urgent need of supplies, she complains, has provided an opportunity for "a small circle of hoarders with crooked noses and a business-sense they carry in their blood to size up the situation and exploit it to their advantage [...] In part deliberately, in part unconsciously, they thereby assist those forces that are working to bring this Volk, heroic beyond all measure and supremely capable of resistance, down to defeat." (p. 80) Those at home, she notes, are more despondent and defeatist than the men in combat at the front. "The body of the people is growing sick: Hatred is beginning to strike its blows internally instead of directing them outward to the enemy." (p. 82) In these circumstances, she feels more and more estranged from her own class. At a large, lavish party to celebrate the von Werths' silver wedding anniversary in the Adlon hotel, the best in Berlin, she feels isolated and imagines what Christian would have thought of the triviality and superficiality of those around her. Yet her own sister is obviously in her element and a cousin, who asks her why she is so withdrawn, is uncomprehending when she responds that she is pondering how even the war has changed nothing in these people. "No doubt he is a brave officer," she reflects with the same compassionate contempt the author of *Gott in mir* expressed for her family or the author of *Nordische Frau und Nordischer Glaube* for women unable to free themselves from Christianity. "One cannot demand more of him." Still, "Kraft and Helmut, her two blond-headed ones, have got to become like their father, not like those people here." (p. 86) To ensure that this will happen she brings them up in freedom, in the country, in a manner directly and deliberately opposed to her own upbringing. Often the freedom she gives them is dangerous, but she accepts that. On the contrary, her aim is to encourage them to be fearless and resolute.

To Irene, what we now refer to as the November Revolution of 1918 is simply an opportunity for every evil human instinct to throw off the inhibiting yoke of discipline. The end of the war is a humiliation: "not even a defeat redeemed by heroic combat, but a voluntary surrender out of weakness of will." The Kaiser's "departure and the abdication of all the princes, not a single one of whom had the strength to put his life on the line in support of the hereditary distinction of spirit [Geistesgnadentum] so often touted in good times," might well, she reflects, be "evidence enough that a certain historical period is – rightly – coming to an end." Hitherto she had hoped that people would be transformed by the war itself and that the inner hollowness of the ruling class would be filled with a new, nobler spirit, its thoughtless self-centeredness replaced by a deeper wisdom. But had she not had to observe over and over again that in all these years nothing had changed fundamentally? Had she not again and again wondered to herself: 'What still needs to happen for these people to recover authentic being?'" [damit diese Menschen wesentlich werden]. She re-reads Christian's letters and is "shattered to discover what he wrote about the nobility and the existing social order. How right he had been [...]. Yes, the old order had to collapse and be swept away so that there would be room for the New, the Greater Order to grow. If the coming time brought hardship, that had to be. Too much wrong had to be atoned for, too much that had been suppressed and buried had to be brought up into the light. But one day Spirit and Soul would be victorious over darkness and selfishness. When would that be? Would she live to experience it – an order in which each would greet the other in the light of the Sun as a brother in equality, in love, and in selfless devotion to a common goal named Germany?" (p. 96)

She now finds the traditional virtues of her class – stoic fortitude and obedience – insufficient, even reprehensible. During the revolutionary days in Berlin, her father is insulted by "two strangers dressed as sailors" It has become dangerous for an officer to walk in the street, she notes. Yet her father continues to serve the Majority Social Democratic government, "even though those currently occupying the seats of power stand for a view of the world directly opposed to his." "Just obey, always and to the letter," she reflects. "The main thing is that someone should be giving orders, it doesn't matter what one thinks of that person. So long, above all, as one doesn't have to make a decision oneself and act accordingly. But they all know how to complain. That they are good at." (pp. 97-98)

To bring up the "blond-headed" twins, as she wants to, and to fulfill what she feels deeply is her promise to her slain hero-husband, Irene has in the meantime gone to Süderhude in Lower Saxony to see whether she can acquire the Overbroocks' ancestral farm. She has come to love the strange, flat landscape, where "one learns to understand the concept of infinity" and has been moved by the tough, hardy inhabitants. She has even tried to learn their Low German dialect. But the farm is now occupied by a Catholic family from Silesia. Even though this does not sit well with the locals, it takes time and perseverance before Irene finally succeeds in buying back the farm and settling on it with her two boys. (pp. 62-73)

Shortly afterwards she receives a visit from an army comrade of Christian's, an officer angered and embittered by the contempt he and his comrades have met with on their return from the front. The officer tells Irene that he has responded by joining in the fight against *Spartakus*, the communist league allegedly at the heart of the 1918 Revolution, and recounts "with hate-filled pleasure the murder of Karl Liebknecht and Rosa Luxemburg." (p. 108) Irene admonishes him not to give up serving Germany: "Now, especially, that Germany is sick and suffering, she needs our love so that the New Order that is about to come can fight its way out of the darkness." Hohmann, the officer, asks what this "New Order" is and protests that he wants the old order back. "If the old order had been so good and had proved its value, it would not have disappeared so quickly from the scene," Irene replies. "I do not think it will ever come back. Moreover I do not wish it to." The officer springs to his feet in anger: "How can you, the widow of Christian Overbroock, who so loved his fatherland, say such a thing!" "I say it precisely because I am the wife of Christian Overbroock," is the answer. "You are very mistaken if you imagine that [Christian] fought and died for what you call the good, old and tried order. He fought for something he expected could only emerge out of the ruins of a dying age, for something brand new and hitherto unknown, for the victory of truthfulness and a better, nobler humanity." (p. 109) The officer begins to read the books in Christian's library – "socialist, philosophical, theological writings that he had hitherto steered clear of." (p. 112) He grows ever closer to Irene and asks her to marry him, but she refuses. "I am the mother of the Overbroocks." She cannot even be his "wife" for one night, though she admits that she is powerfully attracted to him. "There is no genuine love unless there is a readiness to let it bear fruit." How right Christian was to name you "Mother Earth," the officer replies sadly and admiringly. (pp. 109-12)

Meantime Irene is not finding it easy to run the farm. The locals respect her resourcefulness, resilience, and willingness to do hard physical work, but they are wary of her outspokenness, which they are unaccustomed to in a woman, and of her undisguised lack of interest in traditional religion. Though these peasants are by no means devout churchy types

[Betschwestern], the narrator explains – on the contrary, they are "as sober, clear-headed, and heroic" in this area of their lives as in all others – it was a centuries' old tradition among them that children be baptized and raised in religion and they are outraged when Irene demands that her boys be excused from religious instruction in the local school. When she attends a political meeting and speaks out, "it sounded like the purest communism," and they begin to wonder whether "the owner of the Overbroocks' farm might be a Bolshevist." (pp. 119-20) Still, they gradually get used to her. Though she remains the "foreigner," they cease to be suspicious of her independent ways. On her side, Irene becomes more and more attached to the farm; it is not only the home of her sons and the object of a promise made to Christian, she herself feels rooted in the land and her own life seems to her to have adopted its rhythms. It is becoming more and more difficult for her to run the farm, however, for in its dire need of money to pay off the cruelly high reparations debt imposed by the victors, the post-Armistice Weimar regime fleeces its own impoverished population. Moreover, the legal system is weighted against the peasant farmer. (p. 125)

At this difficult point, two young men named Karl and Wilhelm – a student of theology and a student of architecture – arrive at the farm and offer their services to her as farmhands. They explain that they are from the *Artam League*, founded in 1924 with the aim of promoting land settlements and encouraging German men and women to leave the cities and return to their homelands as farmers working the native soil. (p. 127) In defiance of their parents' wishes, Karl and Wilhelm have temporarily abandoned their professional studies and devoted themselves to studying and solving the agrarian problem, as well as the problem of race. "For the first time in all those years," the narrator comments, "Irene found justification of the path on which she had intuitively set out and of her desperate struggle for the native soil." (p. 129) The two idealistic young students seemed to her like a bridge between the time of the pre-war *Wandervögel* and other youth groups, who had already deliberately set out to combat a corrupt bourgeois world-view, and the point in time to which Hartmut and Kraft belonged. (p. 130) Even with the help of the two *Artamans*, however, she has to take out a loan in an effort to save the farm and in the end cannot meet her payments. Before the loan company can repossess the farm, Karl and Wilhelm want to burn it down, but Irene stops them. "That must not be. This farm and this earth, on which it stands, are eternal. We ourselves live only a short span of time, but long after we are gone the farm will still be there, a home for German men and women. What is happening now is only a transition. We [as individuals] do not count. It is the farm that must be preserved. As soon as Germany has re-risen, the farm too will rise again. And it is your task to see that that happens. Your job is to build. Negation is death, affirmation is life." (p. 136)

Having lost the farm, Irene has to move with the twins to a working-class neighborhood of Bremen, where the youngsters attend a Gymnasium and are struck by the contrast between the poor children they live among and "the spoiled sons of wealthy patrician families" they encounter at school. "Are they all part of the same people?" they ask themselves. As the years pass, Irene realizes that her boys have been transformed from children into fighters capable of building Germany's future. She notes with satisfaction that they have chosen to side with the disinherited youth of their own neighborhood and have turned away "almost with repugnance from the spoiled sons of the upper classes." (pp. 140-41)

Around this time, she receives a letter from relatives of Christian who, like many farming families from Lower Saxony, had emigrated to America. Now well-established and well-to-do farmers in Wisconsin, they have heard of her hardships and offer to pay the passage for her and the boys to emigrate and join them in Wisconsin. To Irene's great satisfaction, the boys refuse to leave Germany. At this very point, "something new and important takes center stage in her life": Kraft and Helmut join the *Hitler Youth*. (p. 143) Irene knew of the National Socialist Party, having heard about it from Karl and Wilhelm as early as 1928. She knew what its program was, had read a number of political pamphlets, and was awaiting further developments with eager anticipation. She had been turned off by the political squabbling of the 1920s, but she was still not completely won over to the Party, despite its massive growth. "As a North German born and bred, she looked with suspicion on anything that came from the South." (p. 144) Kraft and Helmut, however, are filled with enthusiasm. To them, "the fight for a Germany without the class hatred and snobbery they had observed in the two worlds they moved in, the Gymnasium and the working-class Bremen neighborhood where they lived, for a Germany in which there would be no more exploitation and no more usurious lending of the kind they had experienced on the Overbroock farm, for a Germany in which the dispossessed and despised proletariat would at long last find the way back to its native soil – to them that struggle seemed worthy of their infinite youthful capacity for dedication and self-sacrifice." (p. 144) It became the most important thing in their lives. They spent so much time with the *Hitler Youth* that in 1932 they were not promoted to the top grade in the Gymnasium. "Their teachers and classmates had felt not the slightest breath of the spirit of a new age." (p. 147) Moreover, the teachers had been displeased by the boys' constantly questioning them and challenging them. Finally Kraft and Helmut ask their mother if she will allow them to leave school in order to devote themselves entirely to the Party. Might they not later hold it against her that she had permitted them to cut short their education, she asks. No, they protest, their work for the *Hitler Youth* is more important than school. Irene grants them their wish. (p. 148)

Then one evening the boys fail to return home. The countryside is combed, every square inch of heath and moorland. Everyone participates in the search, especially the members of the *Hitler Youth*. But no trace of the boys is to be found. Soon winter sets in and snow begins to blanket the earth. A young lad suddenly appears to tell Irene that her boys will never be found. He insists that he himself had "nothing to do with it." But he belongs to a Communist youth group. The inevitable conclusion is drawn: Kraft and Helmut have been murdered by Communist youths. Karl and Wilhelm, who had been models for the twins, return and the search resumes, this time for the boys' bodies, but "the last resting-place of Christian's sons remained unknown, like that of their father, who also had died for Germany." (p. 160) Irene has become like a shell. She is tormented by doubts. Should she not have contented herself with having realized Christian's desire to ensure the continuity of his ancient peasant line? Why did she allow the boys to become involved in politics? On the other hand, she reflects, they had been so carried away by enthusiasm; and had not Christian himself said, "Many must fall"? (p. 161) She contemplates suicide. She has earned the right, she feels, to cast off the burden of life. She is held back by the thought "that it might be said of her that her godlessness and rejection of the Church had deprived her of solid ground beneath her feet and thrust her into the dark night of despair. No," she resolves, she will "not allow those hypocritical weaklings to celebrate a triumph." (p. 162) As she recalls passages from Christian's letters, she hears, like a fanfare sounding in her brain and overcoming everything else. "You, Irene, shall live. You must and will carry on the fight for Good in the world!" (p. 163)

With joy she learns the "great news" of the seizure of power on 30 January 1933. "That evening the bells rang out from every tower and steeple and rejoicing filled the streets." (p. 165) Wilhelm comes to her. She reaches out to him: "After all, it was not all pointless and in vain, Wilhelm," she says, and at last her tears flow freely. The change of regime in 1933 is followed by the arrival of the Overbroock relatives from Wisconsin, Georg and Lina. Though a great sadness clouds their lives – they are childless – they are so thrilled by the new Germany that they contemplate staying. At one point Lina – who, the narrator tells us, looks out on the world like an authentic peasant woman, "through wise eyes [...] firmly and clearly" – tells Irene that she now understands why Christian and his sons gave their lives for Germany. "One could never do that for America," she remarks. (p. 173)

Between Georg and Irene an unusual closeness develops. He feels that "when he takes her hand in his, he is holding Germany," and "when he gazes on her golden-haired beauty at his side, it is Germany that he sees walking in step with him." (p. 174) Lina senses Georg's happiness, but feels no jealousy. Suddenly, Irene wonders whether this man has a right to let his bloodline die out just because his wife is so dear to him that he will not abandon her. Lina herself had said that he should take a woman who can bear him children. (p. 176) As Irene and Georg stand together before Christian's sculpture of "Mutter Erde," she suddenly has a thought "so frightening and monstrous that she instinctively shut her eyes as though blinded by it. 'Not that; anything, but not that,' she feels her whole being cry out." (pp. 179-80) Later, she recalls Christian's words to her: "I consider you capable of taking on an extraordinary destiny." Has my destiny not been extraordinary enough, she asks herself. "Why am I always called on to do more?" Again she hears Christian's voice: "I have chosen you to be my wife and the mother of the Overbroocks." "Is my faithfulness to you worth so little?" she demands. "For nineteen years I have been faithful and God knows it was not always easy." (No doubt she is thinking of Hochmann). Christian's spirit, living within her, responds: "There is a fidelity that is greater than that." After a long, tense conversation with Christian's spirit, she capitulates. "Christian, dear Christian...I will do it all. You are right, a thousandfold." At this point Georg enters the room. She tells him he must buy the farm. "The homeland is calling on its sons." Soon afterwards, she adds, "You must have an heir, Georg." He is taken aback. "Irene!" "The homeland needs the ancient tree. It may not die," she responds. "Only one woman can give me that heir, Irene. Do you love me?" In response she looks directly at him and he "draws back before the bold expression in her eyes, which took in the reality of their present situation clearly and precisely." She explains to him that Lina wanted her to marry him, but that she cannot contemplate it. "I am the wife of the dead man and I cannot be the wife of another, but I can become the mother of the Overbroocks with his blessing [...]. The child will be yours, and Lina will be its mother." (p. 184)

Georg sails back to America to sell the farm in Wisconsin, taking with him the knowledge that Irene is pregnant with his child. (p. 186) Georg and Lina buy the Overbroocks family farm and recover their German citizenship. After three days in labor, Irene brings a son into the world. She spends four weeks in the hospital, recovering only very slowly. As soon as she can, she gives the child to Lina: "This is my and Georg's son and the heir to the Overbroock farm. Accept him, Lina, I beg you, as a gift from me and protect him as best you can. He is now unconditionally yours." (p. 191) Lina is taken aback. She knew nothing. Even Georg had not been informed of the child's birth, since Irene wanted Lina to be the first to learn of it. But Lina weakens. She feels excluded and for the first time experiences jealousy. Irene reasons with her: her readiness to sacrifice her marriage to Georg for the sake of the family has earned her the right to be the mother of the Overbroocks' heir. "Don't spoil everything with silly jealousy. Besides, is this about you, about us? The farm and the family line are far more important than us and our petty feelings, for we are like flies with a lifespan of a day." (p. 192) Lina accepts the child and names him Oldwig – the old term, she says, for the native soil and hearth.

On 21 June, the birthday of Kraft and Hartmut, "the fires of the summer solstice celebration were lighted all over Germany. Hundreds of young voices intoned the old festive songs, swore allegiance to Germany, and leapt as they did so through the flames as a symbol of purification and sloughing off of all everyday pettiness. It was as though in that hour every one was joined in a single chain throughout the entire Reich and a single great sacrificial pyre marked Germany's honor and revival." (p. 196) Irene came on the festivities as she emerged from the woods where she had been walking "and she saw that all was well." "Now I want to sleep, Christian," she murmurs. "I am very, very tired, and I think I have fulfilled my promise." From inside her consciousness, however, Christian tells her that she may yet again be needed. "No one may drop out before the hour has struck." She protests: "What you ask of me is superhuman, Christian." "Nothing is superhuman," he retorts. "Everyone lives the destiny allotted to him. There are no limits, except those that you set yourself through weakness or strength." "I cannot go on any more, Christian," she responds. "I cannot, and I will not." "You should not forget that you are a soldier's daughter,

Irene," he answers. But this time, the narrator tells us, Irene could not obey Christian. It was enough. She had done her duty, fulfilled her destiny. It was so quiet in the woods – how much more peaceful still it would be in eternal sleep. She felt happy, kissed the dewdrops on a wild rosebush, took off her clothes and untied her hair, "so that nothing added by man to nature would remain on her." Slowly she began walking into a lake. Suddenly, however, she is pulled back by the call of a lark, like the cry of a child. She realizes that she cannot simply abandon Oldwig. "No, she had to stand by him, and watch over him from afar." She writes to Karl, Wilhelm's friend, to say that she has decided to accept his invitation to come and live with him and his family.

The novel closes on the greeting "Heil Hitler!" and the signature: "Mutter Irene." (p. 200)

# 8. After 1945: Unrepentant Neo-Nazi

The catastrophic end of the Third Reich in 1945 had no effect on the Princess's outlook; it inhibited but did not change the character of her activities. She had to leave Munich, where she seems to have been living, and seek temporary refuge with the daughter of her former publisher Roselius in Bremen.[1] As nearly a quarter-century had passed since the publication of *Gott in mir*, and Roselius himself had died in 1943, it seems likely that the relationship the author had apparently maintained with the publisher and his family over the years was based on their common devotion to National Socialism and the Nordic idea.[2]

Doubtless the Princess's family fortune had not been completely destroyed, however, for she found her feet again fairly quickly. In 1947 she took part in a conspiratorial meeting of former Nazis in Hameln – known throughout the English-speaking world for its legendary hero, the pied piper – at which it was decided to infiltrate the Free Protestants of Rhine-Hesse and turn their group into a right-wing religious organization to be called the *Deutsche Unitarier Religionsgemeinschaft* [German Unitarian Religious Community]. From the outset, this organization distinguished itself from other Unitarian communities by emphasizing first, that it was German, and second, that it had nothing whatsoever to do with Christianity. As is made clear by the choice of the Hagal rune (already adopted by the author of *Nordische Frau und Nordischer Glaube*) as its emblem and by the ideological genealogy displayed on a "family tree" in a subsequent number of the organization's journal, the *DUR* was in fact a continuation of the *völkisch*, anti-Semitic, neo-pagan religious groups that had been intermittently encouraged, exploited, and held in check or even disbanded in the National Socialist era. As such, it was completely compatible with the pantheistic paganism of *Gott in mir* as well as with the philosophico-religious writings – which continued to be printed after the war – of another eminent *Nationalsozialistin*, Mathilde Ludendorff, the widow of the right-wing General Erich von Ludendorff. It was commonly referred to in the post-war Federal Republic as a "Nazi sect" even though that description was challenged in court on several occasions in an effort to ward off official proscription. What is certain is that its meetings did in fact provide a forum for prominent ex-Nazis and war criminals of all kinds. In the 1950s younger members of the organization were being advised to "choose their spouses only from among those of pure German blood."[3]

The Princess's co-conspirators at Hameln included the "SA poet" Herbert Böhme, the author and publisher Herbert Grabert, and the writer Eberhard Achterberg. Achterberg had been chief editor of Rosenberg's *Nationalsozialistische Monatshefte* and had headed the Department for "Judentum und Freimaurerei" [Jewry and Freemasonry] in Rosenberg's "Dienststelle für die Überwachung der gesamten geistigen und weltanschaulichen Schulung und Erziehung der NSDAP" [Office for Oversight of the Total Spiritual and Ideological Training and Education of the NSDAP]. Böhme, who succeeded the Princess as the organization's theological leader, also went on to found other extreme right-wing associations, such as the *Deutsches Kulturwerk Europäischen Geistes* in 1950, the aim of which was the protection and promotion of "volkhaft-konservative" literature. Grabert had been a leader of the pre-war *Deutsche Glaubensbewegung* and editor of the neo-pagan monthly *Deutscher Glaube*, as well as the author of *völkisch* works such as *Die völkische Aufgabe der Religionswissenschaft* [How the Study of Religion should Contribute to the Culture of the *Volk*] (1938) and *Der Glaube des deutschen Bauerntums: Eine weltanschauungskundliche und glaubensgeschichtliche Untersuchung* [The Religion of the German Peasantry: A Study in the History of Religion and Worldview] (1939). During the War he had served as an official in Rosenberg's Ministry for the Occupied Eastern Lands; in the post-war period, in addition to his participation in the founding of the *DUR*, he established an "Institut für deutsche Nachkriegsgeschichte," which concerned itself principally with the "Kriegsschuldlüge" [the lie about German war guilt], and a publishing house (1953), one of the publications of which – the journal *Deutschland in Geschichte und Gegenwart* – has been judged "the most important organ of 'revisionist' falsification of history in the Federal Republic."[4] The Princess's own role in the *DUR* was crucial, however. Without her early intellectual leadership, her promotion of the organization through frequent lecture tours in West Germany, and her decades-long participation in its activities, it has been said, "there would be no *DUR* today." As late as 1991 the Princess was still publishing in *DUR* affiliated magazines.[5]

Six years after the end of the war in Europe and the collapse of the National Socialist regime, the Princess made a grand heroic gesture in the aristocratic, self-sacrificing mode of the heroine of *Die Overbroocks*, where the chapter that tells of Irene's sacrifice of her twin sons to the National Socialist cause is entitled "Das heilige Opfer" [The Sacred Sacrifice]. Still recorded on several neo-Nazi and neo-Fascist websites over half a century later, this gesture – if the document supporting it is authentic – seems to confirm the claim in *Nordische Frau und Nordischer Glaube* that "even when a woman has been convinced of the unreasonableness of a position, she will hold tenaciously to its forms out of the instinctive need for constancy of her maternally protective nature."[6] In a letter to John McCloy, the American High Commissioner for Germany, dated Bremen, 10 February 1951, the Princess offered herself as a replacement for one of seven SS men from the Landsberg concentration camp who had been condemned to death as "so-called war criminals" – "und zwar für den unter ihnen, der die meisten Kinder durch seinen Tod vaterlos machen würde" [and specifically for the one among them whose death would make the largest number of children fatherless]. "I am an old National Socialist," she informed McCloy, aristocratically disdaining any attempt to conceal a commitment that circumstances alone, in her view, had rendered inopportune, "and it is my obligation, in accordance with a pledge I made to the *SS-Reichsführer* [Himmler] in 1930, to take care of members of the SS wherever and however it is possible for me to do so. I have always done my best to keep a promise made in the happy times of our hope for a better and more beautiful Germany and I want to keep that promise now too, in Germany's hour of deepest suffering. I do so in the spirit of the words of a song we used often to sing together on festive occasions: 'When all are unfaithful, we still keep the faith...'"[7] This astounding document (fig. 20) indicates clearly that, in the Princess's mind, there was nothing wrong with the ideas and actions of the SS. The allied victory and the regrettable (but perhaps not permanent) triumph of Western liberalism – as in the period after World War I – had simply made those ideas and actions inexpedient. And in such times especially it is the moral duty of truly free, independent-minded Nordic men and women, the

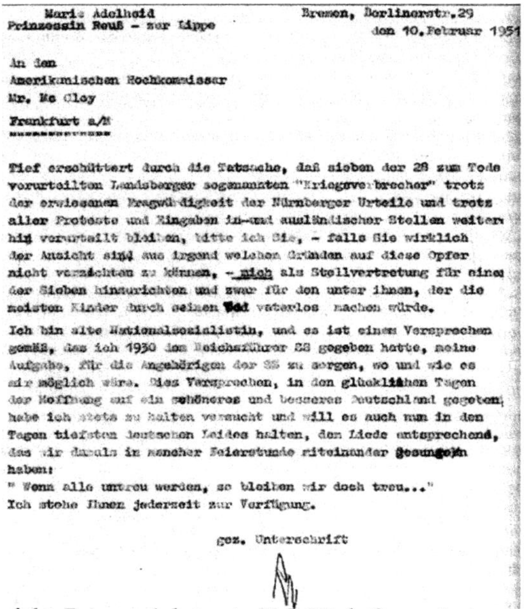

Marie Adelheid
Prinzessin Reuß - zur Lippe

Bremen, Berlinerstr.29
den 10.Februar 1951

An den
Amerikanischen Hochkommissar
Mr. Mc Cloy
Frankfurt a/M

Tief erschüttert durch die Tatsache, daß sieben der 28 zum Tode verurteilten Landsberger sogenannten "Kriegsverbrecher" trotz der erwiesenen Fragwürdigkeit der Nürnberger Urteile und trotz aller Proteste und Eingaben in-und ausländischer Stellen weiterhin verurteilt bleiben, bitte ich Sie, - falls Sie wirklich der Ansicht sind aus irgend welchen Gründen auf diese Opfer nicht verzichten zu können, - mich als Stellvertretung für einen der Sieben hinzurichten und zwar für den unter ihnen, der die meisten Kinder durch seinen Tod vaterlos machen würde.

Ich bin alte Nationalsozialistin, und es ist einem Versprechen gemäß, das ich 1930 dem Reichsführer SS gegeben hatte, meine Aufgabe, für die Angehörigen der SS zu sorgen, wo und wie es mir möglich wäre. Dies Versprechen, in den glücklichen Tagen der Hoffnung auf ein schöneres und besseres Deutschland gegeben, habe ich stets zu halten versucht und will es auch nun in den Tagen tiefsten deutschen Leides halten, dem Liede entsprechend, das wir damals in mancher Feierstunde miteinander gesungen haben:
" Wenn alle untreu werden, so bleiben wir doch treu..."
Ich stehe Ihnen jederzeit zur Verfügung.

gez. Unterschrift

20. Copy of the Princess's letter to U.S. High Commissioner McCloy.

The text reads:

Marie Adelheid
Prinzessin Reuß-zur Lippe

Bremen, Berliner Str. 29
den 10. Februar 1951

An den
Amerikanischen Hochkommissar
Mr. Mc Cloy
Frankfurt a/M

Tief erschüttert durch die Tatsache, daß sieben der 28 zum Tode verurteilten Landsberger sogenannten "Kriegsverbrecher" trotz der erwiesenen Fragwürdigkeit der Nürnberger Urteile und trotz aller Proteste und Eingaben in- und ausländischer Stellen weiterhin verurteilt bleiben, bitte ich Sie, falls Sie wirklich der Ansicht sind aus irgendwelchen Gründen auf diese Opfer nicht verzichten zu können, mich als Stellvertretung für einen der Sieben hinzurichten und zwar für den unter ihnen, der die meisten Kinder durch seinen Tod vaterlos machen würde.

Ich bin alte Nationalsozialistin, und es ist einem Versprechen gemäß, das ich 1930 dem Reichsführer SS gegeben hatte, meine Aufgabe, für die Angehörigen der SS zu sorgen, wo und wie es mir möglich wäre. Dieses Versprechen, in den glücklichen Tagen der Hoffnung auf ein schöneres und besseres Deutschland gegeben, habe ich stets zu halten versucht und will es auch nun in den Tage tiefsten deutschen Leides halten, dem Liede entsprechend, das wir damals in mancher Feierstunde miteinander gesungen haben:
" Wenn alle untreu werden, so bleiben wir doch treu…"
Ich stehe Ihnen jederzeit zur Verfügung.

gez. Unterschrift

heroic elite, not to swim with the tide but to stand up for the "untimely."

As she had been a co-founder of the *DUR*, the Princess was a co-founder in 1958 of the *Ahnenstätte Conneforde*, a burial ground in the district of Ammerland, about 30 kilometers north-west of Bremen, in the countryside in which, years before, she had located the Overbroocks' ancestral farmstead. The term "Ahnenstätte" [ancestral place] in place of the customary Christian term "Friedhof" was intended to underline the site's pagan, Germanic, and non-Christian character. Several such burial grounds, dating from both before and after World War II, still exist, though some have been closed by the civil authorities because of their connection with neo-Nazi movements. They are the favored burial grounds of former local NSDAP leaders. In principle, they are situated far from towns, in areas of wood or heath, weed and wild flowers, approachable only by footpaths. Cut flowers and cultivated gardens are scorned, sometimes expressly forbidden. Dates of birth and death are indicated on the stone grave markers by the runic symbols favored by the SS. (The Old Germanic Algaz-rune or man-rune, which the Nazis interpreted as life-rune, indicates date of birth; turned upside down, it indicates date of death). Swastikas as well as other runic signs can be seen, but no crosses. The *Ahnenstätte* was and is also a favored locale for pagan religious rites like the celebration of summer and winter solstices. Conneforde had in fact already been a cult site for the celebration of the summer solstice under the Nazis.[8]

The message of the *Ahnenstätte* – a Blood and Soil interpretation of the Goethean *Stirb und werde* that the Princess had chosen as the envoy of her *Gott in mir* of 1921 and referred to repeatedly in her subsequent writings – was and is clear: the dead have not vanished, they have rejoined the eternal natural cycle of birth and death in the soil from which they emerged and from which they and their eternally renewable family line are as inseparable as the local trees or grasses.[9] The model *Ahnenstätte*, also in Lower Saxony, was no doubt Hilligenloh, established in 1932 by the *völkisch*, racist, anti-Christian, and neopagan *Verein Deutschvolk* of Erich and Mathilde von Ludendorff.[10]

There is nothing surprising about the Princess's role the founding of *Ahnenstätte Conneforde*. Through her mentor Darré, she had been connected before the War with another institution that was closely related to the *Ahnenstätte*, namely *Ahnenerbe*. Founded in 1935, *Ahnenerbe* was the brainchild of Heinrich Himmler, the head of the SS, his friend Darré, and Herman Wirth, the Dutch-German champion of the Nordic idea and protégé of Roselius. With headquarters at Himmler's Wewelsburg Castle, near Paderborn, and with 46 separate departments, many headed by university professors, *Ahnenerbe* was envisaged by Himmler as the spiritual and scientific center of the SS, which he imagined as a kind of Aryan knighthood, a "Neuer Adel," a new aristocracy of Germanic blood and soil. (Though it was not formally incorporated into the SS until 1940, most of its academic and medical research staff – later responsible for some of the horrendous medical "experiments" of the Nazis – were at least honorary members of the SS.) Research was undertaken into ancient Nordic culture in order to promote the goal – fervently espoused by Himmler, Darré, and the Princess, though for tactical reasons not given very wide publicity – of re-establishing a supposed ancient Aryan religion in Germany as a spiritual basis for the new National Socialist world order, in place of and in opposition to an alien, "Oriental" Christianity.[11] The *Ahnenstätte* thus contributed to the larger aims of *Ahnenerbe*.

Through her writing the Princess continued to play her part in the propagation of right-wing and neo-Nazi ideas. 1960 saw the publication of *Weltfrömmigkeit*, a volume of poems, some borrowed from the earlier *Gott in mir*, in which she again gave lyrical expression to the heroic Nietzschean-aristocratic ideal represented in novelistic form in the figure of Irene in *Die Overbroocks* (and, in the Princess's eyes, in reality in the members of the elite corps founded by "Reichsführer-SS" Heinrich Himmler, to whom she declared in her letter to High Commissioner McCloy that she had sworn an oath of allegiance): that of the strong-willed, free-spirited, unsentimental, hard-thinking, and fearless individual, who has cast aside the illusions and petty consolations of the weak and joyfully assumed his or her destiny. Though its specific character may vary, the general shape of that destiny is always the same: it is to play a willing and active part, without thought of what to others might count as success of failure, in the mysterious course, at once ever changing and unending, of the universe – and not least in the course of human history – in full confidence that the individual participates, through his or her *volk*, in the divine nature of the universe or the "All" and will be reabsorbed into the "All" once his or her destiny has been fulfilled.

In 1961, under the title *Entlarvte Heuchelei* [Hypocrisy Unmasked] (Wiesbaden: Priester), the Princess published her translation into German of *Perpetual War for Perpetual Peace: A Critical Examination of the Foreign Policy of Franklin Delano Roosevelt and its Aftermath*, a collection of essays edited by the American historian Harry Elmer Barnes, including two by the editor himself. Barnes was one of the earliest "revisionist" historians. A study of the Great War, in which he challenged the established account of German responsibility, had been published by Knopf in New York in 1926, and had been accepted as a serious work of scholarship by the historical profession. Subsequently, however, Barnes – who bitterly opposed American action against Germany in the late 1930s and 40s – extended his critique to the Second World War, and then to the generally accepted account of the Holocaust. At that point his scholarship began to be perceived as having been subordinated to an ideological agenda; he lost his standing among his fellow historians; and his work had to be published by an undistinguished far-right press. The text translated by the Princess was published by Caxton Printers in Caldwell, Idaho.[12]

The Barnes translation was followed in 1965 by a translation into German, under the title *Das Drama der Juden Europas: Eine technische Studie* (Hanover: Hans Pfeiffer Verlag), of *Le Drame des juifs européens* (Paris: Les Sept Couleurs, 1964) by Paul Rassinier, a onetime Communist and concentration camp inmate, who was subsequently a Socialist *député* in the French parliament. In the original French this book had in fact been favorably reviewed in the *Journal of Historical Review*, the organ of the Holocaust-denying Institute for Historical Review, by none other than Barnes, whom the Institute characterizes on its website as "the founding father of historical revisionism," and who went on to translate it into English himself. (It was published as *The Drama of the European Jews* [Silver Spring, MD: Steppingstones Publications, 1975]). In the introduction to a 1977 republication of this text, together with translations of other works by Rassinier, under the title *Debunking the Genocide Myth: A Study of the Nazi Concentration Camps and the Alleged Extermination of European Jewry* (Los Angeles: The Noontide Press) the connection between Rassinier and Barnes was clearly spelled out. Rassinier was described here as "an important revisionist historian in the tradition of the late American historian, Harry Elmer Barnes." (p. xvi)

The Princess continued her post-war career as a self-described faithful "alte Nationalsozialistin" by financially supporting the periodical *Die Bauernschaft*, launched in 1969 by Thies Christophersen. Christophersen, a notorious neo-Nazi, was subsequently threatened with imprisonment in Germany for spreading Nazi propaganda and race hatred and finally had to leave Germany and settle in Denmark. His periodical, of which the Princess herself assumed the editorship in 1971, kept alive the *Blut und*

*Boden* ideology fervently promoted both by the Princess's mentor Darré and, as we have seen, by the Princess herself in her pre-War and wartime writings. In 1971 Christophersen launched another publishing venture: *Kritik: Die Stimme des Volkes*, a series of explicitly neo-Nazi writings. Typical titles are *Die Auschwitz-Lüge* [The Auschwitz Lie] (1973) by Christophersen himself, followed shortly afterwards by his *Der Auschwitz-Betrug* [The Auschwitz Deception], a collection of documents and readers' letters relating to the earlier publication,[13] *Ist Rassenbewusstsein verwerflich?* [Is Race Consciousness Reprehensible?] (1975) by G. A. Amaudruz, and *Rassenethik* [Race Ethics] (1977) by René Binet.

In 1978 a collection of fourteen poems by the Princess, entitled *Freundesgruß* (fig. 21), appeared in Christophersen's series, with markedly traditional woodcut illustrations by the popular Nazi artist Georg Sluyterman von Langeweyde, whose mother was from Lower Saxony (where the Overbroocks had their farm) and whose work is largely devoted to celebrating the hard lives of the region's peasants as well as heroic figures from German history and legend. Whereas the typographic layout of the earlier post-war collection of poems, *Weltfrömmigkeit*, had been uncharacteristically modern, somewhat reminiscent of art deco, with *Freundesgruß*, the Princess reverted to *Fraktur*, the typeface usually thought of as characteristically "German" and adopted in all her pre-war writings.[14]

The poems in the new collection range in length from 12 to 58 lines and are of varying structure, as in the two previous collections. Some are made up of traditional four-line, mostly rhyming pentameter verses, others use hexameters, others still mix lines of uneven length. Each poem, with only one exception, carries a date, from 1918 to 1964, along with its title. (In two cases the date *is* the title). Each expresses thoughts and feelings aroused by and associated in the mind of the poet with the historical date in the title. It is, of course, possible that the dates refer to the year of composition of the poem. Two ("Glaube. 1950" and "Glück. 1946") had in fact already appeared, untitled, as the opening poems of the earlier post-war collection, *Weltfrömmigkeit*. It is more likely, however, in my view, that the dates are an integral part of the title of each, so that the collection as a whole, arranged as it is chronologically, should be read as the poet's reflections on and response to fifty tumultuous years of German history, from the disaster of 1918, through the period of triumphant National Socialism, to the Second World War, the defeat of what she continues to regard as a great and noble ideal by the combined hostile forces of the capitalist West and

21. Cover of the Princess's collection of poems *Freundesgruß* in the extreme rightwing series *Kritik: Die Stimme des Volkes* (1978).

the communist East, the efforts of the victors to destroy the unity and break the spirit of her beloved German *volk*, and the irrepressible hope, among a resilient, faithful few, in the ultimate triumph of their cause. By entitling the collection *Freundesgruß* [Greeting from a Friend] the Princess indicates that it is addressed to a readership of "friends" – like-minded former Nazis, neo-pagans, readers of *Kritik* – by whom she can expect her reflections to be immediately understood and shared.

A sampling of these poems, albeit in summary or fairly literal translation, will convey at least some sense of the subject matter and the tone. It will be seen that the dominant themes of the Princess's writing have changed very little: mourning and disillusionment in 1918 at the collapse of the imperial regime, together with willingness to write that old regime off as feeble, corrupt, and having in the end deserved its fate, along with determination to stake everything on building a new Germany; selfless courage, heroism, activism, and readiness to sacrifice what is held most dear as the qualities required for the construction of a New Order that its champions will probably not live to witness; defiant loyalty to the "dream of the Reich" even after its catastrophic destruction in 1945; joyful acceptance of change as the law of the universe and with it the consoling guarantee that no victory is lasting, no defeat final; victory over death through willing surrender of individuality and identification with the *volk* and ultimately with the Cosmos. In a word: *stirb und werde!* And everywhere the pervasive symbolism of fire and light, along with worship of the Sun – the common repertory of neo-Gnostic Christians, neo-pagans, and National Socialists, as well as of those on the Left who also sought to fuse religion and political ideology.

### From *9. November 1918*

[...]

In the west darkness falls and the sun goes down.
Even so does dread sink nightly over Prussia.
Except that the sun smiles anew with the new day,
while here what has been lost will never return.

[Im Westen dunkelt's und die Sonne sinkt.
So sinkt auch nächtlich Graun auf Preußen nieder.
Nur daß mit neuem Tag neu Sonne winkt,
hier aber kommt Verlorenes nicht wieder.]

### *Ausblick. 1918* [Prospect. 1918]

The order of the day is: Be strong,
and, head held high,
proudly bear the inevitable.
It is useless to lament and wail
over that of which by favor of fate we have been robbed!

With fresh resolve look ahead!
Let not your courage flag!
Life helps those alone who bravely battle and fight!
The will to act can alone master the world
and lay hands on the horn of salvation.

[Jetzt heißt es: stark sein,
mit erhob'nem Haupt
das Unabänderliche stolz zu tragen.
Es nützt ja nichts, zu jammern und zu klagen
um das, was uns des Schicksals Gunst geraubt!

Frisch vorwärts schaun!
Den Mut nicht sinken lassen!
Das Leben hilft nur dem, der tapfer kämpft und ringt!
Tatkraft allein ist's, die die Welt bezwingt,
vermag allein das Horn des Heils zu fassen.]

## *Silvesternacht 1918* [New Year's Eve 1918]

This poem describes the last day of a terrible year in Germany's history as marking "the end of a great era, a glorious era that began in victory and joyfulness." But the poet sees streak of light on the horizon and she goes "kämpfend, glaubend" [fighting and firm in faith] toward it. "Good is victorious!" she cries, despite everything. "Let me be its warrior!" The poet's underlying response to the disaster of 1918 is unmistakably the familiar: "Stirb und werde!"

## *Pfingstfeuer in Guteborn 1928* [Whitsun Bonfire in Guteborn 1928]

The point of departure and central image of this poem is the fire that is traditionally lit in many parts of Germany to symbolize the descent of the Holy Spirit at Pentecost. The Pentecost fire is also a symbol of purification and, in some areas, a celebration of the end of winter and the arrival of spring. It is highly likely that it was the pre-Christian origin of that aspect of the "Pfingstfeuer" that attracted the Princess's attention. As we saw earlier, she took part herself in a celebration of the summer solstice in 1930. If the traditional *Pfingstfeuer* adapted pagan customs and rituals to Christianity, the Princess's poem translates the Christian desire for grace, the sloughing off of the old Adam and entry into a *vita nuova*, into a political commitment. The *Pfingstfeuer* that is the occasion of her reflections seems more like a gathering of National Socialists than of Christians. In addition, it is unlikely to have slipped the Princess's mind that the castle at Guteborn was the scene, on 13 November 1918, of the abdication of King Friedrich August III of Saxony. Something new is thus presented as rising from the ashes of the old ("stirb und werde!" yet again) and the place-name helps to anchor the poem in the concrete history that the collection as a whole is intended to evoke.

> [...]
> We stand around the fire hand in hand.
>
> Songs and fine words fill the air.
> Around you there is an intoxicating atmosphere of heroism and honor.
> But within you I sense the weight of earthly concerns,
> A fervent desire to be reconciled with happiness.
>
> Not so, friends! - Here in these flames
> I see a stake raised,
> on it all the best and brightest burn.
> Subhuman hatred destroys the blood of the North.

## Brownshirt Princess

[...]

You and I and all who stand here
will be sacrificed for the sake of New Life,
and must surrender ourselves and all that is dearest to us
without ever witnessing success or reward.

Have you thought of this and taken it to heart?
Are you still defiant and resolved?
Have you, living still, already conquered death?
Does your heart draw you toward sacrifice?

If so, then sing, friends. Nothing can make us afraid.

[...]

From our death God will awaken victory!

[...]

Wir stehn um das Feuer Hand in Hand.

[Lieder klingen auf und Worte tönen,
Um Euch ist ein Rausch von Heldenehre,
In Euch aber fühl' ich Erdenschwere,
Heissen Wunsch, dem Glück sich zu versöhnen.

Nicht so, Freunde! – Hier in dieser Glut
seh ich einen Scheiterhauf sich schichten,
darauf brennen all die Hellen, Lichten.
Untermenschenhaß zerstört des Nordens Blut.

[...]

Du und ich und alle, die hier stehen,
werden Opfer sein für neues Leben,
müssen uns und unser Liebstes geben,
ohne je Erfolg und Lohn zu sehen.

Habt ihr dies bedacht in tiefstem Sinn?
Seid ihr dennoch trotzig und durchdrungen?
Habt den Tod ihr lebend schon bezwungen,
Zieht euch euer Herz zum Opfer hin?

Dann, ihr Freunde, singt! Nichts kann uns schrecken.

[...]

Gott wird Sieg aus unserm Tod erwecken! ]

*Weihelied. 1930* [Song of Consecration. 1930]

    Rise up, you beautiful, solemn flames,
    out of the mysterious depths of night,
    Bring us, who are also born of fire,
    and bound together by a single shared desire,
    at this ceremony the greeting of eternal light.

    We are few, scattered fighters,
    around us storms the unreason of the world;
    Glorious light, we are those who pave the way
    For your brightness to spread further, ever further,
    until it illuminates our people's night.

    May our work, begun in joy,
    glow with an inner fire.
    We know that victory will be ours –
    though our lives may be lost to achieve it –
    that out of us the new Reich will blossom.

    [Steigt empor, ihr schönen, ernsten Flammen,
    aus der Nacht geheimnisvollem Grund,
    Bringet uns, die auch vom Feuer stammen,
    und die gleiches Wünschen band zusammen,
    ew'gen Lichts Gruß zur Feierstund'.

    Wir sind wenige, versprengte Streiter,
    um uns tobt die Unvernunft der Welt;
    Schönes Licht, wir sind dir Wegbereiter,
    Daß dein Schein dringt weiter, immer weiter,
    bis er unseres Volkes Nacht erhellt.

    Unser Schaffen, das wir froh beginnen,
    sei von Feuer innerlich durchglüht.
    Ja, wir wissen's wohl daß wir gewinnen,
    – mag auch unser Leben drob zerrinnen, –
    daß aus uns das neue Reich erblüht! –]

*Schneeflocke. 1944* [Snowflake. 1944]

In this somewhat longer poem of 37 non-rhyming hexameter lines, the snowflake serves as a symbol of an individual human life informed by love – love for and dedication to a loved one and, at the same time, a larger Whole embracing all individuals. More specifically, the date defines the snowflake's errant path, destruction, and resurrection in a new form as the fate of the Princess herself and of her fellowship of committed National Socialists.

> Shimmering flake, you seem to dance your way down from heaven.
> Do you float down impassive, blindly borne by chance?
> Are you aware of beginnings and ends? Did you feel pain and,
> child torn from your origin, as you left for ever
> the cloud that lovingly carried and protected you?
>
> Or, dainty one, are you full of sweet longing
> to see again one who left the cloud before you
> and, bold and fearless, took the path to the unknown? –
> How you hurry after him, good-hearted one, unsuspecting – disregarding
> the eternal universal law that love admits of no return.
>
> Gleaming, a shining star, you saw your friend disappear.
> He still waved laughingly to you as he led, fairer than all,
> his round of well-formed playmates.
>
> But you felt your childlike heart contract in sharp longing.
> You threw yourself after him and foundered, sank into the bottomless
>   abyss. –
> Raging whirlwinds seized hold of you, thrusting you now downwards
> out of the measured path, now up, then suddenly down again into the
>   depths.
>
> Then the loved one slipped hopelessly out of your sight. –
>
> Shimmering, fragile flake, lovely likeness of the stars,
> exhausted, deathly tired, fainting and hurting in every limb,
> you sought shelter for your tender body on my windowsill.
> All around you many others piled up, loved and forgotten like you. –
>
> But the one among them all who had touched your soul,
> drawn you to the earth, the source of your pain and your fate –
> has long since gone under, nameless, and merged with the mass.
> You will never find him again, lovely little sister.
>
> Do not weep now because you are dying, hit by the warm breath of my
>   room.
> Dying is nothing, it is not a final point. Your comrade died too. –
>
> But now your two currents can freely embrace.
> Having cast off all weight and need, they will run down
> deep into the darkening night of the sheltering, cooling realm of earth,
> in order to rise upward again, in fleeting swirls of misty veils,
> until, when divinely measured time has run its unknown course,
> you will again begin your descent, yet this time as one,

and only as a precious silver drop of quietly contented dew
shimmering tenderly in the starry night on satin moss.

[Schimmernde Flocke, im Tanz scheinst du vom Himmel zu schweben.
Gleitest du fühllos hinab, blindlings vom Zufall getragen?
Kennst du Beginnen und Ende? Leidest du schmerzliche Qual,
da aus der Wolke heraus, du losgerissenes Kind,
scheidest für immer von ihr, die liebend dich trug und behütend?

Oder bist, Zierliche du, voll von süßem Verlangen,
einen bald wieder zu sehen, der vor dir die Wolke verließ,
furchtlos und kühn nahm den Weg Unbekanntem entgegen? –
Wie doch du Gute ihm nacheilst, Ahnungslose – mißachtend
ewiges Weltengesetz, daß Rückkehr versagt ist der Liebe.

Leuchtend, ein strahlender Stern, sahst du den Freund dort entschwinden,
winkte noch lachend dir zu, da er führte den Reigen
wohlgestalteter Gespielen, doch so viel schöner als sie.

Aber dein kindliches Herz krampfte sich brennend in Sehnsucht.
Stürzest ihm nach und versankst, sankest ins Bodenlose. –
Faßten dich wütende Wirbel, aus der gemessenen Bahn
jählings dich schleudernd hinab und hinauf und wieder zur Tiefe.

Da deinen Blicken entschwand hoffnungslose der Geliebte. –

Schimmernde, zärtliche Flocke, liebliches Abbild der Sterne,
todesmatt und erschöpft, schwindlig mit schmerzenden Gliedern
bargst du den zierlichen Leib auf meinem Fenstergesims.
Ringsum türmten sich viele, geliebt und vergessen gleich dir. –

Doch von allen der Eine, der deine Seele berührte,
der dich zur Erde gejagt, schmerzhaftes Schicksal dir wurde –
längst ist er untergetaucht, namenlos in der Masse.
Findest ihn nimmermehr, kleine, liebliche Schwester.
Weine nun nicht, weil du stirbst, vom Hauch meiner Stube getroffen.
Sterben ist nichts, ist kein Ziel. Dein Geselle starb auch. –

Aber nun können sich frei euere Ströme umschlingen.
Bar aller Last, aller Not nieder werden sie rinnen
tief in die dunkelnde Nacht bergenden, kühlenden Erdreichs
um alsdann, flüchtig von dort wallend in nebligen Schleiern,
aufwärts zu steigen, hinauf, bis ihr dann, wenn erfüllt sich
göttlich gemessener Zeit unbekannter Verlauf,
wieder den Abstieg beginnt, diesmal gemeinsam jedoch,
einzig des wunschlosen Taus köstlicher, silbriger Tropfen
schimmernd in sternheller Nacht zärtlich auf samtenem Moos.]

## *Wintersonnenwende. 1945* [Winter Solstice. 1945]

In Germany's darkest winter, the faithful National Socialist finds reassurance in the winter solstice that darkness will be followed by light, winter by spring, and death by rebirth. *Stirb und werde* once again brings consolation and an austere confidence.

> Our hope was struck harder
> than any human heart could have imagined.
> We had to carry to the grave everything
> that had made life bright and joyful.
>
> Freezing and starving through the streets
> run those who only yesterday bathed in heroic light,
> foreign hatred has robbed them of their well-earned reward
> and pressed into their hands the beggar's staff.
>
> And yet: today is solstice time,
> ceremoniously announcing, as for a thousand,
> for thousands of years, the eternal truth
> that there is CHANGE, but never an END.
>
> Our little human hearts demand
> that everything should be arranged as we intend,
> thus, much will appear hopeless to us
> only because our timidity makes us shrink from it.
>
> Do we know what lies slumbering
> in the womb of time, pressing for resurrection?
> Our poor, short lives barely capture
> a speck of dust of the vast universe.
>
> Before the miracle of this holy night
> we bend our knees in the courage of faith:
> it will turn out otherwise than we thought,
> but whatever serves change is GOOD.
>
> [Unser Hoffen ward so tief geschlagen,
> wie kein Menschenherz es je gedacht.
> Alles mußten wir zu Grabe tragen,
> was das Leben hell und froh gemacht.
>
> Frierend, hungernd laufen durch die Gassen,
> die noch gestern Heldenglanz umgab,
> den verdienten Lohn raubt' fremdes Hassen,
> drückt in ihre Hand den Bettelstab.
>
> Aber dennoch: heut ist Sonnenwende
> wie vor tausend, abertausend Jahr',

kündet feierlich, was ewig war,
daß es WANDEL gibt, doch niemals ENDE.

Unser kleines Menschenherz verlangt,
daß sich alles fügt, wie wir es meinen,
und so will uns vieles trostlos scheinen,
nur weil uns'rer Zagheit davor bangt.

Wissen wir denn, was im Zeitenschoß
schlummert und zur Auferstehung drängt?
Unsres armes, kurzes Leben fängt
ja ein Staubkorn kaum der Welt so groß.

Vor dem Wunder dieser heil'gen Nacht
beugen wir das Knie in Glaubensmut:
anders wird es wohl als wir's gedacht
aber was dem Wandel dient ist GUT. –]

**From *Glück. 1946* [Happiness. 1946]**

The poem opens on an expression of gratitude for the beauty of the world and continues:

Will the pain we are living through
More deeply and fully submit to us?
Is not every defeat a path to victory,
to greater growth, to the rousing of energy?

Happiness does not mean standstill and satisfied contentment.

Happiness, true happiness without end
is having grown into union with the All, being one with it,
its ups and downs, its mountains and deep ravines, –
it is like music, blessed repose of the heart,
even in the face of death,
indestructible and eternal.

[Will sich das Leid uns ergeben,
das tiefer und voller wir leben?
Jede Niederlage, ist sie ein Weg nicht zum Sieg,
zum größer Wachsen, zum Kräfte erwecken? –

Glück heißt nicht Stillstand und sattes Behagen.

Glück, wirkliches Glück ohne Ende
ist Einssein, ist innig Verwachsensein mit dem All,
seinem Hinauf und Hinab, seinem Bergen und Schluchten, -
ist wie Musik, ist selige Ruhe des Herzens
noch im Angesichte des Todes,
unzerstörbar und ewig.]

### *Die Internierten. 1947* [Those Interned. 1947]

Grieve not that your best years
are slipping away unused behind bars,
that you must stand in the wings, unable to act,
that you are spared no bitterness.

Dear Brothers, our holy Reich
became a pile of ruins without precedent.
Joy had to give place to deepest grief,
fresh cheeks were bleached by care.

Foreign breath blows bitter cold winds.
It has driven away honor, loyalty, and valor,
and the few who stayed true
are like outcasts in the wilderness.

Will there be a resurrection some day?
We here, on the outside, can scarcely hope so,
for our whole land lies exposed to Evil.
and in the darkness no light is to be seen.

You took our beautiful faith with you.
Hold fast to it, hide it away in your ranks,
rescue it for a future tomorrow,
so that one day it may step forward again into the sunlight.

That you exist, that the enemy dishonors you,
is the only guarantee we still retain
that the dream of the Reich to which we dedicated ourselves
cannot fade and will last forever.

We beseech you: whatever you do,
hold fast to the loyalty you once swore;
never let yourself be dishonored by base repentance;
let us know that you are still Germany!

[Trauert nicht, daß Eure besten Jahre
hinter Gittern ungenutzt vergeh'n,
daß Ihr tatlos müßt beiseite steh'n,
man Euch keine Bitternis erspare.

Liebe Brüder, unser heil'ges Reich
ward zum Trümmerhaufen ohnegleichen,
Freude mußte tiefstem Jammer weichen,
Kummer färbte frische Wangen bleich.

Fremder Hauch weht bitterkalten Wind,
Ehre, Treu und Mut hat er vertrieben,

und die Wenigen, die fest geblieben,
wie Verstoß'ne in der Wüste sind.

Gibt es einmal noch ein Aufersteh'n?
Wir hier draußen können kaum noch hoffen,
steht doch alles Land dem Bösen offen,
ist vor Finsternis kein Licht zu seh'n.

Ihr nahmt unsern schönen Glauben mit.
Haltet ihn in Euren Reih'n geborgen,
rettet ihn hinüber in ein Morgen,
daß einst neu ans Sonnenlicht er tritt.

Daß Ihr seid, daß Euch der Feind entehrt,
ist die einzige Gewähr, die uns geblieben,
daß der Traum vom Reich, dem wir verschrieben
nicht vergehen kann und ewig währt.

Wir beschwören Euch: wie man's auch treibt
haltet fest die einst gelobte Treue,
schändet niemals Euch durch nied're Reue,
laßt uns wissen, daß Ihr Deutschland bleibt! –]

### *Glaube. 1950* [Faith. 1950]

This poem, one of the two that were published earlier in *Weltfrömmigkeit*, reads like a verbal equivalent of the popular image *Lichtgebet* [Prayer of Light], first created by the artist Hugo Höppener, better known as Fidus, in the late nineteenth century. Sold as a postcard at the great German youth meeting on the Hoher Meißner in 1913, Fidus's image was reworked many times and hung in inexpensive reproductions of one version or another in hundreds of thousands of German homes. In the *Weltfrömmigkeit* version, each of the three verses is followed by a runic symbol, the first by the "Algiz" or "Life" rune that has the shape of Fidus's praying youth with arms outstretched toward the light. (See Appendix B, Image Portfolio 2)

I have no desire to kneel before God! –
No, I will stand tall and erect,
both arms outstretched upwards,
reaching high into the clouds,

helping to bear the radiant sun,
exultant, fearless, humbly blessed,
having surrendered myself completely
to the eternal cosmic round.

## Brownshirt Princess

I am nothing apart from the All,
nothing apart from its divine workings.
But the world would be lonely and poor
Without me, the loving-seeing soul.

[Nicht zu knieen drängt's mich vor Gott! –
Nein, hoch aufgereckt will ich stehen,
beide Arme gebreitet nach oben,
bis in die Wolken hinauf zu greifen,

helfend die leuchtende Sonne zu tragen,
jauchzend, furchtlos und demutsvollselig,
hingegeben einzig und ganz
an des Weltenlaufs ewigen Reigen. –

Nichts bin ich ohne das All,
nichts ohne sein göttliches Walten.
Aber die Welt wäre einsam und arm
Ohne mich, die liebend erkennende Seele.]

# 9. Some Concluding Reflections on the Brownshirt Princess

Marie Adelheid Prinzessin Reuß-zur Lippe continued to write and publish neo-Nazi texts until 1990, never deviating from the line she had begun to trace in the long poem that Vogeler had illustrated and Roselius had published, seven decades earlier, in his Angelsachsen Verlag. By the time of her death in 1993 she had amply earned the sobriquet of "die braune Prinzessin" [the brownshirt Princess] bestowed on her by posterity.[1]

Even though our tendency is to dismiss Nazi art and literature as kitsch or propaganda – which they most often are – Marie Adelheid's writing bears witness to a degree of earnest conviction that presents a challenge to the present-day reader. There seems to be little reason to doubt the sincerity of her desire to liberate women from traditional domesticity, for instance, or to rehabilitate the natural and physical aspects of human existence, or to resolve the destructive conflicts produced by laissez-faire economics and an oppressive moral code. How was it possible for a regime and an ideology of unparalleled inhumanity and destructiveness to persuade an educated and not unintelligent individual that it offered an answer to the problems of which she was so keenly aware, and to inspire in a writer of modest but real literary talent such fanatical loyalty and dedication? That is the question that seems to me to be raised by this account of the Princess's *Gott in mir* and of her subsequent career.

There is no simple or obvious answer. A part of the answer may, however, be found in the literary work itself. Most readers of the Princess's writings will be struck by the prevalence of cliché formulae and the emphasis on subjective feeling in them. Intellectual analysis and understanding hardly figure in her work; if anything they are rejected as alien and alienating. The focus is at all times on intuited knowledge and understanding, the knowledge and understanding that are transmitted, as it were, through the blood of the community, and on the quality, intensity and authenticity of feeling, on feeling for its own sake. The occasions or objects of feeling are barely described or defined at all, but appear as vague, intuited entities, such as "Volk," "Blood," "Soil," which, despite their seeming earthiness, must strike the reader who does not share the Princess's ideology, as belonging more to the world of the imagination than to that of empirical, physical experience. Death itself loses its empirical reality by being absorbed into the indefinite category of "unending mutation," through which change is conflated with permanence and transitoriness with eternity.

What defines and distinguishes the "free" and "noble" personality in the Princess's world, penetrated as it is by popular Nietzschean notions, is in fact its freedom from any external, objective constraint, such as logic, empirical evidence, religious doctrine or moral law. Religiosity, it has been said, religious *feeling*, is the hallmark of *völkisch* religions. It is certainly what Wilhelm Hauer, the founder of the *Deutsche Glaubensbewegung*, valued most. The specific content of any particular religious faith or doctrine was of secondary importance to him; indeed the less there was of doctrine, the more authentic, the more truly religious, in Hauer's sense, the religion was likely to be. Similarly, in the Princess's world, truthfulness matters more than truth, especially since objective or universal truth (even as the normative goal of an intersubjective concept of truth) is dismissed as a chimera.

In short, the objective universe, standing over against the individual subject and assumed by many to be the creation of a transcendent God, is eclipsed by a universe in constant process of being created and recreated in and by the subject, in and by the *Gott in mir*. The object-universe is eclipsed by the universe as a work of art in never-ending process of self-creation. The world is discovered not by studying a supposedly fixed, created universe distinct from the self, but in the self, in virtue of its participation in the ever-changing universe. Objectivity and objective constraints exist in the Princess's universe only in the form of species and races, which, though subject to mutation and degeneration, are presented as fundamental realities, an inscrutable and unintelligible "fate" or "destiny," a kind of Law of the universe, which the truly noble, free individual does not suffer or submit to as an external imposition but joyfully and freely wills, inasmuch as he or she is an integral part of the larger racial community of the *volk* and, beyond that, of an All or Cosmos which embraces every nation and indeed, every living thing. The law of the Cosmos, destiny, is thus also the law of the individual's own nature.

Given this outlook, it is not surprising that little attention is paid to the characteristics of the objective, external world, except perhaps to certain physical characteristics of human groups and landscapes that supposedly reveal underlying energies and forces of the *Volk* or the Cosmos. This lack of attention to concrete empirical reality is a striking feature not only of the Princess's poetry but, more surprisingly in view of the usual features of the genre, of her novels. The New Man proclaimed by the Nazis – like the New Man proclaimed several decades before them by *Lebensreformers* such as the Hart brothers – does not seek a deep empirical understanding of the moral and physical ugliness he deplores in the world around him in order to effect needed changes to that world. Were he to do so, were he to conduct what passes for a rigorous intellectual or scientific analysis of social and economic reality, he would be sucked, it was charged, into the very baseness, the very rationalizing, interest-driven, utilitarian, politically liberal system he longs to overcome – whereas the overcoming of baseness, it was held, can be achieved only internally, within each individual, by action of the will. Thus it is not necessary to dissect and reconstruct the external social and economic order using rational or scientific instruments of analysis; the attempt to do so would simply reproduce the evil that that order has created in another form, in the way that modern socialism was said by many of its *Lebensreform* critics, including some on the anarchist Left, to be simply another manifestation of the calculating materialism characteristic of modern capitalism, another form of that post-Enlightenment Western "Zivilisation" that was constantly contrasted with holistic, communitarian (and primarily Germanic) "Kultur." The overcoming of materialism, utilitarianism, and egoism, the creation of the New Man and the New World, of the free human personality and the new community would thus be the product not of action guided by observation, reflection, and calculation but of the action of the will on the heart and soul. Such a vision of the New Man and the New World might well have been shared by the Princess and her Left-leaning contemporary Heinrich Vogeler before the latter finally adhered, not without struggle and "backsliding," to the strict doctrine of dialectical materialism.[2]

As feeling itself, the quality of feeling, is what counts, loyalty, heroism, self-sacrifice are released from their usual relation to specific objective and rationally or discursively justifiable goals and values. To the contrary, goals and values are themselves likely to be measured by the quality of the feelings – the intensity of dedication, loyalty, faith, and love of kin – that they inspire. In her tribute to Gobineau in July 1941, the Princess cited with admiration a passage in which Gobineau allegedly asserted that "wherever the greatest things are at stake, we should not weigh or measure our hopes for victory; faith alone must do everything."[3] Thus it was possible, in the end, to view the death and misery of millions and the destruction of Germany itself as secondary to the heroism, the comradeship, and the self-sacrificing devotion that the Party had been able to inspire in its members. How else can one explain the striking response of Hitler, as reported by Albert Speer, to Speer's plea, in the very last days of the Second World War, that, in view of the inevitability of defeat, it was essential not to destroy the entire German infrastructure in order to prevent it from falling into the hands of the victors, as Hitler had ordered, but to preserve as much of it as possible, so that Germany might be able to revive after the War had ended? "It is not necessary to worry about what the German people will need for elemental survival," Hitler is said to have replied. "On the contrary, it is best for us to destroy even these things. […] Only those who are inferior will remain after this struggle, for the good have already been killed."[4]

# Notes

**Introduction.**

1. On the Angelsachsen Verlag, see Herbert Schwarzwälder, *Das Große Bremen-Lexikon* (Bremen: Edition Temmen, 2002), pp. 19-20.

2. The drawing was published under the title *Ekstase* as the cover illustration of *Die Aktion*, vol. 4, no. 22, 30 May 1914. (On *Die Aktion*, described by Pfemfert himself in the first number [February 1911] as "an organ of honest radicalism," see the Afterword in Franz Pfemfert, *Die Revolutions G.m.b.H.*, ed. Knut Hickethier, Wilhelm Heinrich Pott and Kristina Zerges [Wissmar and Steinbach: Anabas Verlag Günter Kampf, 1973], pp. 169-96. Schmidt-Rottluff, Egon Schiele, and two younger men associated with Vogeler and with Worpswede, Georg Tappert and his student Wilhelm Morgner, were among other artists who contributed to the magazine.) Many years later, in an article written in the Soviet Union, after he had become a committed Communist, Vogeler looked back on this work (illustrated in the article and referred to there as *Neugeburt* [Rebirth]). Interpreting it as his own attempt to achieve rebirth by breaking radically with the Jugendstil that had been the hallmark of his art until then, he was also critical of it: "Thus arose, in the midst of severe inner struggle, the etching 'Neugeburt.' Rays of light divide up the little world of the copper plate, illuminating its expressive essence. A hand emerges from the clouds, touching a young mother as if to awaken her. A newborn child lies in her lap. Under heavy clouds that are moving away, in the distance [i.e. in the upper right-hand corner of the picture] a man drags himself along almost crushed under the weight of a cross. Real-life experiences resting on completely abstract forms. For the first time, expressionist techniques are to be seen in the art of this painter. It was his passionate attempt to free himself from everything obsolete in bourgeois art, an attempt to destroy the Old. An attempt made on the level of form. For the content was still individualist, private, abstractly removed from the social. A revolution with no future and no goal. Yet there was something good in this attempt: it brought our painter powerfully back to reality, for his etching was, as he thought, an accounting, a line drawn under the past, marking its end." ("Erfahrungen eines Mahlers: Zur Expressionismus-Diskussion" [Experiences of a Painter: A Contribution to the Debate about Expressionism], *Das Wort* [Moscow], 3, 6: June 1938], pp. 84-94, on p. 86). What the work must have suggested to its early viewers was that salvation and a *vita nuova* will come, but not through Christianity. In the version that was used to illustrate the Princess's poem the child in front of the woman in the original drawing and in etchings made in 1915-16 is unaccountably missing. As Vogeler continued to use the mother-child image or the child alone in many paintings and

## 132   Brownshirt Princess

drawings of this period as a symbol of rebirth, cosmic unity, and a new relationship among human beings, the elimination of the child from the 1921 frontispiece requires explanation. Did the artist intend to concentrate the viewer's attention on the experience of the subject herself, as described in the Princess's poem? Or is there a simple technical explanation? The child is also absent from some of the twenty or so preparatory sketches for the etching. There is unfortunately no answer to this question anywhere in the extensive – and excellent – literature in German on Vogeler.

3.   In addition to the copy in Princeton University's Firestone Library, in which the frontispiece illustration is hand-signed by the artist, *Gott in mir* is listed in the catalogues of Northwestern University Library, the Deutsche Nationalbibliothek in Leipzig, the library of the Museum für Kunst und Gewerbe in Hamburg, and the Stadtbibliothek in Magdeburg. The original owner of Firestone's copy was a German bibliophile whose outstanding library of first editions of then contemporary German literature was acquired by Princeton in 1924. The book appears as no. 228 in the exhaustive catalogue of books illustrated by Vogeler in Theo Neteler's *Heinrich Vogeler, Buchgestalter und Buchillustrator: Mit einer Bibliographie* (Fischerhude: Galerie-Verlag, 1991), pp. 108-47.

4.   *Achtzig Merksätze und Leitsprüche über Zucht und Sitte aus Schriften und Reden von R. Walther Darré* (Goslar: Verlag Blut und Boden, 1940); *Erkenntnisse und Werden: Aufsätze vor der Zeit der Machtergreifung* (Goslar: Verlag Blut und Boden, 1940).

5.   For a rapid overview of the "German Revolution" the German Socialist Party leadership's response to it, see especially Hans Mommsen, *The Rise and Fall of Weimar Democracy*, trans. Elborg Forster and Larry Eugene Jones (Chapel Hill and London: University of North Carolina Press, 1996; orig. German 1989), pp. 15-50; the moving work of Sebastian Haffner, *Failure of a Revolution: Germany 1918-1919*, trans. Georg Rapp (London: André Deutsch, 1973; orig. German *Die verratene Revolution* [Betrayal of a Revolution], 1969); and the still invaluable Harvard Ph.D. of Robert G. L. Waite, *Vanguard of Nazism: The Free Corps Movement in Postwar Germany 1918-1923* (Cambridge, Mass.: Harvard University Press, 1952). For a vivid day-by-day account, see Harry, Graf Kessler's diary, *Berlin in Lights: the Diaries of Count Harry Kessler 1918-1937*, trans. and ed. Charles Kessler (New York: Grove Press, 2000). On the Revolution in Bremen, see Peter Kuckuk, *Bremen in der deutschen Revolution 1918-1919* (Bremen: Bremen Verlagsgesellschaft Steintor, 1986) and Chris Harman, *The Lost Revolution: Germany 1918-1923* (London: Bookmarks, 1982), pp. 99-103.

6.   Vogeler's so-called "Komplexbilder" – montages of realistically painted fragments – were an attempt to combine modernism and realism in an art adequate to the socialist reality the artist believed was in process of construction. See online Appendix B, Image Portfolio 1.

7.   These feelings were already evident in an anti-war tract of January 1918, duplicated on a hectographic copier and illegally distributed in the last months of the War as a "Letter to the Kaiser from a non-commissioned officer." The letter took the form of a fable, in which God appears as a wretched old man on the Potsdamer Platz in Berlin, distributing leaflets that call for peace on earth and invoking the Ten Commandments, is arrested by the Police, and executed as a traitor. To the surprise of the bloodthirsty generals who promise peace and order but aim to do so only by bringing people to their knees at sword point, the old man, whom everyone believed dead, reappears. He briefly thinks he has been recognized, but

in fact the generals and rulers only use his name in their telegrams, dispatches, and proclamations to give these an air of dignity and legitimacy. The letter concluded with an appeal to the Kaiser to become a prince of peace and place himself in the service of truth and humanity instead of violence, lies, and illusions. For his pains, Vogeler was discharged from the army and briefly hospitalized as a "neuropath" – which allowed the authorities to avoid the publicity and potential embarrassment of a court-martial. The little text was printed by the revolutionaries of November 1918 as a flyer with the title "Das Märchen vom lieben Gott: Brief eines Unteroffiziers an den Kaiser im Januar 1918, als Protest gegen den Frieden von Brest-Litowsk" [The tale of the good Lord: a letter from a non-commissioned officer to the Kaiser in January 1918, in protest against the Peace of Brest-Litovsk] (Bremen: Druck Arbeiterpolitik, 1919) and reprinted in S. D. Gallwitz, *Dreißig Jahre Worpswede: Künstler, Geist, Werden* (Bremen: Angelsachsen Verlag, 1922), pp. 33-34.

8. Friedrich Wolf, *Briefwechsel: Eine Auswahl* (Bonn and Weimar: Aufbau Verlag, 1968), p. 9, letter dated 9 June 1921. In his play *Kolonne Hund* (1926), based on his experience as a member of Vogeler's commune, Wolf subsequently exposed the insuperable obstacles, material and psychological, to the viability and efficacy of communist islands in a capitalist sea. Like Vogeler, Wolf – who at one time was seen as a rival of Brecht – emigrated to the Soviet Union.

9. See Bernd Stenzig, *Worpswede Moskau: Das Werk von Heinrich Vogeler*, Exhib. Cat. (Worpswede: Worpsweder Verlag, 1989), pp. 136-38.

10. "Hingabe" – Heinrich Vogeler, *Friede* (Bremen, 1922), p. 41, quoted by Bernd Stenzig in *Heinrich Vogeler: Vom Romantiker zum Revolutionär; Ölbilder, Zeichnungen, Grafik, Dokumente von 1895-1924* (Exhib. Cat., Bonner Kunstverein, 23 June-1 August 1982), p. 127; "Gesetzmäßigkeit des Werdens" – quoted by Zofia Marchlewska, *Eine Welle im Meer: Erinnerungen an Heinrich Vogeler und Zeitgenossen* (Berlin: Buchverlag Der Morgen, n.d. [1968]), p. 63. "Frieden" – from Christmas letter of the Barkenhoff Arbeitsgemeinschaft, 1920, reproduced in Walter Hundt, *Bei Heinrich Vogeler in Worpswede. Erinnerungen*, foreword by Bernd Stenzig (Worpswede: Worpsweder Verlag, Schriftenreihe der Barkenhoff Stiftung, 1981), p. 166.

11. Bernd Stenzig in *Heinrich Vogeler: Vom Romantiker zum Revolutionär*, pp. 126-28; Heinrich Wiegand Petzet, *Von Worpswede nach Moskau: Heinrich Vogeler – Ein Künstler zwischen den Zeiten* (Cologne: M. DuMont Schauberg, 1972), pp. 124-28. Rejecting as a caricature the image of communism presented by her husband's patron Roselius, Martha Vogeler advised Roselius to read "Krapotkin's 'Gegenseitige Hilfe in Tier- und Menschenwelt.'" That work, she wrote, "is closer to our will to life." (Martha Vogeler to Ludwig Roselius, 4 December 1918, in Ludwig Roselius, *Briefe* [Bremen: H. M. Hauschild, 1919], p. 125) Even Vogeler's establishment of an agricultural and artisanal commune on the property of his once elegant Barkenhoff was not in itself an unequivocal sign of commitment to communism. Communes had been planned or founded by critics of the prevailing liberal-capitalist society on the Right as well as the Left: e.g. the "Mittgart" project of the eugenicist Willibald Hentschel, the "Heimland" settlement of the rabidly anti-Semitic Theodor Fritsch, Ernst Hunkel's "Donnershag." (See Ulrich Linse, "Völkisch-rassische Siedlungen der Lebensreform," in *Handbuch zur "Völkischen Bewegung" 1871-1918*, ed. Uwe Puschner, Walter Schmitz, Justus U. Ulbricht [Munich; New Providence; London; Paris: K. G. Saur, 1996], pp. 397-410; also idem, *Zurück, o Mensch zur Mutter Erde: Landkommunen in Deutschland 1890-1933* [Munich: Deutscher Taschenbuch Verlag,

1983]).

12. The form of the figure is that of the "Algiz" or "Life" rune ᛉ. See other, related images in online Appendix B, image portfolio 2 at: www.openbookpublishers.com.

13. See *The Société Anonyme and the Dreier Bequest at Yale University: A Catalogue Raisonné*, ed. Robert L. Herbert, Eleanor S. Apter, Elise K. Kenney (New Haven and London: Yale University Press, 1984), p. 711. For an illustration, see Online Appendix, section B, Image Portfolio 1. Along with the key notion of "Werden" [becoming] and the rejection of dualisms (separating God from Man, Spirit from Nature, etc.), Vogeler's interest in Buddhism was shared by many in the politically opposite camp (e.g. Himmler, Rosenberg, Magda Goebbels); see Victor and Victoria Trimondi, *Hitler-Buddha-Krishna: Eine unheilige Allianz vom Dritten Reich bis heute* (Vienna: Verlag Carl Ueberreuter, 2002).

14. S. D. Gallwitz, *Dreißig Jahre Worpswede*, pp. 34-35. See also Bernd Stenzig, *Heinrich Vogeler: Eine Bibliogaphie der Schriften* (Worpsweder Verlag, 1994), Introduction, pp. VI-IX.

15. Zofia Marchlewska, *Eine Welle im Meer*, pp. 62-63. Harry Graf Kessler makes a similar observation about the entire leftwing orientation of German writers and artists, such as Vogeler. "The weak spot of the Spartacist League [the revolutionary *Spartakusbund*, founded by Rosa Luxemburg and Karl Liebknecht during the First World War, and the matrix of the German Communist Party] is its disregard of economic facts and necessities. In that respect it is at the opposite pole from Karl Marx. It is remarkable that such a well-read and sharp Marxist as Luxemburg failed to see that. Nostitz [Alfred Nostitz, a Minister of the King of Saxony and longtime friend of Kessler] says...that poets like Paul Adler et al. have completely gone over to *Spartakus*. So too Vogeler and the Worpswede group in Bremen. It is the new religion of the young intellectuals and artists." (Harry Graf Kessler, *Das Tagebuch 1880-1937*, vol. 7 (1919-1923), ed. Angela Reinthal [Stuttgart: Klett-Cotta, 2007], pp. 116-17, entry for 31 January 1919) See also Walter Hundt, *Bei Heinrich Vogeler in Worpswede: Erinnerungen* on Vogeler's relations with Richard Wilhelm, the eminent German Sinologist, Rudolf Steiner, and Martin Buber, who enrolled his son Rafael in the Barkenhoff school.

16. Heinrich Vogeler, "Gott," in Gallwitz, *Dreißig Jahre Worpswede*, pp. 79-81.

17. In general, the ideological line between Right and Left was not always clearly delineated. As is well known, there was a "Left" of the "Right," represented within the NSDAP by Gregor Strasser (murdered on Hitler's orders in 1934). Thus, for instance, the *völkisch* (on the term "völkisch," see below, chapter 2 n. 32) artist Hugo Höppener (Fidus), subsequently an ardent National Socialist, provided the illustrations for the German Socialist Party's May Day newspaper in 1905. (The main illustration was a light-shedding God of Spring – possibly intended to evoke the old Germanic Baldur – surrounded by naked figures and figures clad in Old Germanic costume). Wilhelm Schwaner, the *völkisch* author of a *Germanen-Bibel* and co-founder of the *Germanische Glaubensgemeinschaft* [Germanic Faith Community] was an intimate friend of the liberal Jewish statesman Walther Rathenau (see Part II of this essay) and was seen as a like-minded champion of the welfare of the people by Heinrich Vogeler's close friend and patron, the humanitarian-socialist Jewish doctor Emil Löhnberg. Löhnberg's daughter remembers Schwaner in her memoirs as a neighbor of her family with ideas similar to those behind the

British Workers' Educational Association. "Herr Schwaner," she notes, describing a gathering Löhnberg hosted for Schwaner and thirty educationalists at the country house Vogeler had designed for him, "had (I believe at the beginning of the century) adopted the symbol of the sun-wheel, found on very ancient oriental graves: the swastika. It was he who had revived this symbol in Germany. To him it meant that the light of education would shine into the minds of those who had been deprived of it." This naïve judgment of Schwaner tells much about contemporary perceptions of ideological currents now viewed as unequivocally rightwing. Nor was it altered when her father was physically attacked, in the mid-1920s, by two members of the NSDAP (Nazi Party). "The meaning of the swastika had changed," she writes. "It was no longer the symbol of education and enlightenment of a Wilhelm Schwaner, but one of the German Master Race and aggression." (Marianne Walter, *The Poison Seed: A Personal History of Nazi Germany* [Lewes, Sussex: The Book Guild, 1992], pp. 68, 90) A third example of ambivalence is provided by another friend of Vogeler's, the Worpswede sculptor-architect Bernhard Hoetger, who joined the NSDAP in 1934. Twelve years earlier Hoetger had offered an expressionist version of a *Pietà* sculpture to the workers of Bremen to serve as a "Revolutionsdenkmal" [memorial to the Bremen Revolution of 1919], and this gesture was cited against him when he was attacked in several issues of the SS magazine *Das Schwarze Korps* in 1935 for his alleged corrupting influence on German art (his work showed at one point the strong influence of so-called "primitive" African art) and opportunistic relation to the Party, and once again in a 1938 document justifying his expulsion from the Party. As if to respond to the attacks of 1935, Hoetger created a bas-relief of *Michael der Lichtbringer*, which was placed at the entrance to the celebrated Bremen architectural ensemble, the Böttcherstraße, in 1936 in order no doubt to flatter the Führer. In 1939 he received a commission for a bust of Hitler. (*Bernhard Hoetger: Skulptur, Malerei, Design, Architektur*, ed. Maria Anczykowski [Bremen: H. M. Hauschild, 1998], pp. 291, 498-99). To Vogeler, in contrast, the political choice had become clear by the mid-twenties, and Hoetger's refusal to make it placed him, in Vogeler's eyes, in the camp of opportunists and Nazi sympathizers. (Heinrich Vogeler, *Werden: Erinnerungen, mit Lebenszeugnissen aus den Jahren 1923-1942*, new edn. by Joachim Priewe and Paul-Gerhard Wenzlaff [Berlin: Rütten und Loening, 1989], pp. 256, 265-66, 298-99).

18. Ludwig Roselius, *Briefe*, pp. 94-125, letters between Roselius and Vogeler, November and December, 1918; also Petzet, *Von Worpswede nach Moskau*, pp. 135-38, letters between Roselius and Vogeler, July 1920-March 1921.

19. *Wildnis: Geruhsame Abenteuer in Alaska* (Bremen: Angelsachsen Verlag, 1925).

20. See "Wir Bremer" (originally published in the *Deutsch-Amerika Zeitung*, 1923) and other essays in his *Reden und Schriften zur Böttcherstrasse in Bremen* (Bremen: Verlag G. A. v. Hallem, 1932). Ideas similar to Roselius's were of course current also in England and the U.S. In his plans for the resettlement of the conquered territories in the East by Germanic farmer-warriors, Heinrich Himmler likewise allegedly foresaw "calling on the Germanic race in all countries, the Norwegians and the Swedes, the Dutch and the Danes" and even – in the midst of the Second World War – "the English and the Americans." Thus "a great Germanic International" will be "set against the Jewish and Communist one" and "the assault of Asia will break against the Germanic armed peasantry, who will simultaneously drive the plough and shoulder the musket." (Felix Kersten, *The Kersten Memoirs 1940-1945*,

Introduction by Hugh Trevor-Roper, trans. by Constantine Fitzgibbon and James Oliver [London: Hutchinson, 1956], p. 138, entry dated 22 July 1942).

21. On Hitler's public denunciation of "diese Art von Böttcherstraße-Kultur" as degenerate at the Nuremberg "Kulturtag" in 1936, see *Bernhard Hoetger: Skulptur, Malerei, Design, Architektur*, p. 499. Roselius was able to salvage the Böttcherstraße in Bremen – his *Gesamtkunstwerk*, consisting of the Robinson-Crusoe-House, the Atlantis-House, the Paula Becker-Modersohn-House, and the Roselius-House, a 16th-century building converted by Roselius into a museum of North German antiquities – only on condition that it would be preserved, in Hitler's words, as a "horrifying example for posterity of what was presented as culture and architecture in the years before our seizure of power." (Arn Strohmeyer, *Parsifal in Bremen: Richard Wagner, Ludwig Roselius und die Böttcherstrasse* [Weimar: Verlag und Datenbank für Geisteswissenschaften, 2002], p. 168; see also Elizabeth Tumasonis, "Bernhard Hoetger's Tree of Life: German Expressionism and Racial Ideology," *Art Journal*, 1992, 51: 81-91) Roselius also agreed to change the inscription that he had designed in 1926 for the Paula Modersohn-Becker museum from "Errichtet von Bernhard Hoetgers Hand/ Zum Zeichen edler Frau zeugend Werk,/ das siegend steht/ wenn tapfrer Männer Heldenruhm verweht" [Erected by Bernhard Hoetger's hand/ In recognition of a noble woman's productive work/ Which will still victorious stand/ When the fame of bold and heroic men has faded] to "*bis* [until] tapfrer Männer Heldenruhm verweht." (See Herbert Schwarzenwälder, *Berühmte Bremer* [Munich: Paul List Verlag, 1972], p. 142) Doubtless the Nazis found the original inscription – which, according to Roselius himself, was meant to convey that "Ein schwaches Weib ist stärker als ein tapferer Held, wenn ihr Geist sie zum Führer macht" [A weak woman is stronger than a bold hero when her spirit makes her into a leader] (*Reden und Schriften*, p. 47) – too feminist and insufficiently respectful of male heroism. In the end, Roselius conceded that "the Paula-Becker-Modersohn-House and the Tree of Life on the façade of the Atlantis House in no way conform to the artistic point of view of contemporary National Socialism." (Quoted in Susan Henderson, "Böttcherstrasse: The Corporatist Vision of Ludwig Roselius and Bernhard Hoetger," *Journal of Decorative and Propaganda Arts*, 1994, 20: 165-81, at p. 181). Among the reasons cited for Hoetger's expulsion from the Party in 1938, in addition to his allegedly opportunistic embrace of National Socialism, his corrupting influence on art, and his connections with Jewish art dealers and critics, was his promotion of "a so-called Nordic orientation, which has been sharply criticized and rejected by the scholarly world and risks adulterating National Socialist ideas." (quoted in *Bernhard Hoetger: Skulptur, Malerei, Design, Architektur*, p. 498) On Wirth's matriarchal theories and on the scandal provoked by his publication of the so-called *Ura Linda Chronik*, see Michael H. Kater, *Das "Ahnenerbe" der SS 1935-1945: Ein Beitrag zur Kulturpolitik des Dritten Reiches* (Stuttgart: Deutsche Verlagsanstalt, 1974), pp. 14-16; Victor and Victoria Trimondi, *Hitler-Buddha-Krischna: Eine unheilige Allianz vom Dritten Reich bis heute*, pp. 38-39; Eduard Gugenberger and Roman Schweidlenka, *Mutter Erde: Magie und Politik zwischen Faschismus und neuer Gesellschaft* (Vienna: Verlag für Geisteswissenschaftskritik, 1987); Peter Davies, "'Männerbund' und 'Mutterrecht': Hermann Wirth, Sophie Rogge-Börner and the *Ura-Linda-Chronik*," *German Life and Letters*, 2007, 60: 98-115.

22. See Hitler's remarks in *Mein Kampf* (trans. Ralph Mannheim, [Boston: Houghton Mifflin Co., 1943], pp. 326-27): "If anything is un-*völkisch*, it is this tossing around of old Germanic expressions which neither fit into the present period nor represent

anything definite. [...] I had to warn again and again against those *deutschvölkisch* wandering scholars [...] [who] rave about old Germanic heroism, about dim prehistory, stone axes, spear and shield." Hermann Rauschning (admittedly not always reliable) reports hearing Hitler make a similar comment in early 1933: "These professors and mystery-men who want to found Nordic religions merely get in my way. Why do I tolerate them? Because they help to disintegrate, which is all we can do at the moment. They cause unrest. And all unrest is creative. It has no value in itself, but let it run its course." (Rauschning, *The Voice of Destruction* [New York: G. P. Putnam's Sons, 1940], p. 51) It would be a disaster, however, "if ever our movement or the state itself was saddled with unclear tasks as a result of the infiltration of unclear, mystical elements." (From a 1938 speech, quoted in Manfred Ach and Clemens Pentrop, *Hitlers "Religion": Pseudoreligiöse Elemente im nationalsozialstischen Sprachgebrauch* [n.p.: Arbeitsgemeinschaft für Religions- und Weltanschauungsfragen, 1977. Asgard Edition, 3], p. 62). In 1934 the *Nordic Ring*, in which the Princess herself was active, was disbanded by the Party; even the use of the Nordic names for the months (Weinmond, etc.) was banned. (Paul Weindling, *Health, Race and German Politics between National Unification and Nazism* [Cambridge: Cambridge University Press, 1989], p. 478). Later, Hitler also decreed that Roman typeface should be adopted in preference to traditional German *Fraktur*. On the complex relation between the various *völkisch* movements and National Socialism, see Hubert Cancik, "'Neuheiden' und totaler Staat: Völkische Religion am Ende der Weimarer Republik," in H. Cancik, ed., *Religions- und Geistesgeschichte der Weimarer Republik* (Düsseldorf: Patmos Verlag, 1982), pp. 177-209, at pp. 204-06; Geoffrey G. Field, "Nordic Racism," *Journal of the History of Ideas*, 1977, 38: 523-40, at pp. 525, 533-35; Hans-Jürgen Lutzhöft, *Der Nordische Gedanke in Deutschland 1920-1940* (Stuttgart: Ernst Klett, 1971), pp. 155-57, 293-95; Bernard Mees, "Hitler and Germanentum," *Journal of Contemporary History*, 2004, 39: 255-70; Uwe Puschner, *Die völkische Bewegung im wilhelminischen Kaiserreich: Sprache, Rasse, Religion* (Darmstadt: Wissenschaftliche Buchgesellschaft, 2001), pp. 10-12.

23. See Margaret Bourke-White, *"Dear Fatherland, Rest Quietly": A Report on the Collapse of Hitler's 'Thousand Years'* (New York: Simon and Schuster, 1946), pp. 3-10, 134-37. The celebrated journalist and photographer had known Roselius's daughter Hildegard briefly as a student of journalism at Columbia University before the War and looked her up in 1945 in Bremen. She found her unchanged in her approval of Hitler ("The Führer had a strong manly handshake, the sort of handshake you like. A really *good* handshake. Everyone who met him liked him. He was very sincere, very frank. He believed in what he said. Adolf Hitler never knowingly told a lie"), unrepentantly anti-Semitic ("the Jews pushed America into the war"), and completely convinced that it was not Hitler but "England that actually started the War." It had, moreover, been lost because of "treachery" ("too many Poles and foreigners and too many people listening to the foreign radio"). Hitler and Goebbels both paid tribute to Roselius on his death in 1943. See also the text of a glowing verse tribute to Hitler by Hildegard, dated 9 November 1933, cited by Arn Strohmeyer, "Kunst im Zeichen der germanischen Vorfahren und der Wiedergeburt Deutschlands: Ludwig Roselius und Bernhard Hoetger," in Arn Strohmeyer, Kai Artinger, Ferdinand Krogman, *Landschaft, Licht und niederdeutscher Mythos: Die Worpsweder Kunst und der Nationalsozialismus*, p. 79.

## Chapter 1.

1. Rejection of *antiqua* or Latin script and adoption of *Fraktur*, often in a highly stylized form, was a sign of adherence to *völkisch* ideologies (i.e. ideologies based on a racial conception of the people or nation), as was the use of German names instead of Latin ones for the months of the year; see Uwe Puschner, "Die Germanenideologie im Kontext der völkischen Weltanschauung," *Göttinger Forum für Altertumswissenschaft*, 2001, 4: 85-97. Puschner refers to an article entitled "Deutsches Volk, hüte deine deutsche Schrift: ein Erbgut deutscher Art" [German people, defend your German script, an essential legacy of German-ness] in *Kultur und Familie*, 1913/14, 3: 187f. Hitler's decision in 1941 to make Roman script standard was greeted with dismay by some *völkisch* leaders and provided one of them with "evidence" in the post-War period that he had been an opponent of Hitler's policies. In a letter dated 17 January 1954 Ludwig Dessel, then head of the *Germanische Glaubensgemeinschaft*, a neo-pagan, *völkisch* religious group dating back to the end of the Wilhelminian era, claimed that "the moment Hitler made Roman script standard, it became clear to me [nothing else apparently opened his eyes - LG] that I would never be in agreement with him, that his war aims were not as I had seen them, and that what he wanted for the German people was not what I wanted or what the German people wanted for itself. [...] I can truly say that from that time on I hated him, because he freely and deliberately gave up a cultural treasure that was one of the pillars of our national tradition." ("GGG und NS: Zugehörigkeit zur NSDAP," www.germanische-glaubens-gemeinschaft.de/gggundns.htm.) On the notion of "völkisch," see below Ch. 2 n. 32.

2. Schwaner's *Germanen-Bibel* was republished in 1934 and again in 1941. Judging it desirable to preserve a link between the new Germanic religion and German Christianity, Schwaner subsequently distanced himself from Fahrenkrog and the radically pagan *Germanische Glaubensgemeinschaft*. For similar pantheistic longings in the art of the time, see Online Appendix B, Image Portfolio 2.

3. On Hauer, see the well-documented monograph of the sometime National Socialist scholar Margarete Dierks, *Jakob Wilhelm Hauer 1881-1962: Leben, Werk, Wirkung; Mit einer Personalbibliographie* (Heidelberg: Schneider, 1986) and the notably more critical studies of Hubert Cancik, "'Neuheiden'und totaler Staat: Völkische Religion am Ende der Weimarer Republik" in his *Religions- und Geistesgeschichte der Weimarer Republik*, pp. 176-212, Ulrich Nanko, *Die Deutsche Glaubensbewegung: Eine historische und soziologische Untersuchung* (Marburg: Diagonal Verlag, 1993), and Schaul Baumann, *Die Deutsche Glaubensbewegung und ihr Gründer Jakob Wilhelm Hauer (1881-1962)* (Marburg: Diagonal Verlag, 2006). In English, see the references to Hauer in Doris L. Bergen, *Twisted Cross: The German Christian Movement in the Third Reich* (Chapel Hill: University of North Carolina Press, 1996) and Karla O. Poewe, *New Religions and the Nazis* (New York: Routledge, 2006).

4. Theodor Däubler's multi-volume mythic *Nordlicht* (1910) would be a prime example, as would some of the popular poetry of Friedrich Lienhard. For other examples, see Helmut Scheuer, "Zur Christus-Figur in der Literatur um 1900," and Gunter Martens, "Stürmer in Rosen: Zum Kunstprogramm einer Strassburger Dichtergruppe der Jahrhundertwende," in *Fin de Siècle: Zur Literatur und Kunst der Jahrhundertwende* (Frankfurt a.M.: Vittorio Klostermann, 1977), pp. 378-402 and 481-507.

5. See online Appendix A. Also available directly from Princeton University Library on http://libweb5.princeton.edu/visual_materials/Misc/Bib_2934672.pdf

6. *Meister Eckharts Mystische Schriften in unsere Sprache übertragen von Gustav Landauer* (Berlin: Karl Schnabel [Axel Junckers Buchhandlung], 1903); *Meister Eckeharts Schriften und Predigten: Aus dem Mittelhochdeutschen übersetzt und herausgegeben von Herman Büttner* (Leipzig: Eugen Diederichs, 1903), 2 vols. The texts translated by Landauer were selected and rearranged by him on the principle that "everything would be left out that does not speak to us" and that "Meister Eckhart is too good for a [merely] historical reading; he must be resuscitated as a living voice." (Vorwort, p. 5) On Landauer's relation to Eckhart, see Thorsten Hinz, *Mystik und Anarchie: Meister Eckhart und seine Bedeutung im Denken Gustav Landauers* (Berlin: Karin Kramer Verlag, 2000).

7. Diederichs and the so-called *Sera-Circle* around him in Jena seem to have shared Nietzsche's view of Christianity as simply "Judaism to the second power." (Hubert Cancik, *Nietzsches Antike: Vorlesung* [Stuttgart and Weimar: J. B. Metzler Verlag, 1995], pp. 142-43) See also Justus H. Ulbricht, "'Theologia deutsch': Eugen Diederichs und die Suche nach einer Religion für moderne Intellektuelle," in *Romantik, Revolution und Reform: Der Eugen Diederichs Verlag im Epochenkontext 1900-1949* (Göttingen: Wallstein Verlag, 1999), pp. 156-74: "It is impossible not to detect an anti-Semitic undertone of the kind found in the late Nietzsche in the very project of Diederichs and his stable of authors to revive the mystical tradition – which did not prevent a Jewish intellectual like Martin Buber from publishing his 'Ecstatic Testimonies' with Diederichs." (p. 164)

8. Ed. Otto Karrer (Munich: Verlag 'Ars Sacra' Josef Müller, 1926). Sections were devoted to Spanish mysticism, French mysticism, European mysticism in the nineteenth century (Newman and others), visionaries, and poets (Droste-Hülshoff, Lamartine, Verlaine, Newman, Manzoni, among others). On Heidegger, see John D. Caputo, "Heidegger and Theology," in *The Cambridge Companion to Heidegger*, ed. Charles B. Guignon (Cambridge: Cambridge University Press, 1993), pp. 326-44, on pp. 337-38.

9. Maria Carlson, *"No Religion Higher than Truth." A History of the Theosophical Movement in Russia 1875-1922* (Princeton: Princeton University Press, 1993), pp. 5-6.

10. On the social, cultural and ideological basis of opposition, in Germany, to the values of the new commercial and industrial society and on the social milieux in which disaffection and criticism were strongest, see Gerhard Kratzsch, *Kunstwart und Dürerbund: Ein Beitrag zur Geschichte der Gebildeten im Zeitalter des Imperialismus* (Göttingen: Vandenhoek & Ruprecht, 1969), pp. 23-31, 40-41. Kratzsch's breakdown of the membership of the *Dürer-Bund* in 1905 into social and employment categories (pp. 337-38, 467-68) shows that it was overwhelmingly middle-class and professional – churchmen, schoolteachers, and students being disproportionately represented. Of 3,194 members in 1905, only 20 were "Handwerker" [artisans/ tradesmen] and 47 shop or office employees. *The Hammer*, the anti-Semitic Theodor Fritsch's self-proclaimed "parteilose Zeitschrift für nationales Leben" [Independent Journal for National Life], claimed to address itself above all to a "middle class that is less and less respected in the modern state" as the latter increasingly "kneels before two idols, the secret violent power of capital on the grand scale on the one hand, and the threateningly violent proletarian mass on the other." This "Mittelstand" consists not only of artisans and shopkeepers but also of "all who are neither

multimillionaires nor proletarians." (Michael Bönisch, entry on the "Hammer"-Bewegung in *Handbuch zur "Völkischen Bewegung" 1871-1918*, pp. 341-65, on p. 355) Wilhelm Schwaner claimed that the subscribers to his magazine *Der Volkserzieher* were, in addition to schoolteachers, "pastors, post office employees, shopkeepers, artisans and peasants, as well as heads of administrative districts." (*Der Kunstwart*, XXVI, 2nd August issue, 1913, p. 281)

11. Julius Hart, *Der neue Gott: Ein Ausblick auf das kommende Jahrhundert* (Florence and Leipzig: Eugen Diederichs, 1899), p. 26.

12. *Wirtschaft und Gesellschaft*, ed. Johannes Winckelmann (Tübingen, 1980), p. 307, quoted in Justus H. Ulbricht, "'Cogito ergo credo': Religionswissenschaftliche Argumente für ein Museum der Lebensreform," in *Unweit von Eden: Tagung der Konzeption des Museums der deutschen Lebensreform im Fidushaus Waltersdorf*, ed. Ute Grund (Potsdam: Verlag für Berlin-Brandenburg, 2000), pp. 39-54, on p. 43. According to Thomas Nipperdey, religion was an essential component of all *Lebensreform* movements. (*Religion im Umbruch: Deutschland 1870-1918* [Munich: C. H. Beck, 1988], pp. 148 ff.). See Online Appendix B, Image Portfolio 2.

13. Avenarius often opened his magazine to opposing points of view in an effort to make it a truly national forum for discussion and debate: e.g. on the role of Jewish writers in German literature (vol. XXV, 11, 1st issue for March, 1912, pp. 281-94) or on the possibility and desirability of a new "Germanic" religion (vol. XXVI, 22, 2nd issue for August, 1913, pp. 259-64, 280-82). A tribute to Karl Marx on the 100th anniversary of his birth appeared in the number for April-June 1918.

14. Hermann Bahr in the literary magazine "Moderne Dichtung" (January 1, 1890), quoted in Ulbricht, "'Cogito ergo credo'," p. 46.

15. Ludwig Fahrenkrog, *Baldur: Drama* (Stuttgart: Greiner und Pfeiffer, 1908), pp. 46 (Act I, scene 2, set in Stonhenge), 101 (Finale).

16. On the conflation of Christ and Baldur or Odin (Wotan), see Ekkehard Hieronimus, "Zur Religiosität der völkischen Bewegung," in Cancik, *Religions- und Gestesgeschichte der Weimarer Republik*, pp. 159-75, quoting the head pastor of Bremen, J. Bode, author of *Wodan und Jesus: Ein Büchlein vom christlichen Deutschtum* (1920): "In what is most essential and best in them, Wodan and Jesus are in agreement. The faith of both is deep-rooted, farseeing, and generous. In both, there is a striving after spiritual freedom [...]." (p. 162) In the early 1920s Friedrich Döllinger (*Baldur und Bibel*, 1920) and Hermann Wieland (*Atlantis, Edda und Bibel*, 1922) held that Jesus was a prehistoric Germanic king and that the basic texts of the Bible represent ancient Germanic wisdom. (See Eduard Gugenberger and Roman Schweidlenka, *Mutter Erde: Magie und Politik zwischen Faschismus und neuer Gesellschaft*, p. 49) "The Krist and Father Wotan get on well together," according to a contributor to Wilhelm Schwaner's *Volkserzieher* (1913, p. 47); in the view of Klaus Wagner (*Krieg: Eine politisch-entwicklungsgeschichtliche Untersuchung* [1906]), "to brand Jesus, that fighter full of Germanic daring, as a patient lamb, is a lie, an impudent distortion of a Siegfriedian image, of a Baldurian figure." (Both quoted in W. W. Coole and M. F. Potter, *Thus Spake Germany* [London: Routledge, 1941], pp. 6, 7) The Baldur-Christ analogy was taken up even by a poet who was a regular contributor to Pfemfert's *Die Aktion*. As early as 1902, in "Baldur: Bruchstücke einer Dichtung," Ernst Stadler, an early expressionist writer from Alsace, who fell in the first months of World War I, presented Baldur, Christ, and Prometheus as aspects of the same heroic

savior-figure. As in Fahrenkrog's drama, the "Finale" of Stadler's poem points toward a new day, when life will be resanctified and redeemed from the ugliness and darkness of the present: "Baldur = Prometheus = Christus - / Heiliges Leben/ In Licht, in Schönheit,/ Nie sterbender Götterrausch/ Glühendster Trunkenheit!.../ Nur fühlen, atmen, schwelgen. Seligstes/ Nirwana und/ Aus tausend Himmeln tausend Morgensonnen." (Ernst Stadler, *Dichtungen, Schriften, Briefe, Kritische Ausgabe*, ed. Klaus Hurlebusch and Karl Ludwig Schneider [Munich: C. H. Beck, 1983], p. 28) See, in addition, Sylvia Siewert, *Germanische Religion und neugermanisches Heidentum* (Frankfurt; Bern; Berlin; Brussels; NewYork; Oxford; Vienna: Peter Lang, 2002), p. 134; Uwe Puschner, "Weltanschauung und Religion: Ideologie und Formen völkischer Religion," *Zeitenblicke* (2006), 5, no. 1: sec. 13 http://www.zeitenblicke.de/2006/1/Puschner/index.html.

17. On Wachler's theatre, see the contemporary essay by the "Heimatkunst" poet and essayist Friedrich Lienhard, *Das Harzer Bergtheater* (Stuttgart: Greiner & Pfeiffer, 1907). Also George L. Mosse, *The Crisis of German Ideology* (New York: Schocken Books, 1981 [1st edn. 1964]), pp. 80-82.

18. Though not peculiar to Germany, *Lebensreform* does appear to have been more vigorous and influential there than in other major European countries. Its cultural and ideological significance is now fully recognized and there is an extensive literature on it. For a comprehensive overview, see Wolfgang R. Krabbe, *Gesellschaftsveränderung durch Lebensreform* (Göttingen: Vandenhoek & Ruprecht, 1974) and *Die Lebensreform: Entwürfe zur Neugestaltung von Leben und Kunst um 1900*, ed. Kai Buchholz et al., exhib. cat. (Darmstadt: Häusser, 2000). In English, see Matthew Jefferies, "Lebensreform – a Middle-Class Antidote to Wilhelminism?," in Geoff Eley and James Retallack, eds., *Wilhelminism and its Legacies: German Modernities, Imperialism and the Meanings of Reform 1890-1930* (New York and Oxford: Berghahn Books, 2003), pp. 91-106. In Jefferies' brief but comprehensive article, the usual critique of *Lebensreform* by German scholars, namely that it was a form of bourgeois escapism, is challenged on the dubious grounds that many of its agendas (environmentalism, vegetarianism, body culture, etc.) are once again in vogue. It is true that contemporary champions of organic food and "natural" cures might find nothing unfamiliar in Himmler's view, for instance, of the way the food industry (un-natural food) and the pharmaceutical industry (un-natural cures for the maladies resulting from the consumption of the un-natural products of the food industry) work together to undermine the people's health (see *The Kersten Memoirs 1940-1945*, pp. 43-48), but that in itself does not invalidate the argument of the German scholars. The classic study of George L. Mosse, *The Crisis of German Ideology: Intellectual Origins of the Third Reich* (1964), has lost none of its relevance.

19. Janos Frecot, Johann Friedrich Geist, Diethart Kerbs, *Fidus 1868-1948; Zur ästhetischen Praxis bürgerlichen Fluchtbewegungen* (Munich: Rogner & Bernhard, 1972; new expanded edn. with introd. by Gert Makenklott, 1997).

20. Landauer passage cited in Hinz, *Mystik und Anarchie*, p. 18. (Landauer's case was probably less rare than he apparently thought.) On the concept of an "alternative" modernity rather than "anti-modernity," see Arno Klönne, "Eine deutsche Bewegung, politisch zweideutig," in *Die Lebensreform: Entwürfe zur Neugestaltung von Leben und Kunst um 1900*, pp. 31-32; Eva Barlösius, *Naturgemässe Lebensführung: Zur Geschichte der Lebensreform um die Jahrhundertwende* (Frankfurt and New York: Campus-Verlag, 1996), pp. 18-19; Kratzsch, *Kunstwart und Dürerbund*, pp. 15-18; Eley,

"Making a Place in the Nation"; also n. 16 above. Thomas Nipperdey maintains that the rise of alternative beliefs and religions in the wake of the decline of Christianity in Germany was "keine Wendung gegen die Moderne" [not a rejection of modernity]. (*Religion im Umbruch: Deutschland 1870-1918*, p. 152) For the later National Socialist period, the term "autochtonous modernism" has been suggested (Sebastian Graeb-Könneker, *Autochtone Modernität* [Opladen: Westdeutscher Verlag, 1996], pp. 29-37). On the general political and ideological ambivalence of *Lebensreform*, as exemplified by the celebrated international community of Monte Verità in Ascona (Switzerland), see Martin Green, "The Asconian Idea in Politics," in his *The Mountain of Truth: The Counterculture Begins; Ascona, 1900-1920* (Hanover, NH: University Press of New England, 1986), pp. 238-53. See also n. 7 above and n. 1 to Chapter 2 below on the imaginative and influential publishing enterprise of Eugen Diederichs.

21. Max Bruns, *Aus meinem Blute* (Minden/Westfalen: J. C. C. Bruns' Verlag, n.d.), pp. 70-71. A visual equivalent of those lines by the *völkisch* artist Fidus was circulated at the great gathering of German youth and *Wandervogel* groups on the Hoher Meißner in 1913 and became one of the most popular and best-known images in Germany. For a celebration of the artist's 60th birthday fifteen years later, the architect Arno Reutsch composed a poetic tribute to that image that recalls Bruns's verses of three decades before: "Dein Jüngling steigt hinauf/ Zu freier Bergeshöh',/ Tief unter ihm die Welt./ Durch Wolken hinan,/ Er schaut ins All,/ Die Arme breitet er aus,/ Jauchzend grüßt er die Sonne!" (Quoted by Winfried Mogge, "'Jauchzend grüßt er die Sonne!' Fidus und die Jugendbewegung," in Ute Grund, ed., *Unweit von Eden*, pp. 20-38, on p. 30). See Online Appendix B, Image Portfolio 2.

22. Julius Hart, *Triumph des Lebens* (Florence and Leipzig: Eugen Diederichs, 1898), p. 57. The poet Friedrich Lienhard later defined the union of the thrusting vertical and the recumbent horizontal as the fundamental, divine movement of Life, symbolized in many cultures by the figure of the Cross: "Das Leben besteht aus Stoß und Schoß. Der Strahl der Sonne, der Schoß der Erde, die Befruchtung als Ergebnis: so wiederholt sich im Einzelnen und Ganzen immer wieder der erhabene Vorgang. Jenen Strahl oder Stoß darf man als die Senkrechte bezeichnen; den empfangenden Teil als die Wagerecht: und man hat die Kreuzform als bedeutsames Sinnbild alles Lebendigen. Dieses Sinnbild ist uralt und vielen, weit auseinanderliegenden Völkerschaften gemeinsam." (Friedrich Lienhard, "Die Abstammung aus dem Licht: Grundriß einer kosmischen Lebenslehre," 3, in his *Der Meister der Menschheit*, 3 vols. [Stuttgart: Greiner und Pfeiffer, 1919-21], vol. 1, p. 156).

23. See Appendix to Part 1: "The *völkisch* rejection of Christianity."

24. *Meister Eckeharts Schriften und Predigten: Aus dem Mittelhochdeutschen übersetzt und herausgegeben von Herman Büttner* (Leipzig: Eugen Diederichs, 1903), 2 vols., vol.1, p. xiii. For obvious reasons (both his Jewish origins and his universalism), there are few references in the *völkisch* literature to Spinoza, in whose judgment the religion of the Hebrews had been designed to "make sure that men should never act of their own volition, but always at another's behest, and that [...] they should at all times acknowledge that they were not their own masters but completely subordinate to another." (*Tractatus Theologico-Politicus (Gebhardt edition, 1925)*, trans. Samuel Shirley [Leiden; New York; Copenhagen; Cologne: E. J. Brill, 1989], ch. 5, p. 119)

25. Carlson, pp. 28, 116-17, 135-36.

26. Wille's circle of friends included the Hart brothers, Heinrich and Julius, who were prominent in the literary circles of the time, the anarchists John Henry Mackay and Gustav Landauer, the promising young Jewish poet Ludwig Jacobowski, founder of the avant-garde literary and artistic group *Die Kommenden*, and Jacobowski's close friend Rudolf Steiner. In 1920 Wille edited a volume entitled *Deutscher Geist und Judenhaß* (Berlin: Kultur-Verlag), consisting of testimonies about their attitudes to Jews and anti-Semitism from a wide range of public figures on the Left and the Right, including himself. Most of the testimonies, not least his own, were sharply critical of anti-Semitism.

27. Quoted from the Prospectus by Karin Bruns in *Handbuch literarisch-kultureller Vereine, Gruppen und Bünde 1825-1933*, ed. Wulf Wülfing, K. Bruns, Rolf Parr (Stuttgart and Weimar: J. B. Metzler, 1998), p. 163.

28. Wolfgang Kirchbach, *Ziele und Aufgaben des Giordano Bruno-Bund* (Schmargendorf bei Berlin: Verlag Renaissance - Otto Lehmann, 1905), pp. 3-7.

29. Quoted in Gerhard Kratzsch, *Kunstwart und Dürerbund*, p. 93.

30. http://www2.uni-jena.de/biologie/ehh/forum/ausstellungen/monistenbund.htm On Haeckel's enormous influence, see Nipperdey, *Religion im Umbruch*, pp. 126-27; on the *Monisten-Bund* and Ostwald's sermons, ibid., pp. 135-36.

31. Jacobowski, the founder of *Die Kommenden*, was Jewish. The membership included Leo Frobenius, the anthropologist; Rudolf Steiner, the founder of anthroposophy; the poet and critic Wolfgang Kirchbach, a close friend of Avenarius; the Jewish expressionist poetess Else Lasker-Schüler; the anarchist Erich Mühsam (also Jewish), murdered by the Nazis in 1933; and the self-proclaimed "anti-modern" composer Hans Pfitzner, subsequently a supporter of National Socialism. The aim of the *Neue Gemeinschaft*, as stated in its brochure, was to "embrace everything that concerns and excites the life and thought of modern, intellectually free men and women struggling to define a new view of the world, [...] to achieve a new, authentic culture for humanity." (Quoted by Karin Bruns in *Handbuch literarisch-kultureller Vereine, Gruppen und Bünde 1825-1933*, p. 358) Its members included Wilhelm Bölsche, one of the founders of the *Giordano Bruno-Bund*; Adolf Damaschke, the champion of "Bodenreform" [land reform]; Gustav Landauer, the Jewish anarcho-socialist who, as a member of the short-lived Munich revolutionary government, was murdered by the Counter-revolutionaries in 1919; Hugo Höppener (Fidus), the *völkisch* artist and future Nazi; Martin Buber, the Jewish philosopher and theologian; and Magnus Hirschfeld, the physician, sexologist, and champion of homosexual rights, who was also Jewish.

In 1912, those elected to the governing board of the *Dürer-Bund* ranged from left-leaning or liberal (the Social Democratic theorist and politician Eduard Bernstein; the neo-Kantian philosopher Paul Natorp; the writer Ricarda Huch) to right-wing and nationalist or *völkisch* (Henry Thode, a fierce critic of the French influence on German painting and the trend toward Impressionism, represented by the Jewish-born Max Liebermann; Wilhelm Schäfer, a popular writer of short stories, later a supporter of National Socialism; the architect Paul Schultze-Naumburg, an enemy both of pompous imperial neo-baroque and of international modernism, and a champion of a revived, racially determined vernacular style; Wilhelm Schwaner, author of the *Germanen-Bibel*), with most members of the board somewhere in between (e.g. the artist Max Klinger, the architect Heinrich Tesserow, the composers Max Reger and Anton Webern, the historians Friedrich Meinecke and

Karl Lamprecht.) It included a few Jews (the politican Bernstein and the painter Liebermann) and at least two particularly virulent anti-Semites: Adolf Bartels, a supporter of the German Christian movement, a leading champion of *Heimatkunst* [art, architecture, literature, and music rooted in native soil and popular tradition], the author of *Geschichte der deutschen Literatur* [1901-1902], *Heinrich Heine: Auch ein Denkmal* [1906], and *Judentum und deutsche Literatur*, [1912], all of which denounce the corrupting "Jewish influence" on German literature, and the recipient, in 1942, of the NSDAP's Gold Medal; and Arthur Bonus, another supporter of a Germanic Christianity and the author of *Von Stöcker zu Naumann: Ein Wort zur Germanisierung des Christentums* [1896] and *Deutscher Glaube* [1897]. (See Kratzsch, *Kunstwart und Dürerbund*, pp. 467-68)

The membership of the *Verdhandi* – or *Werdandi-Bund*, founded in 1907 to combat international modernism and foster a German style in art and architecture (it took its name from Verhandi, one of the Norns or Fates of Nordic mythology), was more decidedly *völkisch*-nationalist and anti-Semitic (Bartels; the artist Franz Stassen, a close friend of the Wagners; the architect Paul Schultze-Naumburg; the poet Börries von Münchhausen; the art critic Henry Thode) but even it also included the Jewish graphic artist Hermann Struck (Rolf Parr, "Werdandi-Bund (Berlin)," in *Handbuch literarisch-kultureller Vereine, Gruppen und Bünde 1825-1933*, pp. 485-95) and Heinrich Vogeler was among the signers of the Bund"s original Aufruf or statement of purpose in 1908. (Janos Frecot, "Der Werdandibund," in Burkhard Bergius, Janos Frecot and Dieter Radicke, eds., *Architektur, Stadt und Politik. Julius Posener zum 75. Geburtstag* [Giessen: Ananabas Verlag, 1979], Werkbund Archiv Jahrbuch 4, pp. 37-46).

32. There is no English equivalent of the term "völkisch." Since the late nineteenth century it has been used, in German, to describe what properly belongs to the *volk*, the community constituted by race and tradition. It signals opposition to the "bourgeois," liberal, constitutional state, to international trade, industry and finance, to urban and cosmopolitan lifestyles, to democracy, to "international" Jewry and foreign influences on culture and the arts generally, as well as to international socialism and even, often enough, to the Roman Catholic Church on account of its roots in the Jewish Old Testament and its universalist message. In a text of 1928, by Alfred Conn, the author of books with titles like *Rasse statt Heilsplan* [Race instead of Redemption] and *Das eddische Weltbild: Mythos statt Geschichte* [The Worldview of the *Edda*: Myth instead of History], both published in 1934, it is defined as follows: "Völkisch kommt vom Volk und bedeutet den Willen, in arteigenen oder, anders ausgedrückt, blutbedingten Formen zu leben. Arteigen leben heißt völkisch sein [...]. Völkisch sein ist eine Sache des Blutes." [*Völkisch* comes from *volk*, or folk, and signifies the will to live in forms proper to one's own kind or kin, in other words, in forms determined by blood. To be *völkisch* is to live in ways proper to one's own kin. Being *völkisch* is a matter of blood.] (Quoted in Uwe Puschner, "Weltanschauung und Religion," p. 7). George L. Mosse's nuanced account of "Volkish" in his *Germans and Jews: The Right, the Left, and the Search for a 'Third Force' in Pre-Nazi Germany* (New York: Howard Fertig, 1970) remains invaluable.

33. Quoted in Dieter Fricke, "Der 'Deutschbund'," in *Handbuch zur "Völkischen Bewegung" 1871-1918,"* p. 329, from *Was ist und was will der Deutschbund*, Lange's address at the opening meeting, 18 October 1894.

34. Ekkehard Hieronymus in *Handbuch zur "Völkischen Bewegung" 1871-1918*, p. 136,

citing the *Regularium Fratrum Ordinis Novi Templi*. The term "ario-heroic" alludes to the Aryan basis of the heroic world-view. See also on the *Ordo Novi Templi*: Friedrich-Wilhelm Haack, *Wotans Wiederkehr: Blut-, Boden- und Rasse-Religion* (Munich: Claudius Verlag, 1981), pp. 37-47.

35. Quoted in Michael Bönisch, "Die 'Hammer'-Bewegung," in *Handbuch zur "Völkischen Bewegung" 1871-1918*, p. 352.

36. *Runen*, no. 7 (21 July 1918); Rudolf von Sebottendorf, *Bevor Hitler kam* (Munich, 1934), pp. 57-60; both quoted in Markus Osterrieder, "Völkische 'Niebelungei': Das Wiederaufleben der 'Nibelungenströmung' in der deutschen Kultur des 19. Jahrhunderts," *Erziehungskunst*, 2002, 66: 3-10 (also http://www.celtoslavica.de/bibliothek/nibelungelei.html

37. Göring, Heß, Himmler, Rosenberg, Julius Streicher, and other leading figures in the NSDAP, though not Hitler himself, were members of the *Thule Society*. (Friedrich-Wilhelm Haack, *Wotans Wiederkehr*, pp. 7-8). In the 1920s ever more such societies continued to be founded (see sample lists in Haack, *Wotans Wiederkehr*, pp. 48-49), such as the *Edda-Gesellschaft* (1925) of Rudolf John Gorsleben, a member of both the *Ordo Novi Templi* and the *Thule Gesellschaft*, the author of the anti-Semitic (and anti-Christian) *Die Überwindung des Judentums in uns und außer uns* [The Overcoming of Judaism in us and outside of us] (1920), and the publisher and editor of a periodical successively named *Deutsche Freiheit*, *Arische Freiheit*, and – after it became the organ of the *Edda-Gesellschaft* – *Hagal* (after the rune of that name, to which Gorsleben ascribed occult properties). Gorsleben's translation of the *Edda*, which he presented as a kind of Bible of Nordic-Germanic religion, ethics, and customs appeared in 1920 and went through many subsequent editions (1921, 1922, 1923, 1924, 1930, 1933, 1935, 1940). The Princess was probably one of its many readers; the *Edda* figures explicitly in her later fictional writing as just such a source book of wisdom and ethical example. On Gorsleben, see Nicholas Goodrick-Clarke, *The Occult Roots of Nazism: The Ariosophists of Austria and Germany 1890-1935* (Wellingborough, Northhants.: The Aquarian Press, 1985), pp. 155-60.

38. Quoted from *Das Reich der Erfüllung: Flugschriften zur Begründung einer neuen Weltanschauung*, ed. Julius and Heinrich Hart, numbers 1 and 2 (Leipzig, 1901) and Julius Hart, *Der Neue Gott* (Leipzig 1900), in Rolf Kauffeldt, "Die Idee eines 'Neuen Bundes' (Gustav Landauer)," in Manfred Frank, *Gott im Exil: Vorlesungen über die Neue Mythologie*, 2. Teil (Frankfurt a.M.: Suhrkamp, 1988), pp. 131-79, at pp. 139-40.

39. Uwe Puschner, "Weltanschauung und Religion," section 4, quoting from Karl Themel, *Der religiöse Gehalt der völkischen Bewegung und ihre Stellung zur Kirche* (Berlin, 1926).

40. Max Robert Gerstenhauer, *Was ist Deutsch-Christentum?* 2nd edn. (Berlin-Schlachtensee, 1930), quoted in Puschner, "Weltanschauung und Religion."

41. Paul de Lagarde, "Über das Verhältnis des deutschen Staates zu Theologie, Kirche und Religion" (1873), in *Deutsche Schriften*, ed. Wilhelm Rössle (Jena: Eugen Diederichs Verlag, 1944; 1st edn. 1878), pp. 94-156, on pp. 141, 156. See also "Über die gegenwärtige Lage des deutschen Reichs" (1875): "As religion makes an exclusive claim to rule and the fatherland – as distinct from the state – may rightfully make the same claim, conflict between the two can be avoided only by striving […] to achieve a national religion, in which the interests of religion are wedded to those of the fatherland." (ibid., p. 216)

42. W. Maasddorff, *Die Religion und die Philosophie der Zukunft*, 2nd edn. (Lorch-Württemberg: Karl Röhm, 1914; the Foreword is dated 1902), pp. 34-35.

43. Schwaner, cited in *Der Kunstwart*, XXVI, 2nd issue for August 1913, p. 263.

44. Joachim Kurd Niedlich, *Deutsche Religion als Voraussetzung deutscher Wiedergeburt* (Leipzig, 1921). The titles of some other works by this author (see the entry on him by Matthias Wolfes in *Biographisches-Bibliographisches Kirchenlexikon*) are indicative of the direction of his thought: *Das Mythenbuch: Die Germanische Mythen- und Märchenwelt als Quelle deutscher Weltanschauung* [The Book of Myth: The World of Germanic Myth and Folktale as Source of the German Worldview] (Leipzig, 1921; 2nd edn. 1923; 3rd edn. 1927]; *Jahwe oder Jesus? Die Quelle unserer Entartung* [Jahwe or Jesus? The Origin of our Degeneration] (Leipzig 1921; 2nd edn. 1925). See also Puschner, "Weltanschauung und Religion," sec. 7-15.

45. Ottmar Hegemann, "Das Recht des Kristentums," *Heimdall, Zeitschrift für Deutschtum und Altdeutschtum* (1915), 20: 100, quoted in Puschner, "Weltanschauung und Religion," Sec. 8.

46. "Unsere Ziele," *Das Geistchristentum: Monatschrift zur Vollendung der Reformation durch Wiederherstellung der reinen Heilandslehre*, 1932, 5: 329, quoted in Rainer Flasche, "Vom deutschen Kaiserreich zum Dritten Reich: Nationalreligiöse Bewegungen in der ersten Hälfte des 20. Jahrhunderts in Deutschland," *Zeitschrift für Religionswissenschaft*, 1993, 1 (2): 28-49, on p. 43. Dinter's insistence on the need for a new religious foundation for the New Germany was to lead to his expulsion from the Nazi Party (which he had joined at its founding and for which he held card no. 5) when, as efforts were being made to find an accommodation with the established Churches, it proved inopportune.

47. Alfred Rosenberg, *The Myth of the Twentieth Century*, trans. Vivian Bird (Torrance, CA: Noontide Press, 1982; orig. German, 1930), pp. 383, 387.

48. J. W. Hauer, "Die Anthroposophie als Weg zum Geist," *Die Tat*, 12, no. 11, February, 1921, pp. 800-24, on pp. 802-03.

49. Carlson, p. 28; Rudolf Steiner, "Form-Creating Forces" (a lecture given in Berlin, 20 June 1912), in *Earthly and Cosmic Man* (Blauvelt, NY: Spiritual Science Library, 1986), p. 172. As early as 1919, "Steiner and the adherents of anthroposophy were regarded as enemies in nationalist and national socialist circles." Thus Dietrich Eckart, the right-wing nationalist poet who was a mentor to Hitler in his early Munich days, criticized the founding of an anthroposophic Waldorf school in Stuttgart and described Steiner as a Jew in his popular anti-Semitic weekly *Auf gut Deutsch* in 1919. Hitler himself attacked Steiner in the *Völkischer Beobachter*, the Nazi Party newspaper (15 March 1921), as a leading figure in the "destruction of the normal spiritual constitution of peoples." Supporters of Ludendorff disrupted a Steiner lecture in Munich in 1922. A Nazi Party report on anthroposophy, dated May 1936, presented Steiner's movement as philo-Semitic, sympathetic to Communism, linked to freemasonry, and critical of the notion of a deep connection between a people and a race. "It condemns the racial and the *völkisch* to the low sphere of the primitive, and treats them as instincts that have to be overcome by spirit." A further report, drawn up by the Nazi philosopher Alfred Bäumler in 1938 noted Steiner's high regard for "the Jew Ludwig Jacobowski"; see Uwe Werner, *Anthroposophen in der Zeit des Nationalsozialismus (1933-1945)* (Munich: R. Oldenbourg, 1999), pp. 7-8. On Steiner's opposition to racism and attacks on him by the National Socialists,

see also René Freund, *Braune Magie? Okkultismus, New Age und Nationalsozialismus* (Vienna: Picus-Verlag, 1995), pp. 21-23.

50. In demanding a "modern" religion, the publisher Diederichs and many of his authors had a "German" religion in mind. (Justus H. Ulbricht, "'Theologia deutsch'," pp. 167-68) As formulated by the "more moderate wing" of the movement on 16 May 1933, the guiding principles of the *Deutsche Christen* [German Christians], "recognize[ed] the difference between peoples and races as a God-given order for this world" and therefore rejected the whole idea of missionary work. "True" Christianity – i.e. Christianity purged of all Judaic (and Roman) influences – was for Aryans only. (Full document in Peter Matheson, ed., *The Third Reich and the Christian Churches* [Edinburgh: T. & T. Clark, 1981], pp. 21-23).

51. Thomas Westerich, *Orplid das heilige Land: Das Mysterium der Reinheit* (Stade: Zwei Welten Verlag, 1922), p. 12, quoted in Puschner, "Weltanschauung und Religion," sec. 9. In the same vein, Artur Dinter: "Race and religion are one." (*Die Sünde wider das Blut*, [Leipzig: Wolfverlag, 1918], Afterword to $1^{st}$, $2^{nd}$ and $3^{rd}$ eds., quoted by Puschner, *ibid.*) See also Günter Hartung, "Artur Dinter, der Erfolgautor des frühen deutschen Faschismus," in *The Attractions of Fascism: Traditionen und Traditionssuche des deutschen Faschismus*, ed. Günter Hartung (Halle a.d. Saale: Martin-Luther-Universität/ Wissenschaftliche Beiträge, 1988), pp. 55-83, at p. 62.

52. *Foundations of the Nineteenth Century*, trans. John Lees, 2 vols. (London and New York: John Lane, 1911; $1^{st}$ edn. 1910; orig. German 1899), vol. 2, pp. 45-50.

53. Wilhelm Schwaner, *Germanen-Bibel*, 2nd edn. enlarged, 2 vols. (Berlin-Schlachtensee; Volkserzieher-Verlag, 1904-05), vol. 1, p. viii. Ferdinand Avenarius went further, proclaiming the Unconscious the dwelling place of "Volk und Rasse." but also of "das Gemeinsame allen Menschentums" [what is common to all mankind], and warning against xenophobic rejection of everything alien. ("Hodler in unsrer Kunst," *Kunstwart*, 1918, 31: 129-32, on p. 129).

54. J. Wilhelm Hauer, *Deutsche Gottschau: Grundzüge eines deutschen Glaubens*, $4^{th}$ edn. (Stuttgart: Kutbrod Verlag, 1935; $1^{st}$ edn. 1934), p. 240.

55. From document in Matheson, ed., *The Third Reich and the Christian Churches*, p. 23.

56. Quoted in Matheson, ed., *The Third Reich and the Christian Churches*, p. 6.

57. Quoted in Matheson, *The Third Reich and the Christian Churches*, pp. 39-40, 81-82. In the period after World War II some Germanic religious groups denied that the importance they had attached to race had had anything to do with the destructive racism of the National Socialists. According to a text published by the *Germanische Glaubensgemeinschaft* after the end of World War II, Ludwig Fahrenkrog, founder of the *Germanische Glaubensgemeinschaft*, and Otto Sigfrid Reuter, founder of the *Deutscher Orden* and the *Deutsch-religiöse Gemeinschaft*, had failed to unite their organizations because they could not agree on the participation of Ernst Wachler, the director of the open air "Harzer Bergtheater," which Wachler placed at the GGG's disposal for its annual summer *Thing* or General Assembly and at which he also put on Fahrenkrog's Nordic myth-inspired dramatic spectacles. Though a champion of a Nordic-Germanic religion, an advocate of *Aufnordung* (restoring the Nordic racial component in the German people), and an early supporter of the National Socialists, Wachler had a Jewish grandparent. Reuter refused to

participate with him in a proposed "Thing" to be held by the *GGG* and the *DRG* in common in 1914, since, "as a German-Jewish man, Dr. Wachler did not meet the conditions of our agreement [to hold a 'Thing' in common]. [...] You wrote that we planned to be 'among our own kind'," Ernst Hunkel, a leading member of Reuter's organization, told Fahrenkrog, "and yet you propose as one of the main speakers Dr. Wachler, who is personally quite honorable but [...] not 'of our kind.'" The implication is that Fahrenkrog gave up the opportunity to collaborate with Reuter because he was not willing to sacrifice Wachler and was therefore not a racist. It is admitted that a provision was subsequently introduced requiring proof of pure German ancestry as a condition of membership in the *GGG*. An extract from Fahrenkrog's *Das deutsche Buch* (an account of his spiritual itinerary), published as *Die Germanische Glaubensgemeinschaft* (Berlin-Steglitz: Verlag *Kraft und Schönheit*, n.d. [probably 1921]; Kleine Germanenhefte 6) states: "We require blood, just as we require the experience of God in us; i.e., as befits a community of German faith: race and religion!" (p. 6) Likewise the opening clause of the *GGG*'s "profession of faith" in the same booklet: "I solemnly declare that I am of German ancestry and, to the best of my knowledge and in good conscience, free of the blood of a non-Aryan race. I also swear to keep my blood pure through an appropriate marriage and to raise my children in this spirit." (p. 11) This clause was apparently adapted from the 1911 membership form of Reuter's *Deutsch-religiöse Gemeinschaft* which required the incoming member to swear that he or she was "to the best of my knowledge free of the blood of any Semitic or dark-skinned race." (See Uwe Puschner, *Die völkische Bewegung im wilhelminischen Kaiserreich*, p. 236). It is claimed, however, that this provision was never dogmatically enforced and that Fahrenkrog stuck by Wachler even as anti-Jewish measures grew in intensity. Fahrenkrog is quoted as maintaining through the 1930s that the *GGG* was neither anti-Semitic nor anti-Christian, that it was non-political and that it sought only toleration of all creeds and all religious groups. (See www.germanische-glaubens-gemeinschaft.de/gggundns.htm [February 2009]).

58. Following Lagarde (*Deutsche Schriften*, pp. 140-42), it was generally agreed that a national faith could not be created by fiat but had to grow organically from the German spirit. Thus, for instance, Fahrenkrog: "A German faith can come into being only through the German spirit. But who are we? We are the spirit and the religious aspiration of our ancestors and forefathers by way of Eckehart and Goethe down to the present day." Fahrenkrog went on to cite Eckhart, Böhme, Angelus Silesius, Kant, Goethe, Lagarde, and Hartmann in support of the view that an indwelling, an experience, a knowledge of "God in us" is the defining characteristic of the Germans as distinct from other peoples. (*Die Germanische Glaubensgemeinschaft*, pp. 4-5) On the threshold of the Nazi era, the theme was developed by Alfred Rosenberg in *The Myth of the Twentieth Century* (trans. Vivian Bird [Torrance, CA: The Noontide Press, 1982], p. 153).

59. Chamberlain, *Foundations of the Nineteenth Century*, vol. 1, pp. 221-23, 246-47. In the year Chamberlain's book appeared, the journal *Heimdall* wrote of "the Aryan Jesus Christ, the son of a Germanic-Roman official" and presented the Bible as appealing for "pure blood and a higher race." (1901, no. 2, p. 45; see René Freund, *Braune Magie*, p. 27). *Heimdall* described itself as *Monatsschrift für deutsche Art, Zeitschrift für reines Deutschtum und All-Deutschtum* [Monthly magazine for Germanic Kin, Journal for pure Germandom and All-Germandom]. Heimdall was the Norse God of light, the watchman of the Gods, and "the whitest-skinned of all

the Gods" (*Encyclopedia Britannica*). Hitler himself asserted that "Christus war ein Arier." [Christ was an Aryan] (*Tischgespräch*, quoted in Friedrich-Wilhelm Haack, *Wotans Wiederkehr*, p. 61)

60. See Appendix to Part I, "The *Völkisch* rejection of Christianity."

61. Klaus Jeziorkowski, "Empor ins Licht: Gnostizismus und Licht-Symbolik in Deutschland um 1900," in his *Eine Iphigenie rauchend: Aufsätze und Feuilletons zur deutschen Tradition* (Frankfurt a.M.: Suhrkamp, 1987), pp. 152-80; Ernst Osterkamp, *Lucifer: Stationen eines Motivs* (Berlin and New York: Walter de Gruyter, 1979), pp. 226-27; Flasche, "Vom Deutschen Kaiserreich zum Dritten Reich," p. 44; Siewert, "Germanische Religion und neugermanisches Heidentum," p. 135; Hartung, "Artur Dinter, der Erfolgautor des frühen deutschen Faschismus," pp. 64-65.

62. Quoted from Niekisch, *Entscheidung* (Berlin, 1930), in Michael Pittwald, *Ernst Niekisch: Völkischer Sozialismus, nationale Revolution, deutsches Endimperium* (Cologne: PapyRossa Verlag, 2002), p. 143. Niekisch was a leading representative of what is sometimes called the "Left of the Right," the author of a book attacking Hitler, and the editor, until he was banned from publishing and then imprisoned, of a journal entitled *Widerstand* [Resistance]. His differences with Hitler, which allowed him to appear as an opponent of National Socialism, did not prevent him from sharing much common ground with the National Socialists, including their anti-Semitism. See Ernst Niekisch, *Widerstand: ausgewählte Aufsätze*, ed. Uwe Sauermann (Krefeld: Sinus-Verlag, 1982).

63. "Wir Volkserzieher nennen uns Gottsucher; wir anerkennen ein Gotteswesen, das alles durchdringt als das schaffende, erhaltende und regulierende Prinzip, aber wir suchen es nicht über den Wolken, sondern in uns selbst." (Quoted in Schnurbein, "Die Suche nach einer 'arteigenen' Religion in 'germanisch' – und 'deutschgläubigen' Gruppen," in *Handbuch zur "Völkischen Bewegung" 1871-1918*, pp. 172-85, on p. 179). In similar vein, Guido von List had claimed that the racially pure, free-spirited, heroic, Northern, Ario-Germanic man has no need of written law [für den armanisch und rassisch fühlenden Ario-Germanen bedarf es [...] des geschriebenen [...] Gesetzes nicht], for the law, like the divine itself, is alive in him [denn das Natur-Gesetz ist [...] lebendig in ihm]. The Southern, Mediterranean races, in contrast, require the written laws and sanctions of an external, tyrant-God. (Contribution to *Das Eheproblem im Spiegel unserer Zeit*, ed. Ferdinand Freiherr von Paungarten [Munich: Ernst Reinhardt Verlag, 1913], pp. 59-65) On the indwelling of the divine as a recurrent feature of new "German" [i.e. non-Judaic] religions, see also Hieronimus, "Zur Religiosität der völkischen Bewegung," pp. 168-69, and Puschner, "Weltanschauung und Religion," sec. 11.

64. Wilhelm Schwaner, *Germanen-Bibel*, vol. 1, pp. xxxi-xxxii. The likely source of this text is Schmitt's 18-page booklet, *Katechismus der Religion des Geistes* (Budapest: Heisler, 1914); Eberhardt-Humanus in Wilhelm Schwaner, *Germanen-Bibel*, vol. 1, p. xxxi.

65. Ludwig Fahrenkrog, "Germanen-Tempel," *Volkserzieher*, 11 (1907), 42–43, and 12 (1908), 41–42, 77–78, 171–72, quoted in Hieronymus, "Zur Religiosität der völkischen Bewegung," 168–69. *Geschichte meines Glaubens* (Halle a.d. Saale: Gebauer-Schwetschke, 1906; 2nd edn. Leipzig: Hartung, 1926).

66. "Ist aber Gott in allem und also nicht nur in mir, dann bin ich auch der Andere. Ist aber Gott in mir, dann ist auch sein Gesetz in mir, dann bedarf es weder eines

geschriebenen Gesetzes noch eines Mittlers, dann gibt es für mich keine andere Erlösung als die durch mich selber. Meine neugewonnene Weltanschauung kurz in drei Sätze gefasst – Gott in uns, das Gesetz in uns und die Selbsterlösung – fand ich bald darauf." (Quoted in the 1997 Hamburg University Master's thesis of Daniel Junker, self-published as *Gott in uns! Die Germanische Glaubensgemeinschaft: Ein Beitrag zur Geschichte völkischer Religiosität in der Weimarer Republik* [Hamburg: Verlag Daniel Junker, 2002], p. 39, http://www.bod.de/index.php?id=296&objk_id=53833) Cf. Wilhelm Hauer, "We who hold the German Faith are convinced that men, and especially the Germans, have the capacity for religious independence, since it is true that everyone has an immediate relation to God, is, in fact, in the depths of his heart one with the eternal Ground of the world. That is why we reject the whole conception of mediation, whether through a sacred person, a sacred book, or a sacred rite." ("An Alien or a German Faith?" – a lecture given to an audience of ten thousand at the Berlin Sportpalast in April 1933 – in *Germany's New Religion: The German Faith Movement*, trans. T. S. K. Scott-Craig and R. E. Davies [London: George Allen & Unwin, 1937], pp. 36-70, on pp. 47-48) The absence of Spinoza from the religious literature promoting "Gott in uns" is striking; the epigraph of the *Tractatus Theologico-Politicus*, taken from I John 4. 13, reads "Hereby we know that we dwell in God and He in us, because He has given us of his Spirit." Spinoza also provides ample support for the claim by the advocates of a German *völkisch* religion that the Mosaic law applies only to the ancient Hebrews and was designed specifically for a primitive, unruly, and basically unspiritual people as well as for the charge that the chief motivation for observance of the law in Judaism is hope of reward and fear of punishment. (See *Tractatus Theologico-Politicus*, pp. 54-55, 84, 88, 91-92, 118-19).

67. See http://www.germanische-glaubens-gemeinschaft.de/bekenntnis.htm.

68. *Die Germanische Glaubensgemeinschaft* (Berlin-Steglitz: Verlag Kraft und Schönheit, n.d.). See fig. 17.

69. On Bonus, see Rainer Flasche, "Vom deutschen Kaiserreich zum Dritten Reich: Nationalreligiöse Bewegungen in der ersten Hälfte des 20. Jahrhunderts in Deutschland," pp. 39-40; on Diederichs, see Justus H. Ulbricht, "'Theologia deutsch'," pp. 167-68; on Eckart, see Claus-E. Bärsch, *Die politische Religion des Nationalsozialismus* (Munich: Wilhelm Fink Verlag, 1998), pp. 58-63; on Mathilde von Ludendorff, see Hieronimus, "Zur Religiosität der völkischen Bewegung," pp, 172-73; on Hauer, see J. Wilhelm Hauer, *Deutsche Gottschau: Grundzüge eines deutschen Glaubens*, p. 78; on Krannhals, see Hieronimus, "Zur Religiosität der völkischen Bewegung," p. 159 and Flasche, "Vom deutschen Kaiserreich zum Dritten Reich: Nationalreligiöse Bewegungen in der ersten Hälfte des 20. Jahrhunderts in Deutschland," pp. 45-46, citing Krannhals's *Religion als Sinnerfüllung des Lebens* (1933); on Rosenberg, see Alfred Rosenberg, *The Myth of the Twentieth Century*, pp. 130-33, and Clemens Vollnhals, "Völkisches Christentum oder deutscher Glaube: Deutsche Christen und Deutsche Glaubensgemeinschaft," *Revue d'Allemagne*, 2000, 32: 205-17, on pp. 212-13.

70. Peter Matheson, ed., *The Third Reich and the Christian Churches*, p. 40.

**Chapter 2.**

1. On the orientation of Eugen Diederichs' important publishing enterprise, see the excellent essay by Gangolf Hübinger, "Der Verlag Eugen Diederichs in Jena,"

*Geschichte und Gesellschaft* (1996), 22: 31-45. On the "ambivalences" of Diederichs' "alternative Moderne" and the cultural circle around him in Jena, the *Sera-Kreis*, see also Meike G. Werner, *Moderne in der Provinz: Kulturelle Experimente im Fin de Siècle Jena* (Göttingen: Wallstein, 2003); Justus Ulbricht and Meike G. Werner, eds., *Romantik, Revolution und Reform: Der Eugen Diederichs Verlag im Epochenkontext 1900-1949* (Göttingen: Wallstein Verlag, 1999); and Diederichs' own autobiographical sketches and correspondence, *Selbstzeugnisse und Briefe von Zeitgenossen*, ed. Ulf Diederichs (Düsseldorf and Cologne: Diederichs Verlag, 1967).

2. In the Introduction to an edition of texts on Chasidism by Buber, Maurice Friedman noted in Buber's earlier writing on this topic "the suggestion of mystic unity, […] of the self as part of the all, which contrasts with Buber's later philosophy of dialogue." (*Hasidism and Modern Man* [New York: Horizon Press, 1958], p. 14) In general, anti-Semitic writers sometimes professed admiration for those deeply religious, conservative Jews to whom religion and identity as a *volk* were one (e.g. Chamberlain, Langbehn, Börries von Münchhausen); their target was the "modern," emancipated, individualist, and therefore rootless Jews whose cosmopolitanism and very readiness to assimilate threatened to undermine the racial integrity and *völkisch* solidarity of the peoples among whom they lived. Quoting Jewish sources may also have been a rhetorical ploy of racist and anti-Semitic writers. The Princess's husband, Hanno Konopath, refers in his pamphlet *Ist Rasse Schicksal? Grundgedanken der völkischen Bewegung* (published in 1926 by the notorious extreme rightwing press of J. Lehmann in Munich) to "what G. Karpeles writes in the volume commemorating the twentieth anniversary of the Jewish Order of B'nai B'rith: 'Just as the individual stands firmest on the foundation of the heritage of his fathers, to which he is bound by a thousand fine threads, so too a people can find strong roots only in its own history, its own writing. Here is to be found the secret of its strength…'" (3rd edn., 1931, p. 6) On Münchhausen's praise of the ancient Hebrews, see my "Jugendstil in Firestone: The Jewish Illustrator E. M. Lilien," *Princeton University Library Chronicle*, 66, no. 1 (2004), 11–78, at 41–49.

3. See George L. Mosse, "The Influence of the Volkish Idea on German Jewry," ch. 4 of his *Germans and Jews*, especially pp. 85-92; also the excellent article by Bernard Susser, "Ideological Multivalence: Martin Buber and the German Volkish Tradition," *Political Theory* (1977), 5: 75-96.

4. On Buber and Schwaner, see Martin Buber, *Briefwechsel aus sieben Jahrzehnten*, ed. Grete Schaeder, vol. 2: 1918-1938 (Heidelberg: Verlag Lambert Schneider, 1973), pp. 52-53, 264. On Buber and Hauer, ibid., pp. 326-29, 457, 473 and Margarete Dierks, *Jakob Wilhelm Hauer 1881-1962: Leben, Werk, Wirkung, mit einer Personalbibliographie* (Heidelberg: Lambert Schneider, 1986), pp. 202-08, 243-44, 344-45 et passim.

5. J. Wilhelm Hauer, *Deutsche Gottschau: Grundzüge eines deutschen Glaubens*, pp. 4, 22.

6. Karl O. Paetel, *Reise ohne Uhrzeit: Autobiographie*, ed. Wolfgang D. Elfe and John M. Spalek (London: The World of Books; Worms: Verlag Georg Heinz, 1982), pp. 30, 185. Paetel, whose second mentor was Ernst Niekisch, the founder and leader of the "National Bolshevik" movement, quit the NSDAP when it became clear to him that Hitler was not interested in socialism and intended to maintain capitalism. He was subsequently imprisoned by the Nazis.

7. Quoted in Cancik, *Religions- und Geistesgeschichte der Weimarer Republik*, pp. 178-

## 152   Brownshirt Princess

79, n. 12. In 1949, Buber testified to a denazification court that Hauer was "a man of deep and serious religious vision, who, like many other truly intellectual and moral Germans, succumbed to the illusion that the National Socialist project offered the prospect of realizing his ideas in history." (Quoted in Heinz Eduard Tödt, *Komplizen, Opfer und Gegner des Hitlerregimes: zur "inneren Geschichte" von protestantischer Theologie und Kirche im "Dritten Reich"* [Gütersloh: Chr. Kaiser, 1997], p. 186).

8. See the entry on "Deutschgläubige Bewegungen" by Kurt Nowak in *Theologische Realenzyklopädie*, ed. Gerhard Krause and Gerhard Müller (Berlin and NewYork: Walter de Gruyter, 1981), 8: 554-59, on p. 557.

9. Quoted in Ulrich Nanko, *Die Deutsche Glaubensbewegung: Eine historische und soziologische Untersuchung* (Marburg: Diagonal-Verlag, 1993), pp. 89, 139. See also *Deutsche Gottschau*, pp. 10-11, where Hauer claims – following Houston Stewart Chamberlain (*Foundations of the Nineteenth Century*, vol. 2, pp. 41-42) – that while the creativity of the Jews in religious matters cannot and should not be denied, the Nordic and Germanic achievement in this area is equal and indeed superior to that of the Jews.

10. Klaus Jeziorkowski, "Empor ins Licht: Gnostizismus und Licht-Symbolik in Deutschland um 1900," p. 153.

11. Geoff Eley, "Making a Place in the Nation," in Eley and James Retallack, eds., *Wilhelminism and its Legacies: German Modernities*, pp. 16-33, on p. 31. No doubt rapidly evolving social and economic conditions alone cannot account for the enormous popularity of the idea of *Werden* [Becoming] in Germany. In an age of industrial expansion vitalist philosophies were popular in many countries, as the impact of Bergson in France demonstrates. Moreover, many adepts of the new *Lebensphilosophie* were as scornful of the rising industrial, commercial, and technocratic culture of the new Germany as of diehard old conservatives. As has been pointed out, however, opponents of "modern" liberal-capitalist culture often espoused a "modern," Nietzschean-Darwinian cult of "energy" and "struggle." They may thus be seen, not implausibly, as part of the very social and economic conditions they rejected.

12. Avenarius, "Stirb und werde! In der Zeit der Totenfeste," *Deutscher Wille: Des Kunstwarts 32. Jahr*, October-December 1918, pp. 103-04.

13. Peter Kratz, *Die Götter des New Age* (Berlin: Elefanten Press, 1994), p. 307. Wirth claimed to have demonstrated that "the course of the development of human culture is the opposite [of what it is usually held to be]: from North and West to East." (Herman Wirth, *Der Aufgang der Menschheit: Untersuchungen zur Geschichte der Religion, Symbolik und Schrift der Atlantisch-Nordischen Rasse* [Jena: Eugen Diederichs, 1928], p. 16)

14. The report was published by the press of Diederichs at Jena in 1931. (See Siewert, "Gemanische Religion und neugeranisches Heidentum," p. 135; Hieronimus, "Zur Religiosität der völkischen Bewegung," p. 167).

## Chapter 3.

1. Pantheism is by no means identical with Gnosticism; in some respects the two are opposed. (See Hans Jonas, *The Message of the Alien God and the Beginnings of Christianity: The Gnostic Religion*, 3rd edn. [Boston: Beacon Press, 2001], pp. 262-

64). Opponents of the established religions, however, seem to have borrowed indiscriminately from both. On the startling success of Indo-Germanic scholars in winning acceptance for the idea of a deep, race-based historical connection between ancient Nordic beliefs and those of Buddhism and Hinduism – and in laying the foundations of an Aryan National Socialist religion, see Victor and Victoria Trimondi, *Hitler-Buddha-Krishna: Eine unheilige Allianz vom Dritten Reich bis heute*. Research into this issue was the main business of Himmler's *Ahnenerbe* foundation until the outbreak of war. Just as those who wished to salvage the New Testament for the new National Socialist Germany claimed that Jesus was an Aryan, those who wished to discard Christianity altogether in favor of a race-based Aryan religion argued that Buddha had been a fair-skinned, blue-eyed Nordic type (p. 62 et passim).

2. Cf. the similar tone, a decade earlier, of the poem "Sehnsucht" by Wilhelm Spohr, who managed to be both a patron of the future Nazi Fidus and a collaborator of the anarcho-socialist Gustav Landauer: "Auf die Berge möcht' ich fliehn,/ Fort aus dieser dumpfen Welt,/ Wo der Staub der Erdenmenschen/ Geistesflug gefangen hält./ Fort aus diesen engen Mauern,/ Aus der Stätte düstrer Qual,/ Auf den Bergen, auf den Bergen,/ Da ist Freiheit überall/ [...] Um mich her der Geister Weben,/ Und in mir des Geistes Kraft,/ Der zu tatenfrohem Leben/ Weg und Mittel selbst sich schafft." (*Bilder und Stimmungen: Gedichte* [Berlin and Leipzig: Modernes Verlagsbureau-Curt Wiegand, 1909], pp. 21-22) Walls and fences, along with the contrast between "das Wir" (the We) and "das häßliche Ich" (the ugly I), are likewise a recurrent theme in both the novels and the extremely popular fairy tales of a writer whose career stands in vivid contrast to that of the Princess – the gifted and undeservedly forgotten Hermynia Zur Mühlen, sometimes known as "die rote Gräfin." Born Countess Hermine Isabella Maria Viktoria Folliot de Crenneville-Poutet into an old Austrian noble family, Zur Mühlen broke with her family and background to devote herself to the cause of social and economic justice, was a member of the German Communist party in the 1920s, and fought tirelessly all her life against National Socialism, anti-Semitism, and oppression and discrimination of every kind. The impulse to break with the past and the longing for community could lead in diametrically opposed directions, as the contrast between Vogeler and Reuß zur Lippe has already indicated.

## Chapter 4.

1. Ludwig Gurlitt, "Der Fluch der toten Religion," *Die Aktion*, 1/8 (10 April 1911), col. 233-235 (233); see Joes Segal, *Krieg als Erlösung: Die deutsche Kunstdebatten 1910-1918* (Munich: Scaneg, 1997), p. 33. According to George L. Mosse, Gurlitt repeated his critique of Christianity at a teachers' meeting the following year (*The Crisis of German Ideology*, new edn. (New York: Schocken Books, 1981), pp. 154-55). For an excellent, still relevant overview of völkisch and National Socialist opposition to Christianity, see Edmond Vermeil, *Hitler et le Christianisme* (Paris: Gallimard, 1939)..

2. Letter dated 18 September, 193, quoted in Arn Strohmeyer, "Kunst im Zeichen der germanischen Vorfahren und der Wiedergeburt Deutschlands: Ludwig Roselius und Bernhard Hoetger," p. 69. See also Elizabeth Tumasonis, "Bernhard Hoetger's Tree of Life," pp. 89-90.

3. Ernst Wachler, *Über die Zukunft des deutschen Glaubens*, 1930 ed., pp. 6-8, quoted

## 154 Brownshirt Princess

in Uwe Puschner, *Die völkische Bewegung im wilhelminischen Kaiserreich*, pp. 226-27; *Die Armanenschaft der Ario-Germanen* (Vienna, 1908), quoted in Sylvia Siewert, *Germanische Religion und neugermanisches Heidentum*, p. 146.

4. Ernst Reuter, *Schriften, Reden*, ed. Hans E. Hirschfeld and Hans J. Reinhardt, 4 vols. (Berlin: Propyläen Verlag, 1972-75), vol. 1, p. 451, vol. 2, p. 486.

5. *Sigfrid oder Christus? Kampfruf an die germanischen Völker zur Jahrtausendwende* (Leipzig, 1910), quoted in Stephanie von Schnurbein, "Die Suche nach einer 'arteigenen' Religion in 'germanisch' – und 'deutschgläubigen' Gruppen," in *Handbuch zur "Völkischen Bewegung" 1871-1918*, p. 180. The anti-heroic strain in Christianity was a common theme of anti-Christian writing; cf. the complaint by Wilhelm Kusserow, leader of the *Nordisch-religiöse Arbeitsgemeinschaft* that "das Christentum verlangt die Zerknirschung und Beugung des stolzen Menschen. Es lehrt sogar die Feindesliebe" [Christianity demands remorse and submission from the proud-hearted man. It even teaches love of one's enemies]. (*Das nordische Artbekenntnis*, 1934, quoted in Friedrich-Wilhelm Haack, *Wotans Wiederkehr*, p. 27). In 1935, according to Hermann Ullstein, the head of the great Berlin publishing house, "in the centers of Berlin and Munich, certain shops displayed huge posters in the windows: *Down with a Christ who allows himself to be crucified! The German God cannot be a suffering God! He is a God of power and strength!*" The shops, Ullstein explains "were the propaganda centers of General Ludendorff and his fanatical second wife, whose pamphlets attacking Christianity were on sale there." (Hermann Ullstein, *The Rise and Fall of the House of Ullstein* [New York: Simon and Schuster, 1943], p. 282).

6. Quoted in Coole and Potter, *Thus Spake Germany*, p. 6.

7. Ernst Eberhardt-Humanus in Wilhelm Schwaner, *Germanen-Bibel*, 2nd edn, vol. 1, pp. xxx-xxxi.

8. Quoted from *Aufsätze zum Germanenglauben* (Leipzig, 1937), p. 7, in Claus Wolfschlag, *Ludwig Fahrenkrog: Das goldene Tor* (Dresden: Verlag Zeitenwende, 2006), pp. 14-15. A similar note was struck in a Christmas article in the official SS newspaper *Das schwarze Korps* on 22 December 1938: "The religions of the world may well call themselves universal and preach what they call the one-ness of the Christian people, but the peoples of foreign blood have never properly understood the profound symbolism of Christmas. The Magi of the East today cast frightened glances in the direction of the bright flame that we are lighting on the nights of the Winter Solstice. This flame for us is not the flame of sacrifice; it is not the same old buried custom. This flame is for us the clear sign of life; it is God smiling over the earth, a God who has called his creation to life and not to death. The flame burns throughout the night. For us, this hour is not one of bewitched obscurity. This flame lighting up the starry vault is for us the symbol of the unity of nature and life. Day and night, body and soul, light and shade, all is comprehended in the eternal cycle of the fertility of Time. Watch over this flame, comrades, for fire, light, and sun are the most sacred of our possessions." (Quoted in Frederic Reider, *The Order of the SS* [Tucson, AZ: Aztex Corporation, n.d.], p. 156).

9. Hieronimus, "Zur Religiosität der völkischen Bewegung," p. 172. On a visit to some well-heeled Ludendorff supporters in Hamburg in the mid-1920s, Hubertus, Prinz zu Loewenstein, heard his hosts assert that "the Jews are rather overrated," that "nobody realizes how dangerous the Jesuits are," and that the Jesuits, the Bolsheviks,

and the Jews and Freemasons constitute three purely tactical subdivisions of a single force bent on the destruction of the German people. (Prince Hubertus zu Loewenstein, *Conquest of the Past: An Autobiography* [Boston: Houghton Mifflin Company, 1938], pp. 189-92) Eighteen years later, with the National Socialists in power, Heinrich Himmler lumped Jews, Freemasons, Marxists, and the Churches together as enemies of Germany. The coming struggle, he warned in a speech to his SS *Gruppenführer* (8 November 1938), will be not only a struggle among the nations, but a struggle of world-views, in which the whole "Juden-, Freimaurer-, Marxisten- und Kirchentum" is aware that it must destroy Germany or be itself destroyed. (*Heinrich Himmler: Geheimreden 1933 bis 1945*, ed. Bradley F. Smith and Agnes Peterson, introd. Joachim Fest [Berlin: Propyläen Verlag, 1974], p. 37)

10. Oskar Michel, "Wie lange noch," *Ringendes Deutschtum*, 2 October 1921.

11. Quoted in Puschner, "Weltanschauung und Religion," sec. 4. On Wolzogen, who had been associated with the Hart brothers and who, like the Princess (though in a lighter, more satirical mode), was a rebel from his class, see Amelia von Ende, "A representative 'Young German': Ernst Freiherr von Wolzogen," *New York Times*, book review section, 7 January 1911. Wolzogen's step-brother Hans, a well known Wagnerite and editor of the *Bayreuther Blätter*, followed in the footsteps of his master by seeking to detach Christianity from its Jewish roots. He invited Franz Overbeck, Nietzsche's theologian friend and colleague in Basel, to contribute to a special issue of the journal on the topic "Entjudung des Christentums" [Dejudaising of Christianity], but was rebuffed. From the start the theme was unacceptable to him, Overbeck replied. "I do not believe in Schopenhauer's interpretation of Christianity [i.e. that it was closer to Buddhism than to Judaism - L.G.] even though I acknowledge that he had a keen eye for a certain element in it [...]. But the historical explanation offered by Schopenhauer is completely false and the consequences of his errors are particularly visible in some of Wagner's ideas, "for example his questioning of Jesus's Jewish descent." He and Rohde "and probably Nietzsche too" had clearly discerned the weakness of Schopenhauer's argument about a family connection between Christianity and Buddhism and the resulting "misconstruing of the family connection of Christianity and Judaism." (See Andreas Urs Sommer, "Weltentsagung, Skepsis und Modernitätskritik: Arthur Schopenhauer und Franz Overbeck," *Philosophisches Jahrbuch*, 107 [2000]: 192-205, on pp. 202-03).

12. *Zur Germanisierung des Christentums* (1911), quoted in Hieronimus, "Zur Religiosität der völkischen Bewegung," p. 164.

13. Prince Hubertus zu Loewenstein, *Conquest of the Past: An Autobiography*, p. 160. On the popularity among *völkisch* writers of the idea that Germanic fairytales, folktales, and ancient sagas served as a sanctuary in which the ancient wisdom and religious worldview of the Nordic peoples was preserved for centuries from the destructive attacks of an alien, "Judaic" Christianity, see Puschner, *Die völkische Bewegung im wilhelminischen Kaiserreich*, pp. 228-30.

14. "Unser Ziel," *Das Geistchristentum* (1932), 4: 329 f., quoted in Rainer Flasche, "Vom Deutschen Kaiserreich zum Dritten Reich: Nationalreligiöse Bewegungen in der ersten Hälfte des 20. Jahrhunderts in Deutschland," p. 44.

15. Quoted in Hieronimus, "Zur Religiosität der völkischen Bewegung," p. 174.

16. *Der Wahn vom völkischen Staat auf christlicher Grundlage* [The Illusion of a *Völkisch* State on Christian Foundations] (1928), quoted in Puschner, "Weltanschauung und

# 156   Brownshirt Princess

Religion," p. 23. In one of the conversations recorded by his doctor Felix Kersten, Himmler expressed a similar view of the incompatibility of authentic German-ness and Christianity. "The Church had a great interest in preventing the formation of a true Germanic type, for she had need of the inferior racial type, the only one ready to accept her teaching. The real hundred-per-cent German, on the other hand, was the born enemy of clerical doctrine." (*The Kersten Memoirs 1940-1945*, pp. 78-79) Likewise, the peasant-soldiers of Germanic race who will be settled in the conquered territories of the East will soon abandon the Church. "The more our training takes root and men become infused with our spirit, the less will they depend on the churches – and one day they will be empty. [...] It will be a particular satisfaction to me when we take over these churches and turn them into Germanic holy places." (ibid., p. 136)

## Chapter 5.

1.   Curiously, in view of her activities on behalf of the National Socialist regime, there is scant published information about the Princess. She is not mentioned in the standard books on women under National Socialism (e.g. Rita Thalmann [1982], Florence Hervé [1983], Georg Tidl [1984], Renate Wiggershaus [1984], Angelika Ebbinghaus [1987]).

2.   It was an idiosyncratic Reuß custom to name all male children Heinrich and number them, regardless of whether they were sovereign princes or not, in chronological order of their birth within a particular century. Thus, Heinrich XXIII (b. 1878) was the son of Heinrich VII (b. 1825) and elder brother of Heinrich XXXV (b. 1887), yet uncle/father of Heinrich V, Marie Adelheid's son (b. 1921).

3.   Konopath is listed on the website of an amateur English genealogist, along with hundreds of others, as a descendant of William the Conqueror. It is not clear, however, what credence if any should be given to this claim or whether Konopath himself ever made it. He did contribute a short article, entitled "Adel, eine politische Forderung" [Nobility: A Political Necessity], to the *Deutsches Adelsblatt*, 1924, 42: 328-29, probably in the same spirit as his friend Darré's *Neuadel aus Blut und Boden* of 1930.

4.   See the richly documented work of Stephan Malinowksi, *Vom König zum Führer* (Berlin: Akademie Verlag, 2003). Malinowski demonstrates that the attraction of the nobility to a different Right from that of traditional conservatism dates back to the Imperial period itself and to associations like the *Deutsche Kolonialgesellschaft* [German Colonial Society] and the *Deutsche Adelsgenossenschaft* [League of German Nobles] (pp. 175-97). The former was unavoidably racist; Malinowski notes (pp. 214-19) that the nobility was disproportionately represented in the brutal genocidal campaign against the Hereros in South-West Africa. The latter, founded in 1874, was anti-Semitic from the start but became "biologically" racist after 1918. A short summary of Malinowski's main findings is available in English: "From King to Führer: The German aristocracy and the Nazi movement," *Bulletin of the German Historical Institute of London*, 2005, vol. 27, pp. 5-28; on the close links between the Nazis and the nobility, see pp. 21-26. On "Rebellinnen" (women rebels) in the nobility, of whom the most celebrated is doubtless Franziska von Reventlow, see Monika Wienfort, "Adelige Frauen in Deutschland 1890-1939," in *Adel und Moderne*, ed. Eckart Conze and Monika Weinfort (Cologne; Weimar; Vienna: Böhlau, 2004),

pp. 197-203. Rebellious and adventurous, mostly upper-class women, ranging from Nancy Cunard, Gertrude Bell, and Hermynia Zur Mühlen to Magda Goebbels and the Mitfords, seem to have been a feature of the age. Of approximately 150 members of princely families who had joined the NSDAP by the end of 1934, 30% were women, whereas women made up only 5-8% of the general membership of the Party. (Werner Bräuninger, *Hitlers Kontrahenten in der NSDAP 1921-1945* [Munich: F. A. Herbig Verlagsbuchhandlung, 2004], p. 123)

5. See Malinowski, "From King to Führer," pp. 18-20 on the (illusory) belief in noble circles, which the Nazis never actively discouraged, that the restoration of a reformed monarchy and nobility might yet be the end result of Hitler's rise to power. On Crown Prince Wilhelm's relation to National Socialism, see Klaus W. Jonas, *Der Kronprinz Wilhelm* (Frankfurt a.M.: Heinrich Scheffler Verlag, 1962), pp. 222-79. In 1940 Wilhelm sent Hitler a telegram congratulating him on the "geniale Führung" that in barely five weeks had resulted in the capitulation of Belgium and Holland and the driving of the "ruins of the English expeditionary force into the sea" (reproduced in Jonas, p. 224).

6. Malinowkski, *Vom König zum Führer*, p. 541.

7. The Prince's book is a dull, systematically arranged compendium of the ideas of Clauß and Hans F. K. Günther. Its basic thesis is that a people's "common will is racially determined." (p. 4) According to one source, eighteen members of the House of Lippe joined the NSDAP. (Jonathan Petropoulos, Royals and the Reich: the Princes von Hessen in Nazi Germany [New York: Oxford University Press, 2000], p. 100).

8. In the early 1940s Clauß came under a cloud in some Nazi circles for allegedly giving precedence to "Geist" [spirit] or "Seele" [soul or psyche]) over "Blut" [blood]. One participant in a discussion at the Institute for the Study of the Jewish Question in March 1941 objected that "Clauß professes the view that an individual's physical racial configuration is no more than the expression of that individual's spiritual being, [...] that spirit and soul determine physical form." Though Clauß denied that this was his position, the discovery that Margarete Landé, his assistant over many years and allegedly his lover, had been a full-blooded Jewish woman, whom he had protected and hidden and whom he refused to give up, sealed his disgrace. (Leon Poliakov and Josef Wulf, *Das Dritte Reich und seine Diener: Dokumente* [Berlin-Grünewald: Arani-Verlag, 1959], pp. 413-15) Clauß himself apparently claimed in his defense that he had kept Landé on, in accordance with his so-called *mimetic* method of studying other races, in order to study her racial characteristics as a living object, so to speak, just as he had lived as a Bedouin with Bedouins when preparing his 1933 study of that people. According to a recent scholar, Clauß "did not intend any kind of racial (or other) equality between Aryans and Jews. He claimed to be the founder of the NS race-psychology and in a letter to the dean of the Berlin philosophy department [...] stated that his books are rightly esteemed anti-Semitic. His 'Rassenseelenkunde' was an important variety of National Socialist racism and not an alternative. Clauß never argued or acted against National Socialism. He delivered his inaugural lecture at Berlin University in a brownshirt and during the war he worked for the secret service of the SS." (Horst Jünginger, "Sigrid Hunke: Europe's New Religion and its Old Stereotypes" [1998] at http://homepages.uni-tuebingen.de/gerd.simon/hunke.htm)

9. *Die Tagebücher von Josef Goebbels*, ed. Elke Fröhlich, part I, vol. 2/1, December 1929-

May 1931 (Munich: K. G. Saur, 2005), p. 159 (19 May 1930) and p. 333 (26 January 1931). On Viktoria von Dirksen's salon as a meeting place of monarchist nobility and Nazis, see Malinowski, *Vom König zum Führer*, pp. 554-55; Fritz Günther von Tschirschky, *Erinnerungen eines Hochverräters* (Stuttgart: Deutsche Verlagsanstalt, 1972), pp. 130-31.

10. As late as 1975-77 he was still producing pamphlets justifying the Nazi regime and incriminating the Allies. *Wer von der Lüge lebt, muss die Wahrheit fürchten* was published in the "Gelbe Reihe" of a small extreme right-wing publisher, ATB Die Büchermacher, in 1976 (see www.books-hotopic.de/GELBE_REIHE/gelbe_reihe.html); *War Hitler ein Diktator?*, written in 1977, appeared in 1994 in vol. 86 of the neo-Nazi journal *Kritik: Die Stimme des Volkes*, which also regularly published work by the Princess. (An English translation of this text can be found at http://www.wintersonnenwende.com/scriptorium/english/archives/dictator/dictator00.html)

11. The legitimacy of the zur Lippe-Biesterfeld line had been challenged by the zur Lippe-Weißenfelds while the Schaumburg-Lippe line had challenged the legitimacy of both, alleging marriages to women of less than sufficiently noble birth in the early years of the nineteenth century. This had led to a protracted succession struggle over the principality of Lippe lasting from 1895 until 1905 and supposedly involving the Kaiser himself. See Helmut Reichold, *Der Streit um die Thronfolge im Fürstentum Lippe 1895-1905* (Münster i.W.: Aschendorffsche Verlagsbuchhandlung, 1967).

12. Friedrich Christian Prinz zu Schaumburg-Lippe, *Als die goldene Abendsonne: Aus meinen Tagebüchern der Jahre 1933-1937* (Wiesbaden: Limes-Verlag, 1971), p. 73, fn. 1; cf. Graf zu Solms-Laubach, "Der Adel ist tot – es lebe der Adel" in *Wo war der Adel?*, ed. Friedrich Christian Prinz zu Schaumburg-Lippe (Berlin: Zentral Verlag, 1934), p. 8: "The German nobility miserably missed its last opportunity to demonstrate its right to exist. Exceptions here only prove the rule. The question the people puts to you today is harsh and clear: Where were you noble gentlemen when Germany was in its last throes? [...] Where did you fight, and what sacrifices did you make? You thought of yourselves and how you could save your skins. You thought of yourselves and of the welfare of your families. Maybe you lamented the wretchedness of the people, maybe it distressed you, but you did nothing! Nothing! And you still dare today to claim a leadership role?"

13. On the Prince's education, see his *Verdammte Pflicht und Schuldigkeit: Weg und Erlebnis 1914-1933* (Leoni am Starnberger See: Druffel-Verlag, 1966), especially pp. 21-23, 42-43, 77, 79; on his disillusionment with the nobility, ibid., pp. 72-74, 131-33 ("The nobility as such lost its justification for existing in my eyes when it failed to fight for the preservation of the monarchy after 1918. And it truly gave up when it immediately came to terms with the Marxist-controlled social order of the Weimar Republic" [p. 131]); on the nobility's need to transform itself and on his own first encounter with and attraction to National Socialism, pp. 114-23, 126-36. For photographs of the Prince and his family with Hitler and Goebbels, see his published diaries, *Als die goldene Abendsonne: Aus meinen Tagebüchern der Jahre 1933-1937*. See also Malinowski, *Vom König zum Führer*, pp. 439, 551; Malinowski quotes ("From King to Führer," pp. 25-26) from a noble contributor to *Wo war der Adel?* (1934), the collection of texts edited by the Prince: "From the start, National Socialism was the sole legitimate heir of the entire past tradition of the nobility; the forefathers we have revered all our lives continued to act in and through it."

(p. 584). In the same spirit, Friedrich von Bülow in an after-dinner speech to the Bülow family association in 1935: "Upon blood and soil the Führer is building his Reich. We have understood blood selection for seven centuries and have built our bloodstream on an age-old race and culture. [...] All the great ideals which the Führer has established for the German people originate from the deepest treasure chambers of the German aristocracy. Thus in its very foundations the German aristocracy is akin both in nature and origin to National Socialism." [...] Likewise Wolf Heinrich, Graf von Helldorff, S.A. Leader of Berlin, then Police Chief of Berlin: "A new aristoracy is forming under National Socialism. If the old aristocracy stands aside from the great aristocratic popular movement fate will overrun it; in that case, it would be better if it resolved now to renounce its worthless patents of nobility." ("Adel und Nationalsozialismus," in Das neue Deutschland, October 1935, p. 11, quoted in David Schoenbaum, *Hitler's Social Revolution: Class and Status in Nazi Germany 1933-1939* (New York. W.W. Norton, 1980), p. 70.

14. On the Princess's presence at Dirksen's gatherings, see Rüdiger Jungbluth, *Die Quandts: Ihr leiser Aufstieg zur mächtigsten Wirtschaftsdynastie Deutschlands* (Frankfurt a.M. and New York: Campus Verlag, 2002), p. 108; Anja Klabunde, *Magda Goebbels*, trans. Shaun Whiteside (London: Little Brown, 2001; orig. German 1999), p. 111.

15. Ludwig Wilser, *Die Germanen: Beiträge zur Völkerkunde* (Eisenach and Leipzig: Thüringischer Verlags-Anstalt, 1903) sums up the findings of late nineteenth-century scholarship on the supposed origins of culture among the Nordic peoples. For the erosion of the Nordic strain in the German population Hans F. K. Günther, the leading exponent of the Nordic idea in the 1920s through the 1940s, offers a variety of reasons: emigration of the most enterprising and adventurous; migration from the land to the cities, where intermarriage with racially less dynamic immigrant races, attracted by employment opportunities in factories and in petty commerce had become common; self-imposed limits on the number of children in Nordic families in response to the heavy tax burden they have to bear, as the most successful element in the population, in order to fund social welfare programs for the poor; corresponding rapid population increase in the inferior proletarian population as a result of those very welfare programs; heavy loss of life in the predominantly Nordic officer class in the wars of the nineteenth and twentieth centuries; and so on. (*Kleine Rassenkunde des deutschen Volkes* [Munich and Berlin: F. J. Lehmanns Verlag, 1943;1st edn. 1929], pp. 125-37) The idea that the superior, aristocratic race is constantly under threat from the teeming animal-like masses of the inferior races was common currency in the late nineteenth and early twentieth centuries and is almost certainly a mirror image of upper-class fear of the expanding urban proletariat. In articles in his journal *Ostara* in 1906 and 1912, the Viennese Jörg Lanz von Liebenfels claimed that this idea was the true, hidden content of all the great religious myths, including those of the Old and New Testaments; see Peter Emil Becker, *Zur Geschichte der Rassenhygiene: Wege ins Dritte Reich* (Stuttgart and New York: Georg Thieme Verlag, 1988), pp. 341-49. See also on the fear – and the alleged causes – of racial and national decline, Uwe Puschner, *Die völkische Bewegung im wilhelminischen Kaiserreich*, pp. 115-23.

16. On Harden's "neoconservative" politics, see *Walther Rathenau-Maximilian Harden Briefwechsel 1897-1920*, ed. Hans-Dieter Hellige (Munich: Gotthold Müller; Heidelberg: Lambert Schneider, 1983; vol. 4 of Walther Rathenau, *Gesamtausgabe*), Introduction, pp. 111-23. On the basis of oral testimony by former Chancellor

Heinrich Brüning, Robert G. L. Waite claims that Rathenau, ironically, had been a strong supporter of the *Freikorps* (by whose members he was murdered), raised large sums of money for them, and even donated funds from his own pocket. (*Vanguard of Nazism*, pp. 219-20)

17. Walther Rathenau, *Gesamtausgabe*, vol. 2, "Hauptwerke und Gespräche," ed. Hans-Dieter Hellige and Ernst Schulin (Munich: Gotthold Müller; Heidelberg: Lambert Schneider, 1977), p. 288. Cf. this passage from his *Aphorismen* (1902): "The epitome of the history of the world, of the history of mankind, is the tragedy of the Aryan race. A blond and marvelous people arises in the north. In overflowing fertility it sends wave upon wave into the southern world. Each migration becomes a conquest, each conquest a source of character and civilization. But with the increasing population of the world the waves of the dark peoples flow ever nearer, the circle of mankind grows narrower. At last a triumph for the south; an oriental religion takes possession of the northern lands. They defend themselves by preserving the ancient ethic of courage. And finally the worst danger of all: industrial civilization gains control of the world, and with it arises the power of fear, of brains and of cunning, embodied in democracy and capital." (Quoted in Harry Graf Kessler, *Walther Rathenau: His Life and Work* [New York: Harcourt Brace and Company, 1930], pp. 36-37) On the extensive literature spawned in Germany by the enthusiasm for Nordic race and culture and promoted by major publishers and publishing houses like Eugen Diederichs, Julius F. Lehmann, and the Hanseatische Verlagsanstalt of Hamburg, see Gary D. Stark, *Entrepreneurs of Ideology: Neoconservative Publishers in Germany, 1890-1933* (Chapel Hill: University of North Carolina Press, 1982), pp. 190-93.

18. An intense, intimate, homoerotic friendship between Rathenau and the *völkisch* ideologue Wilhelm Schwaner, co-founder of the *Germanische Glaubensgemeinschaft*, compiler of the *Germanen-Bibel*, and editor of the *völkisch*-oriented *Volkserzieher* (to which Rathenau took out a subscription), has rightly occasioned much commentary. (See Peter Berglar, "Exkurs: Walther Rathenau und Wilhelm Schwaner," in his *Walther Rathenau: Ein Leben zwischen Philosophie und Politik* [Graz; Vienna; Cologne: Verlag Styria, 1987], pp. 266-71; Wolfgang Brenner, *Walther Rathenau: Deutscher und Jude* [Munich and Zurich: Piper, 2005], pp. 336-41; Udo Leuschner, "Walther Rathenau: Ein Dissident seiner Klasse, seiner Rasse und seines Geschlechts," in his *Zur Geschichte des deutschen Liberalismus* [http://www.udo-leuschner.de/liberalismus/liberalismus0.htm].) An illustration in Leuschner's article shows the letterhead in Schwaner's letters to Rathenau decorated with swastikas (already well established as a *völkisch* symbol) and inscribed with the motto: "Treu leben, todtrotzend kämpfen, lachend sterben." [Be true in life, struggle in defiance of death, die with laughter on your lips.] It is unlikely that Rathenau was offended. He himself had declared in his "Address to the Youth of Germany" (*An Deutschlands Jugend*, Berlin, 1918): "I am a German of Jewish descent. My people is the German people, my fatherland is Germany, my religion that Germanic faith which is above all religions." (Quoted in Waite, *Vanguard of Nazism*, p. 219)

19. The relation of National Socialism to religion and of the various religious churches and sects – both Christian and pagan – to National Socialism is extraordinarily complex and has been the object of much investigation: e.g. Hans Buchheim, *Glaubenskrise im Dritten Reich: Drei Kapitel nationalsozialistischer Religionspolitik* (Stuttgart: Deutsche Verlags-Anstalt, 1953); Ernst Christian Helmreich, *The German*

Churches under Hitler (Detroit: Wayne State University Press, 1979); Peter Matheson, ed., The Third Reich and the Christian Churches (Edinburgh: T. & T. Clark, 1981) – a collection of documents with brief commentaries; Hubert Cancik, ed., Religions- und Geistesgeschichte der Weimarer Republik (Düsseldorf: Patmos Verlag, 1982); Doris Bergen, Twisted Cross: The German Christian Movement in the Third Reich (Chapel Hill: University of North Carolina Press, 1996); Heinz Eduard Tödt, Komplizen, Opfer und Gegner des Hitlerregimes: Zur 'inneren Geschichte' von protestantischer Theologie und Kirche im Dritten Reich (Gütersloh: Chr. Kaiser-Gütersloher Verlagshaus, 1997); Richardt Steigmann-Gall, The Holy Reich: Nazi Conceptions of Christianity 1919-1945 (Cambridge: Cambridge University Press, 2003); Karla Poewe, New Religions and the Nazis (New York and London: Routledge, 2006). Some Christians wanted to create a new syncretism that would preserve a Christian core while excluding the Judaic component of traditional Christianity and integrating elements of the allegedly old Nordic religions; others wanted to exclude the Judaic element but vehemently opposed neo-paganism; some of those to whom race was the defining element of humanity and history wished to revive pagan cults; others (including Hitler himself in Mein Kampf) derided these cults as Romantic Germanentümelei [Germanomania]. One of the leading exponents of the Nordic Idea, Professor Hans F. K. Günther, insisted that his focus was on planning scientifically for the future, not reviving early Germanic culture and customs – a task "impossible in itself" and capable only of "producing nonsense." "The Nordic movement has nothing to do with Romanticism or looking back or trying to revive what has become history; it is about looking forward, about restoring to the German people that seed of Nordic race, on the continuation of which its 'German-ness' depends." (Kleine Rassenkunde des deutschen Volkes, p. 142)

20. On Ploetz, see Becker, Zur Geschichte der Rassenhygiene, pp. 58-136.

21. Quoted in Becker, p. 83.

22. Quoted in Puschner, Die völkische Bewegung im wilhelminischen Kaiserreich, p. 177.

23. Quoted in Becker, p. 113. It should be noted that race theory did not necessarily imply anti-Semitism, even though it usually was anti-Semitic in fact. The young Martin Buber and others in his "cultural Zionist" circle (as distinct from the followers of the more pragmatic Herzl) aimed to create a culture expressive of the Jewish "race." Equally, it did not necessarily have as its objective racial purity. (Günther, for instance, acknowledged that only a tiny fraction of the German population was of pure Nordic race). Its basic principle was that the racial element was of primary importance in culture and history. It also claimed that specific races had specific characteristics, some of which public policy might seek, through "Rassenhygiene," to nurture in the general population, while others were reduced or eliminated. Even Clauß at least professed the view, adapted from Herder's conception of individual peoples, that each race has a value of its own ("Jede Rasse stellt in sich selbst einen Höchstwert dar") and a value system of its own, by which alone it can be judged ("Jede Rasse trägt ihre Wertordnung und ihren Wertmaßstab in sich selbst und darf nicht mit dem Maßstab irgendeiner anderen Rasse gemessen werden. Es ist sinnwidrig und unwissenschaftlich, die mittelländische Rasse mit den Augen der nordischen Rasse zu sehen. […] Vielleicht kennt Gott eine Rangordnung der Rassen, wir nicht" [Every race carries its own system of values and standards in itself and may not be judged by the standards of another race. It is absurd and unscientific to view the Mediterranean race with the eyes of the Nordic race. […] Perhaps God

has a hierarchy of races. We do not]). Rejecting criticism of his work in the Vatican *Osservatore Romano*, Clauß insisted that it implied no scale of superior and inferior races. (*Rasse und Seele: Eine Einführung in den Sinn der leiblichen Gestalt* [Munich and Berlin: J. F. Lehmanns Verlag, 1943; orig. 1926], p. 16) In his celebrated collection of poems, *Juda* (1900), which was illustrated by the Jewish artist E. M. Lilien (see my article in *Princeton University Library Chronicle*, 2004, 66: 11-78), Börries von Münchhausen, a future anti-Semitic NSDAP member, actually sang the praises, not, to be sure, of contemporary Jews, but of the ancient warlike Hebrew people, which conformed to his idea of a heroic *race*. It was even argued that, in so far as racial improvement was a desideratum, it might in some cases be more effectively achieved by judicious mixing of races than by attempts to preserve what racial purity remained. Ploetz, for instance, held in his early years that the Jewish race had some desirable characteristics and that the German race might benefit from some infusion of Jewish blood. His anti-Semitism became virulent only after the NSDAP came to power (a development he explicitly welcomed) and showered honors on him. (Becker, pp. 86-87) Later so-called race scholars [*Rassenforscher*], like Clauß and Günther, made the point that the Jews are a people, not a race, and that like other peoples, including the Germans, they are the product of specific racial mixing; see, for instance, *Kleine Rassenkunde des deutschen Volkes*, pp. 12, 55-57.

24. Peter Kratz, *Die Götter des New Age*, p. 307; Becker, p. 84. On Konopath-Konopacki, Walter Laqueur notes that in certain extreme right-wing branches of the *Wandervogel* movement a preponderance of members "of mixed Slavonic blood" had disquieted some native Germans: "For the Nordic purists it must have been disconcerting to find that many, perhaps most of their spokesmen had names that had not been in use either in Valhalla or in Midgard." In a note he adds: "Among those favoring the Nordic orientation of the youth movement of the Reich, names like Luntowski, Konopacki-Konopath or Pudelko were frequent." (*Young Germany: A History of the German Youth Movement* [New York: Basic Books, 1962], pp. 91-92 and note) On individuals of mixed nationality as prophets of nationalistic creeds, see Emil Franzel, *Das Reich der Braunen Jakobiner* (Munich: J. Pfeiffer, 1964), pp. 25-26.

25. *Ist Rasse Schicksal?*, p. 4.

26. According to Winifred Wagner, the Princess ran "a Nordic exchange for job-seekers, people in need of rest and recreation, those seeking marriage partners, etc., etc." (Quoted in Brigitte Hamann, *Winifred Wagner: A Life at the Heart of Hitler's Bayreuth*, trans. Alan Bauce [London: Granta Books, 2005; orig. German 2002], p. 121).

27. Volkmar Weiss, "Die Vorgeschichte des arischen Ahnenpasses," Part III, *Genealogie*, 2000, 50: 615-27 (also available at http://www.v-weiss.de/publ7-pass.html - 3); on Lanz von Liebenfels's encouragement of family genealogical trees, see Becker, p. 351; on the *Edda*, see Malinowski, "From King to Führer," pp. 10-13. Competitions were commonly advertised in racist publications; e.g. a competition for photographs of "the best male and female head of Nordic race, to be illustrated frontally and in profile," for which the *Werkbund für deutsche Volkstums- und Rassenforschung* offered a first prize of 500 Marks, a second prize of 100 Marks and 10 prizes of copies of Hans Günther's *Rassenkunde des deutschen Volkes* (*Volk und Rasse*, 1926, 2: 116-17).

28. On the *Münchner Post* article, see Georg Franz-Willing, *Die Hitler-Bewegung 1925 bis 1934* (Preussisch Oldendorf: Deutsche Verlagsgesellschaft, 2001), p. 252.

29. On the Gobineau celebration, see Hans-Jürgen Lutzhöft, *Der Nordische Gedanke in Deutschland 1920-1940*, p. 65. On Konopath's contributions to the *NPK*, see Florian Odenwald, *Der nazistische Kampf gegen das 'Undeutsche' in Theater und Film 1920-1945* (Munich: Münchner Universitätsschriften Theaterwissenschaft, vol. 8, 2006), p. 51.

30. Becker, p. 85, quoting from *Die Sonne*, 1930, 7: 376. Such celebrations were no longer unusual. The *Sera-Circle* around the publisher Eugen Diederichs had begun organizing similar festivities on a hilltop near Jena before the First World War. For an eye-witness description, see http://www.eiwatz.de/_1589148299_27701416 8_61542248_61542248.html. By the mid-1930s, under the National Socialists, they had become part of the education of German schoolchildren; see the outline of a celebration of the summer solstice in a handbook for public schools reproduced and analysed in Christa Kamenetsky, *Children's Literature in Hitler's Germany: The Cultural Policy of National Socialism* (Athens, Ohio and London: Ohio University Press, 1984), pp. 218-33.

31. *Die Tagebücher von Joseph Goebbels*, Teil 1, vol. 2/1, p. 155 (13 April 1930).

32. Alan Bullock, *Hitler: A Study in Tyranny* (London: Odham's Press, 1952), p. 126. Bullock gave 1928 as the date of Konopath's appointment, but more recent writers have revised that date. See note 35 below.

33. "Leiter der Abteilung für Rasse und Kultur," cited in Georg Franz-Willing, *Die Hitler-Bewegung 1925 bis 1934*, p. 227. On Hitler's choice of Konopath, "an unknown outsider, who had as yet contributed nothing," see Reinhard Bollmus, *Das Amt Rosenberg und seine Gegner* (Stuttgart: Deutsche Verlagsanstalt, 1970), pp. 34-36; Lionel Richard, *Le Nazisme et la culture* (Brussels: Editions Complexe, 2006), p. 95. On Konopath's positions in the Party, see also *Hitler: Reden, Schriften, Anordnungen, Februar 1925 bis Januar 1933*, vol. 4, pt. 1 (October 1930-June 1931), ed. Constantin Goschler (Munich: K. G. Saur, 1994), p. 403, note 1 and vol. 5, pt. 1 (April 1932-September 1932), ed. Klaus A. Lankheit (Munich: K. G. Saur, 1996), p. 201.

34. Florian Cebulla, "Die Rundfunkpolitik des Stahlhelms, 1930-1933," *Rundfunk und Geschichte*, 1999, 25: 101-07.

35. On Konopath's role in the founding of the *Deutsche Christen* movement, see Hans Buchheim, *Glaubenskrise im Dritten Reich*, pp. 75, 77; Klaus Scholder, *The Churches and the Third Reich*, vol. 1: "Preliminary History and the Time of Illusions 1918-1934," trans. John Bowden (London: S.C.M. Press, 1987 [orig. German, 1977]), pp. 205-07; *Biographisch-Bibliographisches Kirchenlexikon*, art. "Wilhelm Kube (1887-1943); Kurt Meier, *Die Deutschen Christen: Das Bild einer Bewegung im Kirchenkampf des Dritten Reiches* (Göttingen: Vandenhoeck & Ruprecht, 1964), pp. 11-13, 315, n. 38. On the movement itself and on the politics and ideology of the various factions within the German Protestant Church (Evangelische Kirche) see Doris Bergen, *Twisted Cross: The German Christian Movement in the Third Reich*. Konopath survived the war and seems to have gotten off lightly. In 1952, he was living in Hamburg and submitted a design for a new European flag to the Hamburg-based *Europa-Union-Deutschland* in response to the interest shown by the Council of Europe in such a flag. Konopath's design – a circle of 15 four-pointed gold stars against a blue background, remarkably similar to today's European Union flag of 12 five-pointed stars – apparently reached the desk of Paul-Henri Spaak, the President of the Council, but was dropped as soon as the designer's past became known. A signed copy has been preserved in the Council Archives and can be viewed by searching under 'Konopath' at http://www.

ena.lu/; see also *Le Point*, 20 October 2005, p. 413, and Markus Kutter, "Europa zeigt Flagge," at http://markuskutter.ch/print/europa6_print.htm.

36. Slightly different figures are given by Gary D. Stark, *Entrepreneurs of Ideology: Neoconservative Publishers in German, 1890-1933*, p. 242. Figures here are taken from the 1943 edition of the popular version, *Kleine Rassenkunde des deutschen Volkes*, and from the advertisement in that work for other works by Günther. Ludwig Ferdinand Clauß's *Rasse und Seele* was also a publishing success, going through 18 editions and selling 122,000 copies between 1927 and 1943.

37. Excerpt in English translation in Heinz-Georg Marten, "Racism, Social Darwinism, Anti-Semitism and Aryan Supremacy," in J. A. Mangan, ed., *Shaping the Superman: Fascist Body as Political Icon* (London and Portland, OR: Frank Cass, 1999), pp. 23-41, on p. 30.

38. Hans F. K. Günther, *Deutsche Köpfe nordischer Rasse: 50 Abbildungen mit Geleitworten von Prof. Dr. Eugen Fischer und Dr. Hans F. K. Günther* (Munich: J. F. Lehmanns Verlag, 1927), Introduction; cf. Ida H. Schlender, *Germanische Mythologie: Religion und Leben unserer Urväter*, 4th edn. (Dresden: Alexander Köhler, 1925; later editions 1934, 1937), p. 109: "The basic principles of the North Germans emerge clearly for us from the *Hávamál* [a collection of wise saying from the *Edda*, most recently translated into English as "The Words of Odin the High One"—L.G.]: savvy, reserve, and courage in every situation." Other works by this popular author include *Was lehren Religion und Leben unserer Urväter der Jetztzeit?* (Dresden, 1920) [What do the Religion and Life of our Ancestors Teach us Today?] and *Germanische Mythologie: Zum Selbststudium und zum Gebrauch an höheren Lehranstalten* [Germanic Mythology: For Self-Study and Use in Higher Education Establishments] (Dresden, 1904 and 1912).

39. Günther apparently saw no advantage, however, in mixing European and non-European races. The "Hither-Asiatic" or "Near-Eastern" race in particular, the dominant strain among Jews and increasingly prominent among Greeks of the later period, was characterized by strongly negative features, such as "cunning," "crafty calculation," "treachery," and "corruptibility." ("'Like a Greek God...,' translated by Vivian Bird from Hans F. Günther's *Lebensgeschichte des hellenischen Volkes*," *Northern World* [Calcutta], 1961, 6, i: 5-16).

40. Dr. Gustav Paul, *Grundzüge der Rassen- und Raumgeschichte des deutschen Volkes* (Munich: J. S. Lehmanns Verlag, 1935), cited from the 4th edition, 1943, p. 208.

41. *Kleine Rassenkunde des deutschen Volkes*, pp. 145-46.

42. Peter Kratz, *Die Götter des New Age*, pp. 305-06.

43. See especially Lutzhöft, *Der nordische Gedanke*; Geoffrey G. Field, "Nordic Racism," *Journal of the History of Ideas*, 1977, 38: 523-40; and Bernard Mees, "Germanische Sturmflut: From the Old Norse Twilight to the Fascist New Dawn," *Studia Neophiloligica*, 2006, 78: 184-98. Scholarly legitimation was eagerly sought by racist propagandists. Professors figure prominently on the editorial boards of two of the most rabidly racist and right-wing journals of the 1920s, for instance: *Volk und Rasse* (1926-1944) and *Deutschlands Erneuerung* (1917-1944), both published by the radical right-wing press of J. S. Lehmann in Munich.

44. A Prospectus bearing the title "Nordisch-Germanisches Kulturerbe" and illustrated by a stone carving of runic letters and a warrior on horseback was issued

by the Diederichs Verlag in April 1933. The announcement read: "What would be a better place to start promoting awareness of the innermost strengths of German being than the Nordic-Germanic literary monuments from which the unbroken strength of German being speaks so powerfully. The books that bring those times closer to us thus arouse a new view of life and have a special role to play in our time." (Fig. 19)

45. One woman scholar argued that philosophy itself is racially determined. Since "blood" determines the entire character of a community and links its members in an undying "bloodstream," no general philosophy of the nature and being of "Man" is possible. While "Man" may be distinguished from the animal realm by general characteristics, "it is very questionable that this general condition of *Menschsein* [being human] is the most essential thing about a human being, i.e. constitutes his or her ultimate metaphysical definition, for the ultimate metaphysical definition of a human lies in his/her bond to his/her community and in his/her obligation toward his/her blood." Hence, "the philosophy of the future, if there is to be one, must be a philosophy of blood. Every philosophy will have value and meaning only for human beings of the same blood community [...] and that means that the philosophy of blood will be accessible to us only in its particular form of *Nordic* blood." (Dr. Erika Emmerich, "Die Philosophie des Blutes," *Nationalsozialistisches Bildungswesen*, 1937, pp. 389-90, repr. in *Das Dritte Reich und seine Diener*, p. 287) In an article in the *Süddeutsche Monatshefte* for 1933-34, Franziska von Porembsky, picking up from Günther, notes that Nordic women are less immediately attractive than others, come to maturity later, and are not submissive but strong and fiercely independent, all of which makes them less desirable to men formed by modern urban culture and contributes to the dangerous decline of the Nordic element in the German population. ("Die nordische Frau, nach Günther," repr. in *Das Dritte Reich und seine Diener*, pp. 407-08).

46. Joachim Fest, *The Face of the Third Reich*, trans. Michael Bullock (London: Weidenfeld and Nicolson, 1970; orig, German, 1963), p. 167.

47. The history of the neo-pagan groups active in the early decades of the nineteenth century is extremely complex and hard to reconstruct. Most appear to have had memberships in the hundreds or low thousands at best. Even so, or because of that, they were beset by inner tensions, broke up and reformed frequently, and competed with one another. The *Nordische Glaubensbewegung* was itself a splinter group that had seceded around 1927, under the leadership of Wilhelm Kusserow, from Otto Sigfrid Reuter's *Deutsch-gläubige Bewegung* (originally known as *Deutsch-religiöse Gemeinschaft*) – which in turn alternately competed and collaborated with Ludwig Fahrenkrog's contemporary, similarly inclined *Germanische Glaubensgemeinschaft* (founded in 1913). (See note 57, Chapter 1 above). It then incorporated the *Nordungen*, another, probably slightly larger neo-pagan group and in 1931 it joined with the *Germanische Glaubensgemeinschaft* to form the *Nordisch-religiöse Arbeitsgemeinschaft* [Nordic-Religious Working Association]. In 1933 this group in turn merged with Reuter's organization in Hauer's *Arbeitsgemeinschaft deutscher Glaubensbewegung* [Working Association of the German Faith Movement]. In 1934, however, when Hauer restructured the loosely bound *Arbeitsgemeinschaft deutscher Glaubensbewegung* into the more tight-knit *Deutsche Glaubensbewegung*, the *Nordische Glaubensbewegung* refused to co-operate and withdrew from the association, alleging that Hauer's new organization was too eclectic and insufficiently committed to specifically Nordic

religious and racial goals. These had been summarized in the first number of the journal *Nordungen* (1932): "We commit to struggle until the essential character of the North German race asserts itself and becomes once again pure in our people and in all areas of interest to it. [...] We have a strong sense that Baldur-Sigfrid still lives today in the best of our people; his sun-like, liberating nature is our highest goal and the object of the longing of us all." (Quoted in Buchheim, *Glaubenskrise*, p. 169) On disputes about the Nordic idea within the *völkisch* and National Socialist camps, see Christopher M. Hutton, *Race and the Third Reich: Linguistics, Racial Anthropology and Genetics in the Dialectic of 'Volk'* (Cambridge: Polity Press, 2005), ch. 7-10.

48. On Hauer, see pp. 16, 44-45 and Chapter 1, note 3. Hauer later complained that radical elements in the *Deutsche Glaubensbewegung* had introduced a polemical, aggressive, and hate-filled tone that was foreign to his intentions and had subordinated his interest in fostering religion in the German people to a purely political agenda. In 1936 he was obliged by then SS *Gruppenführer* Reinhard Heydrich to step down from the leadership of the movement he himself had founded. (See especially Buchheim, *Glaubenskrise*, pp. 194-95).

49. That view had been expressed forcefully in the Prince's address to the reader in *Vom Rassenstil zur Staatsgestalt* (Berlin-Neu Finkenkrug: H. Paetel, 1928): "Do you not *want* to read the signs of the times? Or are you no longer capable of *understanding* them? Do you not *hear* the call for liberation from the suffocating alien ways all around us, the voice appealing for a Nordic form of faith, a faith in which Jesus is not experienced in the oriental mode as a passive, humble sufferer, but as a heroic champion in the Nordic manner, leading the way and answering to none but his conscience. To *his* conscience – not to the God who lords it over all my energies and to reach whom a mediator is required, but to the God that dwells within me. [...] The Nordic soul in the German people is struggling to win freedom from alien ways and to establish its own Nordic form of faith so that the deepest moral energies of Nordic being will be freed to create Nordic forms in every domain." (p. 126)

50. Quoted in Buchheim, *Glaubenskrise*, p. 170.

51. See Ulrich Nanko, *Die deutsche Glaubensbewegung: Eine historische und soziologische Untersuchung*, pp. 143, 237-38. It seems not unlikely, however, that both the Prince and Konopath sided with Kusserow when the latter withdrew from Hauer's *Deutsche Glaubensbewegung* and reconstituted the *Nordische Glaubensbewegung* in 1934. (See Chapter 5, note 47). The Princess's pamphlet *Nordische Frau und Nordischer Glaube* appeared in that same year as the second of the publications of the *Nordische Glaubensbewegung*.

52. Michael H. Kater, "Die Artamenen – Völkische Jugend in der Weimarer Republik," *Historische Zeitschrift*, 1971, 213: 577-638, at pp. 600, 626.

53. On the *Artamans* – mostly young, lower middle-class men and women from the cities, aged between 17 and 30, whose numbers rose from 100, working on six farms, in 1924, when the movement was founded, to 2000, working on 300 farms in 1929 and 70,000 by 1932 – see Michael H. Kater, "Die Artamanen – Völkische Jugend in der Weimarer Republik," and Volkmar Weiss, "Die Vorgeschichte des arischen Ahnenpasses," Part III, *Genealogie*, 2000, 50: 615-27. The name "Artaman" derives from that of the Indian sun-god, Artam, deemed by the *Artamans* to be the true deity of the Aryans. It may also have been intended to evoke the *Hoher Armanen-Orden* [Order of the Heirs of the Sun-King], the elitist association created in 1911 by the

Viennese-born *völkisch* publicist Guido von List (1848-1918). The Viennese *völkisch* movements (headed by List and Lanz von Liebenfels) were motivated almost as much by fear and hatred of the "inferior" Slavs as by anti-Semitism. See Nicholas Goodrich-Clarke, *The Occult Roots of Nazism: The Ariosophists of Austria and Germany 1890-1935*, pp. 7-16.

54. To Darré, the old *Lebensreform* movement's attempts to cure the ills of society through changes in lifestyle were mere romantic tinkering that left basic structures intact. His own "back to the land" ideology was far more radical, in rhetoric at least. "In Germany today," he wrote in 1932, "we are still at the stage of peasant romanticism, i.e. we have already become an urban people aware that its downfall is certain once its peasantry has been destroyed. And as always in history, so too today, recipes for curing the evil are recommended. But these are the products of urban intellectualism and the urban intellectuals for the most part fail to understand that they are circling around symptoms instead of attacking the evil at its roots. It was thought that the evil could be checked through allotments and individual houses with gardens, through small settlements and peasant romanticism, through vegetarianism and nudism, guitars and bare feet, and no one noticed the diabolical smirk of capitalism, which it suits very well for people to settle comfortably [...] into its system with their allotments and [...] garden cities." (Quoted in Hermann Bausinger, "Zwischen Grün und Braun: Volkstumsideologie und Heimatpflege nach dem Ersten Weltkrieg," in Hubert Cancik, ed., *Religions- und Geistesgeschichte der Weimarer Republik*, pp. 215-29, at p. 225).

55. Darré also appears to have been replaced at this time as the editor of *Odal: Monatsschrift fur Blut und Boden*, the journal he had founded in 1932. As of July 1942 (vol. 11, no. 7), his name disappears from both the front cover and from the contents page, where it had regularly figured until then. In addition, he was ousted from leadership of RuSHA (*Rasse- und Siedlungshauptamt*) [Race and Settlement Office], which he himself had founded in 1931. (See Frederic Reider, *The Order of the SS* [Tucson, AZ: Aztex Corporation, n.d.; translated from *L'Ordre SS*, Paris: Editions de la Pensée moderne, 1975], pp. 141-45. This mysterious publication is probably the work of an extreme right-wing writer and should be used with caution.)

56. Munich: J. F. Lehmanns Verlag, 1929. New editions of this book appeared in 1933, 1934, 1935, 1937, 1938, 1940, and 1942. On the literature dealing with the alleged threat to racial vigor and integrity from urbanization, see Uwe Puschner, *Die völkische Bewegung im wilhelminischen Kaiserreich*, pp. 115-19 et passim. Glorification of the German peasantry had already become a commonplace of anti-liberal *völkisch* ideology by 1900 when the culturally avant-garde Leipzig firm of Eugen Diederichs published *Der Bauer in der deutschen Vergangenheit* by Adolf Bartels – subsequently an honorary member of the NSDAP and the recipient of several honors from it (e.g. the "Adlerschild" in 1937, the Gold Medal of the *Hitler Youth* in 1942; see Stephen Nyole Fuller, *The Nazis' Literary Grandfather: Adolf Bartels and Cultural Extremism, 1871-1945* [New York: Peter Lang, 1996], pp. 175-81).

57. R. Walther Darré, *Neuordnung unseres Denkens* (Reichsbauernstadt Goslar: Verlag Blut und Boden, 1940), pp. 11, 56. This was an extremely popular work apparently. The copy in Princeton's Firestone Library comes from the 157-167,000 printing of the 1940 edition and there were further editions in 1941 and 1942.

58. See in particular his popular *Neuadel aus Blut und Boden* (Munich and Berlin: J. F. Lehmanns Verlag, 1930), pp. 12-13. In *Adel und Rasse* (Munich: J.F. Lehmann, 1926)

## 168  Brownshirt Princess

Günther had already claimed that a pure Nordic peasant's daughter was superior to the daughter of a non-Nordic king (pp. 82-86), and earlier still, Julius Langbehn, the author of the celebrated and wildly popular *Rembrandt als Erzieher*, had claimed in a book allegedly written in 1887 that "no one is more aristocratic than the authentic peasant; and the Low German never renounces the peasant in himself even when he becomes a nobleman and a king." (Julius Langbehn, "Niederdeutsches," *Volk und Rasse*, 1926, 1: 257-62, at p. 257; extracted from the posthumously published *Niederdeutsches: Ein Beitrag zur Völkerpsychologie*, ed. Benedikt Momme Nissen [Buchenbach-Baden: Felsen Verlag, 1926]) On Darré, see Clifford R. Lovin, "*Blut und Boden*: The Ideological Basis of the Nazi Agricultural Program," *Journal of the History of Ideas* (1967), 28: 279-88; Anna Bramwell, *Blood and Soil: Richard Walther Darré and Hitler's 'Green Party'* (Bourne End, Bucks.: Kensal Press, 1985); and the entry in Robert Wistrich, *Who's Who in Nazi Germany* (London: Weidenfeld and Nicolson, 1982), pp. 36-37.

59. "Innere Kolonisation" (dated April 1926) in R. Walther Darré, *Erkenntnisse und Werden: Aufsätze aus der Zeit der Machtergreifung*, ed. Marie Adelheid Reuß-zur Lippe, 2nd edn. (Goslar: Verlag Blut und Boden, 1940), pp. 18-46. Inevitably Darré, to whom the German was above all sedentary, rooted in his native soil, found himself opposed to his sometime friend Himmler, who came to view the German as a conqueror, a Viking. The conflict with Himmler resulted, as noted earlier, in Darré's fall from favor in 1942. (See Anna Bramwell, *Blood and Soil*, pp. 129-35 et passim).

60. The Odal rune was also the sign favored by the Germanic neopagan movements of the early twentieth century. It was subsequently adopted by the ethnic Germans in the 7th SS Volunteer Mountain Division, by the Afrikaner Student Federation in South Africa, and by the contemporary neo-Nazi "British National Party." An extensive literature invoked Odal during the Nazi period; see, for instance, Otto Behaghel, *Odal* (Munich: Bayerische Akademie der Wissenschaften, Philosophisch-Historische Abteilung, 1935, Heft 80), and Johann von Leers, *Odal: Das Lebensgesetz eines ewigen Deutschlands* [Odal: the Vital Law of an Eternal Germany] (Goslar: Blut und Boden Verlag, 1935). Von Leers, a regular contributor to Darré's *Odal*, was the Nazi scholar to whom Huizinga, in a famous incident, refused the hospitality of the University of Leiden, on the grounds that he had knowingly contravened historical evidence in asserting the historical reality of the medieval tales of ritual murder of Christian children by Jews. (See William Otterspeer, "Huizinga before the Abyss: The von Leers incident at the University of Leiden, April 1933," trans. with introduction and afterword by Lionel Gossman, *Journal of Medieval and Early Modern Studies*, 1997, 27: 385-444).

61. Janet Biehl, "'Ecology' and the Modernization of Fascism in the German Ultra-right," *Ökologie und Kapitalismus Seminarreader*, pp. 91-119, (on p. 109) (http://jd-jl-rlp.de/themen/13-oeko-und-atompolitik/53-oekologie-und-kapitalismus-sept2006.html); see also Janet Biehl and Peter Staudenmeaier, *Ecofascism: Lessons from The German Experience* (Edinburgh and San Francisco: AKL Press, 1995) and Bramwell, *Blood and Soil*, p. 47. According to Petropoulos (*Royals and the Reich*, pp. 266-67)), Prince Ernst zur Lippe, another member of the Princess's family was working as Darré's assistant (not, however, her brother, as claimed; the Princess's brother Ernst fell in the early days of World War I).

62. "Ein Bahnbrecher rassischen Denkens: Zum 125. Geburtstag Gobineaus," *Odal*,

July, 10: 535-38. To vol. 10 (1941) alone, in addition to the Gobineau article, the Princess contributed a short story ("Dunkle Gewalten," issue no. 4 [April], pp. 329-32) and a column under the rubric "Zucht und Sitte" on the way democracy had undermined the peasant character of Swiss society ("Ein Bauernvolk als Opfer der Demokratie," issue no. 12 [December], p. 863).

63. Peter Kratz, *Die Götter des New Age*, p. 307.

64. Malinowski, *Vom König zum Führer*, pp. 520-27.

65. It may not be coincidental that a short pamphlet by the Princess entitled *Entscheidungsstunde der nordischen Frau* [Moment of Decision for the Nordic Woman] appeared in 1930 (Berlin-Köpenick: Flugschriftenreihe der Nordungen, 5).

66. On the marginalizing of old *völkisch* groups and organizations, see Hubert Cancik, "'Neuheiden' und totaler Staat," in Hubert Cancik, ed., *Religions- und Geistesgeschichte der Weimarer Republik*, pp. 176-212; Uwe Puschner, *Die völkische Bewegung im wilhelminischen Kaiserreich*, pp. 10-12; Friedrich-Wilhelm Haack, *Wotans Wiederkehr*, pp. 12-13. On different attitudes to Hauer's *Deutsche Glaubensbewegung* in NSDAP leadership circles, some demanding outright prohibition, others toleration, see Buchheim, *Glaubenskrise*, p. 193. For a study of a single exemplary case, see Michel Fabréguet, "Arthur Dinter, théologien, biologiste et politique (1876-1948), *Revue d'Allemagne*, 2000, 32: 233-44. Dinter, one of the earliest supporters of Hitler, was expelled from the Party in 1928 because of his anti-Catholic zeal and his insistence that the New Germany required a Germanic religious foundation – independent not only of the established Catholic and Lutheran Churches but, in the end, also of the Party, for which Dinter expected it to provide a religious underpinning. The old youth organizations, whose disaffection from "bourgeois" conventions and vague aspirations toward a new order based on comradeship had helped prepare the ground for National Socialism, were similarly suppressed in favor of the *Hitler Youth* after 1933. Youth leaders who failed to make the transition might find themselves in a concentration camp. (See Hans Siemsen, *Hitler Youth*, trans. Trevor and Phyllis Blewitt [London: Lindsay Drummond, 1940], especially pp. 195-210). After 1945, some *völkisch* religious cults used their partial or total prohibition by the NSDAP and the humiliation or punishment suffered by a few individual leaders as evidence that they were not guilty of the crimes of the Hitler regime. See the website of the *Germanische Glaubensgemeinschaft* http://www.germanische-glaubens-gemeinschaft.de under the heading "GGG und NS" for some disingenuous arguments in this vein.

67. R. Walther Darré, *Erkenntnisse und Werden: Aufsätze aus der Zeit der Machtergreifung*, ed. Marie Adelheid Reuß-zur Lippe, 2nd edn. (Goslar: Verlag Blut und Boden, 1940), p. 7.

68. Helene Bechstein, the wife of the piano-manufacturer, and Elsa Bruckmann, the wife of the Munich publisher, are two other well-known female supporters of Hitler. In concert with their spouses, who, for business reasons perhaps, preferred to remain in the background, they provided money and helped to groom him for his leadership role. (See Joachim Köhler, *Wagner's Hitler: The Prophet and his Disciple*, trans. Ronald Taylor [Cambridge: Polity Press, 2000], pp. 157-60). In the brief family history with which Herbert von Dirksen prefaced his memoirs, written in English in the late 1940s, the former ambassador managed to make no mention of his stepmother; see his *Moscow, Tokyo, London: Twenty Years of German Foreign Policy*

(Norman, OK: University of Oklahoma Press, 1952).

69. Werner Mases, *Adolf Hitler: Eine Biographie* (Munich and Berlin: Herbig Verlag, 1978; orig. Munich: Bechtle Verlag, 1971), p. 311; Henry Picker, *Hitlers Tischgespräche im Führerhauptquartier* (Stuttgart: Seewald, 1977; 1st edn. 1963), pp. 91-92, editorial note; James Pool and Suzanne Pool, *Who Financed Hitler: The Secret Funding of Hitler's Rise to Power 1919-1933* (New York: Dials Press, 1978), p. 422; Klaus W. Jonas, *Der Kronprinz Wilhelm*, pp. 222-23; Bella Fromm, *Blood and Banquets: A Berlin Social Diary* (New York: Carol Publishing Group, 1990; orig. London, 1943), pp. 59-60 (entry for 19 October 1932). Fromm adds, however (entry for 15 December 1933), that at a gala opera performance at La Scala in Milan in 1933, Hitler was annoyed to find Frau von Dirksen in the box next to his: "Hitler is said to be sick and tired of finding himself so frequently next to 'that old hag'" (p. 143). As a staunch monarchist, whose support for the NSDAP was related to her hope that it would bring about a restoration of the monarchy, Dirksen had probably outlived her usefulness to Hitler.

70. After drinking a little too much at one of the Baroness's evening gatherings, it seems, the wealthy and attractive young divorcee – Magda Friedländer at the time of her marriage to Quandt, her surname being that of the Jewish man who had married her single mother and by whom she had asked to be adopted – confessed that she found her life intolerable and was bored to death, whereupon Auwi urged her to attend a National Socialist Party meeting. Goebbels was a speaker at that meeting at the Berlin Sportpalast, and Magda Quandt was immediately seduced by his eloquence. The next day she joined the Party. Soon she was contributing financially to it and by the fall of the year she had met and charmed Hitler himself. The following year she and Goebbels married. See Anja Klabunde, *Magda Goebbels*, pp. 113-14; Rüdiger Jungbluth, *Die Quandts*, pp. 108-09. Bella Fromm gives a slightly different account. According to her, Goebbels had been hired as tutor to Magda's son, the young Harald Quandt. Magda occasionally accompanied him to Party meetings and persuaded Quandt to donate money to the NSDAP as the only reliable bulwark against Communism. (*Blood and Banquets*, pp. 65-66) Fromm does not question that Dirksen and Magda Goebbels were friends.

71. Entry in von Levetzow's diary for 20 November 1930. (Gerhard Granier, *Magnus von Levetzow: Seeoffizier, Monarchist und Wegbereiter Hitlers* [Boppard a. R.: Harald Boldt Verlag, 1982], pp. 194, 293) An intermediary between the former Kaiser and the National Socialists, von Leventzov fell out of favor with the latter in 1935 when, as Berlin chief of police, he intervened against mobs attacking Jewish-owned cafés.

72. *Die Tagebücher von Josef Goebbels*, Part 1, vol. 2/1, p. 183 (25 June 1930).

73. Reinhard Merker, *Die bildenden Künste im Nationalsozialismus* (Cologne: DuMont, 1983), pp. 84-87, 91-93; Barbara Miller Lane, *Architecture and Politics in Gemany 1918-1945* (Cambridge, MA: Harvard University Press, 1968), pp. 156-57; Franz-Willing, *Die Hitler-Bewegung*, p. 185; Reinhard Bollmus, *Das Amt Rosenberg und seine Gegner*, pp. 33-34.

74. *Die Tagebücher von Josef Goebbels*, Part 1, vol. 2/1, p. 175 (11 June 1930). The foreword to the first edition of Günther's *Kleine Rassenkunde des deutschen Volkes* is dated "Saaleck bei Bad Kösen, im Herbst 1928"). Saaleck had long been a showpiece of the vernacular style in architecture that "progressive" architects in the early 1900s favored in place of the pompous eclecticism of the time. It was featured in a major, profusely illustrated article, "Mein Landhaus in Saaleck" by Schultze-Naumburg

himself, in the journal *Dekorative Kunst*, 1906, 14: 11-27.

75. Sebastian Haffner, *Failure of a Revolution: Germany 1918-1919*, pp. 175, 192-93. On Epp and on the "White Terror" in Munich, see also the rich documentation in Robert G. L. Waite, *Vanguard of Nazism*, pp. 85-93.

76. According to Brigitte Hamann (*Winifred Wagner: A Life at the Heart of Hitler's Bayreuth*, p. 121), the "Konopackis" were also friends of Siegfried and Winifred Wagner, possibly through the artist Franz Stassen, an old friend of Siegfried's and a member, according to Hamann, of the Konopaths' Nordic Ring. The close relation of the Wagners to Hitler himself is well known.

77. *Die Tagebücher von Josef Goebbels*, Part 1, vol. 2/1 [December 1929-May 1931] (Munich: K. G. Saur, 2005), pp. 183 (25 June 1930), 175 (11 June 1930), 250 (29 September 1930).

78. *Die Tagebücher von Josef Goebbels*, Part 1, vol. 2/1 [December 1929-May 1931], p. 155 (13 April 1930). The NSDAP's intolerance of rival and potentially divisive ideological groups is illustrated by a semi-official statement issued by the NS Press Bureau on 27 November 1933, in the aftermath of the *Deutsche Christen* group's claim to be the religion of National Socialism: "National Socialism," it was stated, "is the outlook of the whole *volk*; consequently anything that claims to be National Socialist must be able to claim that it is valid for the whole *Volk*." (Quoted in Buchheim, *Glaubenskrise*, p. 134)

79. *Die Tagebücher von Josef Goebbels*, Part 1, vol. 2/1, p. 307 (20 December 1930). Claus-E. Bärsch notes that Goebbels rarely resorts to "biological arguments in the spirit of Social Darwinism. So too in his contributions to *Die Zweite Revolution* (1926) and *Wege ins Dritte Reich* (1927), he does not go on about the nature of race. He appears not to have been interested in either eugenics or euthanasia. And [for rather obvious reasons, in view of his own physical handicap – L.G.] he does not enthuse about the blond superman or Old Germanic grandeur." (*Die politische Religion des Nationalsozialismus* [Munich: Wilhelm Fink Verlag, 1998], p. 110)

80. See Malinowski, *Vom König zum Führer*, p. 396 on a debate, as early as 1926, between Friedrich Wilhelm and Gottfried von Bismarck-Kniephof on the question whether "die Vermehrung der rassisch Wertvollen" and the "Reinhaltung des Blutes" were to be achieved solely by "züchterische Maßnahmen" or whether the broader "Kampf um die rassische Seele" should take precedence. On Himmler's views, see Felix Kersten's record of one of his conversations with him: "He always maintained the theory that men could be bred just as successfully as animals and that a race of men could be created possessing the highest spiritual, intellectual and physical qualities. It was only necessary to face the problem seriously, above all to make a start without being put off by the violent prejudices which men had had ingrained in them from their upbringing and in particular from the teaching of the Church." (*The Kersten Memoirs 1940-1945*, pp. 78-79 [18-19 January 1941])

81. *Die Tagebücher von Josef Goebbels*, Part 1, vol. 2/2 (Munich: K. G. Saur, 2004), p. 112 (30 September 1931).

82. Ibid., pp. 132-33 (25 October 1931).

83. Arnd Krüger, "Breeding, Rearing and Preparing the Aryan Body," in J. A. Mangan, ed., *Shaping the Superman*, pp. 42-68, n. 25. Against Konopath's crude "blond racialism" (Rosenberg also insisted that Nordic blood is always manifested

## 172   Brownshirt Princess

as blond hair and blue eyes) Goebbels maintained that "race lies in a person's being and that external characteristics are mostly unreliable" (*Tagebücher*, pp. 132-33; 25 October 1931). Goebbels' "anti-materialist" position was shared by others, and not only by some prominent figures in the traditional *völkisch* movement, such as Friedrich Lienhard [1865-1929], Theodor Fritsch [1852-1933], and Albrecht Wirth [1866-1936] – who did not possess the much touted physical features of the noble Aryan – but by no less an authority than Paul de Lagarde himself, according to whom "das Deutschtum liegt nicht im Geblüte, sondern im Gemüte" (Uwe Puschner, *Die völkische Bewegung im wilhelminischen Kaiserreich*, pp. 71-76, 124-31; Lagarde quoted p. 124). H. Stewart Chamberlain, while rejecting Lagarde's point that "German-ness does not lie in the blood," nonetheless warned against judging race by external physical characteristics such as blue eyes, fair hair, and shape of the skull (*Foundations of the XIXth Century*, vol. 1, pp. 520-42). In Arthur Dinter's hugely popular anti-Semitic novel *Die Sünde wider das Blut* (1918) the half-Jewish woman who seduces the hero into marrying her and corrupting his "blood" is blond and blue-eyed. Many in the rank and file of the Party also had misgivings about blond hair and blue eyes as indispensable signs of German-ness. The *Frankfurter Zeitung* for 1 June 1937, reported that a certain "SS Chief Group Leader Jeckeln attacked the 'blond craze' at a Party meeting: Blond hair and blue eyes by themselves, he said, were not convincing proof that one belongs to the Nordic race" (quoted by George L. Mosse, *Nazi Culture: Intellectual, Cultural and Social Life in the Third Reich* [New York: Grosset & Dunlap, 1978; orig. 1966], p. 43). On disagreements on the question of race within the National Socialist Party, see Christopher M. Hutton, *Race and the Third Reich*, pp. 3-4 and chapters 7-10.

84. On the conflict between Goebbels and Rosenberg over modern art, see Hildegard Brenner, *Die Kunstpolitik des Nationalsozialismus* (Reinbeck bei Hamburg: Rowohlt Taschenbuchverlag, 1963), pp. 65-83; Barbara Miller Lane, *Architecture and Politics in Germany 1918-1945*, pp. 175-84; Peter Paret, *An Artist against the Third Reich: Ernst Barlach 1933-1938* (Cambridge: Cambridge University Press, 2003), pp. 17-19, 62, 64, 72 et passim. On Goebbels' attack on "National Kitsch" (ashtrays with the legend "Germany awake!", cigarette cases with Hitler's portrait, etc.), see Franz-Willing, *Die Hitler-Bewegung*, p. 185.

85. Claudia Koonz, *The Nazi Conscience* (Cambridge, MA, and London: Harvard University Press, 2003).

## Chapter 6.

1.   The "Nordic" view of woman is also demonstrated in the response of Ludwig Roselius, the publisher of the Princess's 1921 poem and her lifelong friend, to a criticism of the inscription he had designed for the Paula Modersohn-Becker House in the Böttcherstraße (see note 20 above) from a Bremen merchant resident in New York: "Sehr geehrter Herr Strohmeyer! Zu Zeiten unserer Vorväter nahm die deutsche Frau die Stellung ein, welche ihr gebührte, sie wurde verehrt, und man stellte eine edle Frau grundsätzlich höher als den Mann, selbst als den Helden. Überall, wo das Germanentum freie Entfaltung hat, bildet sich eine ähnliche Einstellung heraus. [...] Mir ist es deshalb unfaßbar, daß meine Verehrung für die größte Malerin, die die Welt jemals getragen hat, ausgelegt werden kann als eine Beeinträchtigung des Verdienstes oder des Ruhmes männlicher Helden. Ein solcher Gedanke läßt fast vermuten, daß Sie und Ihre Freunde, die über den Sinn

(oder Unsinn) der Gedenktafel gesprochen haben, sich noch nicht frei gemacht haben von dem jeder germanischen Gefühlswelt fremden Gedanken, die Frau als Haustier und als Sklavin zu betrachten." [Dear Herr Strohmeyer: In the days of our forefathers, the German woman occupied the place that is rightfully hers. She was revered, and a noble woman was regarded as fundamentally superior to a man, even to a hero. Wherever German-ness has been able to develop freely, a similar conception has been formed. That is why it is incomprehensible to me that my reverence for the greatest woman painter the world has ever produced can be interpreted as detracting from the achievements or the fame of male heroes. Such a notion leads one to suspect that you and the friends among whom the meaning (or meaninglessness) of the plaque has been discussed have not yet freed yourselves from a view of woman as domestic animal and slave that is alien to every Germanic sensibility.] (From an article in the *Weserzeitung*, 5 December 1926, in Roselius, *Reden und Schriften*, p. 56). A sentence from Roselius's speech at the opening of the Modersohn-Becker House in 1927 anticipates both the ideas of *Nordische Frau und Nordischer Glaube* and the role of the heroine of *Die Overbroocks*: "Ohnmächtig ist der Mann in seinem Schaffen, steht ihm nicht das Weib zur Seite" [Impotent is the man in his creative work without a woman standing by his side] (ibid., p. 52). In similar vein Ernst Bergmann, *Die 25 Thesen der Deutschreligion: Ein Katechismus* (Breslau: F. Hirt, 1934): "Die Ethik der Deutschreligion ist eine heldische, eine heroische Ethik. Sie beruht auf den drei altgermanischen Tugenden, der Tapferkeit, Ritterlichkeit und Treue, die alle aus der Ehe fliessen" [The ethics of our German religion are heroic ethics, resting on the three old Germanic virtues of courage, chivalry, and fidelity, all of which derive from the marriage bond]. Woman in the old Germanic world is the one being that stands higher than the hero and inspires his reverence: "Heldisch ist der Mensch, der vor keinem anderen Gott kniet als vor dem ewig-Mütterlichen, das uns gebar. Denn das Muttersymbol ist das einzige Bild in der Welt, vor dem auch der Held knien darf" [The heroic man is one who kneels before no other god but the eternal mother that bore us. For the mother-symbol is the only image in the world before which the hero may kneel]. (Quoted in Ilse Erika Korotin, *"Am Muttergeist soll die Welt genesen:" Philosophische Dispositionen zum Frauenbild im Nationalsozialismus* [Vienna; Cologne; Weimar: Böhlau Verlag, 1992], pp. 164-65).

2. Page references are to Marie Adelheid Konopath Prinzessin zur Lippe, *Nordische Frau und Nordischer Glaube* (Berlin: Verlag von Struppe & Winckler, 1934 [Flugschriften der Nordischen Glaubensbewegung, Heft 2]).

3. The Princess's views on this point were not uncommon among *völkisch* critics of the established Christian churches. Generally, Luther was lauded as a hero and Protestantism itself was seen as authentically Germanic in its rejection of "Roman" authoritarianism. But it was the Protestant impulse that was praised, not the established Protestant churches. Thus to Alfred Bäumler – Nazi philosopher, editor of Bachofen, ardent Nietzschean, and sometime correspondent of Thomas Mann – "Protestantism is strong when it finds itself engaged in struggle, when it does what its name implies. [...] Outside the context of struggle Protestantism degenerates very quickly into brittle orthodoxy or effeminate pietism." (From a text of 1936, quoted and translated by Steigmann-Gall, *The Holy Reich*, p. 106) A text of 1940, published as no. 16 of a series entitled "Nordland Bücherei," reviews the age-long struggle between Christianity, in particular Rome, and native Germanic culture in a spirit very close to that of the Princess, and concludes that, as Germans and National Socialists, "we have no right to claim a leadership role in Europe as long

as we lack the courage and revolutionary zeal to confront and overcome the power of an almost two-thousand-year-old idea of spiritual and political community and to replace it with the new National Socialist idea. [...] I am not unaware that those powers that have placed the whole imaginative side of life under their protection and, beyond that, claim to possess access to the Other World, cannot be removed overnight from the spiritual life of our people. We have to work with enormous patience and equally enormous prudence toward the point at which the people of our Reich finally appreciate in its true meaning the natural and therefore divine priority of belonging to a particular people over optional, arbitrarily chosen membership in a confession or church. We must constantly make clear to the German people that no individual can eliminate his or her participation in the being of the people [*Volkspersönlichkeit*] into which, through his or her destiny, he or she has been born. No one can be transferred by a free act of will to another people [...]. Man is bound to his own people by a divine law" (Friedrich Schmidt, *Das Reich als Aufgabe* [Berlin: Nordland Verlag, 1940], pp. 63, 67-68).

## Chapter 7.

1. Page references are to Marie Adelheid Prinzessin Reuß-zur Lippe, *Die Overbroocks*, 2nd edn. (Berlin: Verlag C. V. Engelhard, 1943).

2. The Princess may have read the contribution of Jörg Lanz von Liebenfels, founder of the *Ordo Novi Templi* in 1900 and one of the leading Viennese advocates of restoring racial purity in the period before World War I, to a volume on the problems of modern marriage: "Das Wesen, der Begriff, und der Zweck der Ehe ist: Rassenreinzucht" [The essence, concept, and goal of marriage is the raising up of a pure race]. "Love" is secondary and "cannot be the goal or central feature of marriage" (in Ferdinand Freiherr von Paungarten, ed., *Das Eheproblem im Spiegel unserer Zeit*, pp. 55-56). Such notions cannot, of course, have been unfamiliar to her as a member of one of the great princely families of Germany.

## Chapter 8.

1. Margaret Bourke-White, *"Dear Fatherland, Rest Quietly": A Report on the Collapse of Hitler's 'Thousand Years'*, pp. 130-32. In conversation with Bourke-White, the American reporter and photographer, the Princess tells of having traveled to Berlin in the final months of the war to see her son, who was severely wounded, and gives a graphic description of the fire-bombing raids on the city.

2. See note 22 above.

3. See Jens Mecklenburg, ed., *Handbuch deutscher Rechtsextremismus* (Berlin: Elefanten Press, 1996), pp. 378-79 et passim. For a more detailed and nuanced account of the origins of the movement in an English-administered camp for former Nazis, its internal divisions and splits, and the relations of its various factions to *völkisch* and neo-Nazi ideologies on the one hand, and to Anglo-American Unitarianism on the other, see Ulrich Nanko, "Religiöse Gruppenbildungen vormaliger 'Deutschgläubiger' nach 1945," in Hubert Cancik and Uwe Puschner, eds., *Antisemitismus, Paganismus, Völkische Religion* (Munich: K. G. Saur, 2004), pp. 121-34.

4. Jens Mecklenburg, ed., *Handbuch deutscher Rechtsextrimsmus*, pp. 411-13.

Another of Grabert's publications, the *Deutsche Hochschullehrer-Zeitung* (founded in 1953), aimed chiefly at the rehabilitation of Nazi college teachers. His own postwar writings, all published by his *Verlag der deutschen Hochschullehrer-Zeitung* in Tübingen – *Sieger und Besiegte: Der deutsche Nationalismus nach 1945* (1966), *Das Geschichtsbuch als Umerzieher* (1967), *Volk und Führung: Deutschlands Ringen um Einheit und Bestand* (1977) – are attempts to displace war guilt on to the Allies, to challenge accounts of the Holocaust, etc. These themes are also developed in an unabashed rehabilitation of Goebbels published by the Grabert-Verlag, Tübingen, in 1974 – Wilfrid von Oven's 662-page, illustrated *Finale Furioso: Mit Goebbels bis zum Ende*.

5. Kratz, *Die Götter des New Age*, pp. 307-08. On the DUR and its founding, see *Handbuch deutscher Rechtsextremismus*, pp. 378-79; Peter Kratz, *Die Götter des New Age*, pp. 294-95, 318-72.

6. *Nordische Frau und Nordischer Glaube*, p. 3.

7. See http://www.ladestra.info/?p=6285. The line the Princess quoted is the opening line of a popular poem of 1814 by the nationalist poet Max von Schenkendorf: "Wenn alle untreu werden, so bleiben wir doch treu,/ Daß immer noch auf Erden für euch ein Fähnlein sei./ Gefährten unsrer Jugend, ihr Bilder bessrer Zeit,/ Die uns zu Männertugend und Liebestod geweiht." As American High Commissioner in Germany in 1949, John McCloy had in fact pardoned or commuted the sentences of many war criminals.

8. Andreas Speit, "Fieses unterm Findling: Der Nazi-Kultort 'Ahnenstätte Conneforde' hat einen prominenten Grabredner: Bundeslandwirtschaftsminister Karl-Heinz Funke," *Jungle World*, 21 April 1999 http://www.nadir.org/nadir/periodika/jungle_world/_99/17/12b.htm

9. Peter Kratz, *Die Götter des New Age*, p. 256, quotes Sigrid Hunke, a neo-Nazi philosopher, in her *Europas andere Religion*: "Generation and destruction, growing and withering, birth and death – both have their right and their divine meaning for the Whole. [...] Hence nothing disappears entirely. Hence death is not a complete stop, not an end, not an annihilation." Hunke herself claims to have found the elements of her vision, which Kratz compares to Ernst Jünger's "Heroic Realism" (i.e. the desire to rejoin the Great All by "leaping into the air") in the *Elegien* of Heinrich Vogeler's sometime friend, the poet Rainer Maria Rilke. Rilke she claims, "does something enormous: he lowers the barrier between life and death, he tears down the wall between the living and the dead, he crosses the boundaries between present and past, present and future."

10. See Peter Kratz, *Die Götter des New Age*, pp. 249-51.

11. Archaeological excavations were conducted at various sites in Germany and archaeological and anthropological expeditions were sent to Tibet, Iceland, and the Canary Islands with a view to finding "scientific" support for various theories of Aryan or Nordic racial superiority, such as that human culture had its origin in ancient Thule (Iceland-Greenland) or in the lost continent of Atlantis or that the culture of the ancient Far East had been an Aryan culture. See Victor and Victoria Trimondi, *Hitler-Buddha-Krishna*, part 1.

12. On Barnes, see Deborah E. Lipstadt, *Denying the Holocaust: The Growing Assault on Truth and Memory* (New York: The Free Press, 1993), pp. 30-34, 67-83. According

to Gill Seidel, *The Holocaust Denial: Antisemitism, Racism and the New Right* (Leeds: Beyond the Pale Collective, 1986), "the Holocaust denial movement owes a debt to Harry Elmer Barnes (1889-1968), American historian and sociologist, whom it hails as the father of revisionism." (p. 66).

13. English translations of Christophersen's *Auschwitz-Lüge* appeared with the Liberty Bell Press of Reedy, West Virginia, in 1975 and 1979, and in Toronto and Quebec, Canada.

14. In accordance with a 1941 decree of Hitler, the novel *Die Overbroocks* (1942) was printed in Roman type. The typeface issue appears to have been considered a serious one in *völkisch* circles. See Introduction, note 22 above.

## Chapter 9.

1. Peter Kratz, *Die Götter des New Age*, pp. 307, 362.

2. In several chapters of his *Germans and Jews: The Right, the Left, and the Search for a "Third Force" in Pre-Nazi Germany* (New York: Howard Fertig, 1970) – especially chapter 5: "The Corporate State and the Conservative Revolution in Weimar Germany" – George L. Mosse explores with remarkable even-handedness the implications of the *völkisch* revolutionaries' preoccupation with ideology, with finding an "idea" for Germany, and their accompanying contempt for empirical analysis of social and economic problems. As in the Princess's novel *Die Overbroocks*, there was criticism of usury and finance but no comprehensive economic theory. Paul Krannhals, for instance, deplored the enslavement of man through money and credit. "Just as the state had been separated from the *volk* by parliamentary government, so the economic system had been detached too, because money had become a value in itself and for itself alone. 'Money and blood [the *volk*] are contrasting elements which could not be in greater opposition.' Capitalist finance must be abolished and money made once again a reward for real work. Credit was the essence of unproductive capital – so thought the conservative revolutionaries. They were attracted by the clause in the first program of the National Socialist Party, which called for emancipation from the 'slavery of interest charges.'" (Mosse, *Germans and Jews*, p. 131, citing Krannhals, *Das organische Weltbild*, 1928, p. 238) Economic problems would be resolved once individuals rediscovered the underlying unity of the *volk* and based their actions on it. The society "beyond capitalism and Marxism," in Mosse's words, "was basically a society held together not by an explicit social or economic aim, but by a romantic ideology." (p. 136).

3. *Odal: Monatsschrift für Blut und Boden*, 10: 536 (Heft 7, July 1941).

4. Albert Speer, *Inside the Third Reich*, trans. Richard and Clara Winston (New York: Avon Books, 1971; orig. German 1969), p. 557.

## Bibliography.

1. While Hewins condemns anti-Semitism, his book, written in the shadow of Bernadotte's assassination at the hands of the Stern Gang, is strongly critical both of the fledgling state of Israel and of Jews. Together with the author's relatively sympathetic portrayal of Himmler (pp. 118-20 et passim), this aspect of the book must have appealed to the Princess. Hewins went on to publish a 400-page revisionist biography of Quisling (*Quisling: Prophet without Honour*, London: W. H.

Allen, 1965), in which the Norwegian puppet ruler is presented favorably as "a good man who took the wrong course."

A letter from Hewins, published in *The Times* of 21 September 1948, and cited in full in an appendix to the biography of Bernadotte, conveys the author's tone, recognizably that of the well-bred anti-Semite in its rapid shift from disclaimers of anti-Semitism to a relentless listing of the evils perpetrated on the world by "the Jews." In a move similar to the rhetoric used by neo-Nazis, such as Thies Christophersen or Friedrich Christian, Prinz zu Schaumburg-Lippe, these evils are compared with and judged worse than those of the Nazis:

> Sir, – In common with most Englishmen I have had a number of Jewish friends.
> I have visited Auschwitz, the liquidation camp which will ever stand as one of the supreme infamies in world history. I have wandered aghast over what was once the Warsaw ghetto. Near Danzig I have handled soap manufactured by Germans from Jewish corpses. [...] I have seen the pioneer work done by Jews in Palestine. I know and respect a number of their leaders. I hope, therefore, that nobody will accuse me of being anti-Semitic.
> Yet in this hour of Jewish shame, it is hard to remain objective and to fight the virus of anti-Semitism [...].
> My friends in the Mandatory Government, with whom I had been a few days earlier in the King David Hotel, Jerusalem, were blown up in the midst of their thankless duties by Jews. Two British sergeants have been hung like dogs by Jews, although these simple soldiers were non-political and doing irksome duties far from home. The harmless brother of a Palestine police officer has been murdered by a Jewish infernal machine in his English home. The Jews have vilified the British, their best friends, who fought Hitler for one year alone and made the very idea of the National Home feasible. The Jews have turned much of the great American republic, on whom we lean for our very bread and butter, against us. The Jews have embroiled us with our teeming Arab friends, who substantially paved the way for the destruction of the Hohenzollern confederation against us in the First World War. They threaten openly to engulf our trustiest Arab friend, King Abdulla in Transjordania, which alone in the Middle East never for a second wavered against us in the late war [...]. This, and more, is a lot for the most tolerable [*sic*!] Englishman to bear. It is almost enough to turn a saint anti-Semitic.
> Now the Jews have murdered Folke Bernadotte. No more infamous (nor more unjustified) crime was, in my opinion, committed throughout the war. The Germans could argue that the shooting of innocent hostages and the razing of defenseless towns and villages was 'war,' and that these measures were 'necessary politically'. No such vestige of excuse can be offered for this, the supreme Jewish atrocity of modern times.

Reuß-zur Lippe's translation, listed in only two German library catalogues, could not be consulted directly. At this point, therefore, I am unable to say whether she retained the second, third, and fourth sentences of the passage quoted above.

# Bibliography

## Works by Marie Adelheid Prinzessin Reuß-zur Lippe

### Poetry:

*Gott in mir* (Bremen: Angelsachsen Verlag, 1921), 48 pp. and frontispiece plate.

*Weltfrömmigkeit* (Hameln: Soltsien, 1960), 23 pp. ["Die gute Gabe," vol. 1].

*Freundesgruß* (Mohrkirch: Kritik-Verlag, 1978). Illustrated with woodcuts by Georg Sluyterman v. Langeweyde. 41 pp. [*Kritik: Die Stimme des Volkes*, no. 46].

### Novels:

*Mutter Erde* (Berlin: Verlag 'Neue Nation,' 1935), 191 pp. Published under name of Marie Adelheid Konopath.

*Die Overbroocks* (Berlin: Ährenlese Verlag, 1942; 2nd edn. Berlin: C. V. Engelhard, 1943), 200 pp.

### Essays:

*Das bist du* (Bremen: Friesen-Verlag, 1924), 63 pp. ill.

*Deutscher Hausrat* (Leipzig: A. Strauch, 1938), 22 pp. ill.

*Nordische Frau und nordischer Glaube* (Berlin: Struppe und Winckler, 1935). [Flugschriften der Nordischen Glaubensbewegung, Heft 2]

*Feiern im Jahresring: 6 Feiersprachen* (Düsseldorf-Garath: Verlag Neues Denken, 1968), 67 pp.

Short contributions to the monthly magazine *Odal. Monatsschrift für Blut und Boden* (1932-1942).

### Translations:

*Bernadotte: Sein Leben und Werk* (Frankfurt a. M.: Parma Edition, 1952), 369 pp. ill. [Trans. of Ralph Hewins, *Count Folke Bernadotte: His Life and Work* (London: Hutchinson, [1950]), 264 pp. ill.][1]

*Glückliche Fügung: Die treue Liebe der Mary Conroy* (Mainz: Matthias-Grünewald Verlag, 1955), 248 pp. [From Lenora Mattingly Weber, *My True Love Waits* (New York: Crowell, 1953). Weber was the author of the popular Beany Malone books for girls].

*Entlarvte Heuchelei* (Wiesbaden: Priester, 1961), 257 pp. [From *Perpetual War for Perpetual Peace: A Critical Examination of the Foreign Policy of Franklin Delano Roosevelt and its Aftermath*, ed. Harry Elmer Barnes, with the collaboration of William Henry Chamberlin et al. (Caldwell, ID: Caxton Printers, 1953), 679 pp. [This is the work that confirmed Barnes's reputation as a "revisionist" historian].

*Das Drama der Juden Europas: Eine technische Studie* (Hanover: Pfeiffer, 1965), 271 pp. [From Paul Rassinier, *Le drame des Juifs européens* (Paris: Les Sept Couleurs, 1964). The classic work of Holocaust denial].

**Edited works:**

Richard Walther Darré, *Erkenntnisse und Werden: Aufsätze aus der Zeit vor der Machtergreifung* (Goslar: Verlag Blut und Boden, 1940), 240 pp.

*80 Merksätze und Leitsprüche über Zucht und Sitte aus Schriften und Reden von R. Walther Darré* (Goslar: Verlag Blut und Boden, 1940). [Extracts selected by Reuß-zur Lippe from Darré's *Das Bauerntum als Lebensquelle der nordischen Rasse* and *Neuadel aus Blut und Boden*].

# General Bibliography of Works Cited

Ach, Manfred, and Clemens Pentrop. *Hitlers "Religion": Pseudoreligiöse Elemente im nationalsozialstischen Sprachgebrauch* ([Munich]: Arbeitsgemeinschaft für Religions- und Weltanschauungsfragen, 1977. Asgard Edition, 3).

Anczykowski, Maria, ed., *Bernhard Hoetger: Skulptur, Malerei, Design, Architektur* (Bremen: H. M. Hauschild, 1998).

Avenarius, Ferdinand, ed., *Der Kunstwart*, later *Der Kunstwart und Kulturwart*, and briefly *Deutscher Wille* (Dresden, 1887-94; Munich, 1894-1923). Continued under other editors until 1932, when it appeared under a new name, *Deutsche Zeitschrift: Monatshefte für die politische und geistige Gestaltung der Gegenwart*. In October 1933 the subtitle was changed to *Zweimonatsschrift für eine deutsche Volkskultur*. Publication ceased in 1937.

— "Hodler in unsrer Kunst," *Deutscher Wille: Des Kunstwarts 31. Jahr*, April-June 1918, pp. 129-32.

— "Stirb und werde! In der Zeit der Totenfeste," *Deutscher Wille: Des Kunstwarts 32. Jahr*, October-December 1918, pp. 103-04.

Barlösius, Eva. *Naturgemäße Lebensführung: Zur Geschichte der Lebensreform um die Jahrhundertwende* (Frankfurt and New York: Campus-Verlag, 1996).

Bärsch, Claus-E. *Die politische Religion des Nationalsozialismus* (Munich: Wilhelm Fink Verlag, 1998).

Baumann, Schaul. *Die Deutsche Glaubensbewegung und ihr Gründer Jakob Wilhelm Hauer (1881-1962)* (Marburg: Diagonal Verlag, 2006).

Bausinger, Hermann. "Zwischen Grün und Braun: Volkstumsideologie und

Heimatpflege nach dem Ersten Weltkrieg," in Hubert Cancik, ed., *Religions- und Geistesgeschichte der Weimarer Republik*, pp. 215-29.

Becker, Peter Emil. *Zur Geschichte der Rassenhygiene: Wege ins Dritte Reich* (Stuttgart and New York: Georg Thieme Verlag, 1988).

Bergen, Doris L. *Twisted Cross: The German Christian Movement in the Third Reich* (Chapel Hill, NC: University of North Carolina Press, 1996).

Berglar, Peter. *Walther Rathenau: Ein Leben zwischen Philosophie und Politik* (Graz; Vienna; Cologne: Verlag Styria, 1987).

Bergmann, Ernst. *Die 25 Thesen der Deutschreligion: Ein Katechismus* (Breslau: F. Hirt, 1934).

Biehl, Janet. "'Ecology' and the Modernization of Fascism in the German Ultra-right," *Ökologie und Kapitalismus Seminarreader*, pp. 91-119 (p. 109) http://jd-jl-rlp.de/themen/13-oeko-und-atompolitik/53-oekologie-und-kapitalismus-sept2006.html

— and Peter Staudenmaier. *Ecofascism: Lessons from the German Experience* (Edinburgh and San Francisco: AK Press, 1995).

*Biographisches-bibliographisches Kirchenlexikon*, ed. Friedrich Wilhelm Bautz, 28 vols. (Hamm [Westf.]: Verlag T. Bautz, 1970-2008).

Bollmus, Reinhard. *Das Amt Rosenberg und seine Gegner* (Stuttgart: Deutsche Verlagsanstalt, 1970).

Bönisch, Michael. "'Hammer'-Bewegung," in *Handbuch zur "Völkischen Bewegung" 1871-1918*, pp. 341-65.

Bourke-White, Margaret. *"Dear Fatherland, Rest Quietly": A Report on the Collapse of Hitler's 'Thousand Years'* (New York: Simon and Schuster, 1946).

Bramwell, Anna. *Blood and Soil: Richard Walther Darré and Hitler's 'Green Party'* (Bourne End, Bucks.: Kensal Press, 1985).

Bräuninger, Werner. *Hitlers Kontrahenten in der NSDAP 1921-1945* (Munich: F. A. Herbig Verlagsbuchhandlung, 2004).

Brenner, Hildegard. *Die Kunstpolitik des Nationalsozialismus* (Reinbeck bei Hamburg: Rowohlt Taschenbuchverlag, 1963).

Brenner, Wolfgang. *Walther Rathenau: Deutscher und Jude* (Munich and Zurich: Piper, 2005).

Bruns, Max. *Aus meinem Blute* (Minden [Westf.]: J. C. C. Bruns' Verlag, n.d.).

Buber, Martin. *Briefwechsel aus sieben Jahrzehnten*, ed., Grete Schaeder, vol. 2, [1918-1938] (Heidelberg: Verlag Lambert Schneider, 1973).

— *Hasidism and Modern Man*, ed., Maurice Friedman (New York: Horizon Press, 1958).

Buchheim, Hans. *Glaubenskrise im Dritten Reich: Drei Kapitel Nationalsozialistischer Religionspolitik* (Stuttgart: Deutsche Verlags-Anstalt, 1953).

Buchholz, Kai et al., eds. *Die Lebensreform: Entwürfe zur Neugestaltung von Leben und Kunst um 1900*, exhib. cat., 2 vols. (Darmstadt: Häusser, 2000).

Bullock, Alan. *Hitler: A Study in Tyranny* (London: Odhams Press, 1952).

Büttner, Herman, ed. *Meister Eckeharts Schriften und Predigten: Aus dem Mittelhochdeutschen übersetzt und herausgegeben von Herman Büttner*, 2 vols. (Leipzig: Eugen Diederichs, 1903).

Cancik, Hubert, and Uwe Puschner, eds. *Antisemitismus, Paganismus, Völkische Religion* (Munich: K. G. Saur, 2004).

— *Nietzsches Antike: Vorlesung* (Stuttgart and Weimar: J. B. Metzler Verlag, 1995).

— ed. *Religions- und Geistesgeschichte der Weimarer Republik* (Düsseldorf: Patmos Verlag, 1982).

— "'Neuheiden' und totaler Staat: Völkische Religion am Ende der Weimarer Republik," in H. Cancik, ed., *Religions- und Geistesgeschichte der Weimarer Republik*, pp. 176-212.

Caputo, John D. "Heidegger and Theology," in *The Cambridge Companion to Heidegger*, ed. Charles B. Guignon (Cambridge: Cambridge University Press, 1993), pp. 326-44.

Carlson, Maria. *"No Religion Higher than Truth": A History of the Theosophical Movement in Russia 1875-1922* (Princeton, NJ: Princeton University Press, 1993).

Cebulla, Florian. "Die Rundfunkpolitik des Stahlhelms, 1930-1933," *Rundfunk und Geschichte*, 1999, 25: 101-07.

Chamberlain, Houston Stewart. *Foundations of the Nineteenth Century*, trans. John Lees, 2 vols. (London and New York: John Lane, 1911; 1st pub. 1910; orig. German 1899).

Clauß, Ludig Ferdinand. *Rasse und Seele: Eine Einführung in den Sinn der leiblichen Gestalt*, 18th edn. (Munich: J. F. Lehmann, 1943; orig. 1926).

— *Die nordische Seele: Eine Einführung in die Rassenseelenkunde*, 7th edn. (Munich; Berlin: J. F. Lehmann, 1939; orig. 1923).

Coole, W. W. and M. F. Potter. *Thus Spake Germany* (London: Routledge, 1941).

Darré, R. Walther. *Neuordnung unseres Denkens* (Reichsbauernstadt Goslar: Verlag Blut und Boden, 1940).

— *Achtzig Merksätze und Leitsprüche über Zucht und Sitte aus Schriften und Reden von R. Walther Darré* (Goslar: Verlag Blut und Boden, 1940).

— *Erkenntnisse und Werden: Aufsätze aus der Zeit vor der Machtergreifung*, ed. Marie-Adelheid Prinzessin Reuß-zur Lippe (Goslar: Verlag Blut und Boden [1940]).

— *Neuadel aus Blut und Boden* (Berlin: J. F. Lehmann, 1938; orig. 1930).

— *Das Bauerntum als Lebensquelle der Nordischen Rasse* (Munich: Lehmann, 1935; orig. 1929).

Davies, Peter. "'Männerbund' und 'Mutterrecht': Hermann Wirth, Sophie Rogge-Börner and the *Ura-Linda-Chronik*," *German Life and Letters*, 2007, 60: 98-115.

Diederichs, Eugen. *Selbstzeugnisse und Briefe von Zeitgenossen*, ed. Ulf Diederichs (Düsseldorf; Cologne: Diederichs Verlag, 1967).

Dierks, Margarete. *Jakob Wilhelm Hauer 1881-1962: Leben, Werk, Wirkung, mit einer Personalbibliographie* (Heidelberg: Lambert Schneider, 1986).

Dinter, Arthur. *Die Sünde wider das Blut* (Leipzig: Wolfverlag, 1918).

Dirksen, Herbert von. *Moscow, Tokyo, London: Twenty Years of German Foreign Policy* (Norman, OK: University of Oklahoma Press, 1952).

Ebbinghaus, Angelika. *Opfer und Täterinnen: Frauenbiographien des Nationalsozialismus* (Nördlingen: F. Greno, [1987]). Schriften der Hamburger Stiftung für Sozialgeschichte des 20. Jahrhunderts, 2.

Eley, Geoff and James Retallack, eds. *Wilhelminism and its Legacies: German Modernities, Imperialism and the Meanings of Reform 1890-1930* (New York and Oxford: Berghahn Books, 2003).

— "Making a Place in the Nation," in Geoff Eley and James Retallack, eds., *Wilhelminism and its Legacies*, pp. 16-33.

Fabréguet, Michel. "Artur Dinter, théologien, biologiste et politique (1876-1948)," *Revue d'Allemagne*, 2000, 32: 233-44.

Fahrenkrog, Ludwig. *Geschichte meines Glaubens* (Halle a.d. Saale: Gebauer-Schwetschke, 1906; 2nd edn. Leipzig: Hartung, 1926).

— *Die Germanische Glaubens-Gemeinschaft* (Berlin-Steglitz: Verlag *Kraft und Schönheit*, [1921]). Kleine Germanenhefte, 6.

— *Baldur: Drama* (Stuttgart: Greiner und Pfeiffer, 1908).

Fest, Joachim. *The Face of the Third Reich*, trans. Michael Bullock (London: Weidenfeld & Nicolson, 1970; German orig. 1963).

Field, Geoffrey G. "Nordic Racism," *Journal of the History of Ideas*, 1977, 38: 523-40.

Flasche, Rainer. "Vom deutschen Kaiserreich zum Dritten Reich: Nationalreligiöse Bewegungen in der ersten Hälfte des 20. Jahrhunderts in Deutschland," *Zeitschrift für Religionswissenschaft*, 1993, 1 (2): 28-49.

Franzel, Emil. *Das Reich der Braunen Jakobiner* (Munich: J. Pfeiffer, 1964).

Franz-Willing, Georg. *Die Hitler-Bewegung 1925 bis 1934* (Preussisch Oldendorf: Deutsche Verlagsgesellschaft, 2001).

Frecot, Janos, Johann Friedrich Geist, Diethart Kerbs. *Fidus 1868-1948: Zur ästhetischen Praxis bürgerlichen Fluchtbewegungen* (Munich: Rogner & Bernhard, 1972; new expanded edn. with introd. by Gert Makenklott, 1997).

— "Der Werdandibund," in Burkard Bergius, Janos Frecot and Dieter Radicke, eds., *Architektur, Stadt und Politik. Julius Posener zum 75. Geburtstag* (Gießen: Ananabas Verlag, 1979), pp. 37-46.

Freund, René. *Braune Magie? Okkultimsus, New Age und Nationalsozialismus* (Vienna: Picus-Verlag, 1995).

Fricke, Dieter. "Der 'Deutschbund'," in *Handbuch zur "Völkischen Bewegung" 1871-1918*, pp. 328-40.

Fromm, Bella. *Blood and Banquets: A Berlin Social Diary* (New York: Carol Publishing Group, 1990; 1st edn. London, 1943).

Fuller, Stephen Nyole. *The Nazis' Literary Grandfather: Adolf Bartels and Cultural Extremism 1871-1945* (New York: Peter Lang, 1996).

Gallwitz, S. D. *Dreißig Jahre Worpswede: Künstler, Geist, Werden* (Bremen: Angelsachsen Verlag, 1922).

Goebbels, Joseph. *Die Tagebücher von Joseph Goebbels*, ed. Elke Fröhlich, 9 vols. (Munich and New York: K. G. Saur, 1998-2005).

Goodrick-Clarke, Nicholas. *The Occult Roots of Nazism: The Ariosophists of Austria and Germany 1890-1935* (Wellingborough, Northants.: The Aquarian Press, 1985).

Gossman, Lionel. "Jugendstil in Firestone: The Jewish Illustrator E. M. Lilien," *Princeton University Library Chronicle*, 2004, 56: 11-78.

Granier, Gerhard. *Magnus von Levetzow: Seeoffizier, Monarchist und Wegbereiter Hitlers* (Boppard a. R.: Harald Boldt Verlag, 1982).

Green, Martin. *The Mountain of Truth: The Counterculture Begins; Ascona, 1900-1920* (Hanover, NH: University Press of New England, 1986).

Gugenberger, Eduard, and Roman Schweidlenka. *Mutter Erde: Magie und Politik zwischen Fascismus und neuer Gesellschaft* (Vienna: Verlag für Geisteswissenschaftskritik, 1987).

Günther, Hans F. K. *Lebensgeschichte des hellenischen Volkes* (Pähl: Verlag Hohe Warte – Franz von Bebenburg, 1956).

— *Kleine Rassenkunde des deutschen Volkes* (Munich and Berlin: J. F. Lehmann, 1943; orig. 1929).

— *Deutsche Köpfe nordischer Rasse: 50 Abbildungen, mit Geleitworten von Prof. Dr. Eugen Fischer und Dr. Hans F. K. Günther* (Munich: J. F. Lehmann, 1927).

— *Adel und Rasse* (Munich: J. F. Lehmann, 1926).

Gurlitt, Ludwig. "Der Fluch der toten Religion," *Die Aktion*, 1/8 (10 April 1911), col. 233-235.

Haack, Friedrich-Wilhelm. *Wotans Wiederkehr: Blut-, Boden- und Rasse-Religion* (Munich: Claudius Verlag, 1981).

Haffner, Sebastian. *Failure of a Revolution: Germany 1918-1919*, trans. Georg Rapp (London: André Deutsch, 1973; orig. German *Die verratene Revolution* [Betrayal of a Revolution], 1969]).

Hamann, Brigitte. *Winifred Wagner: A Life at the Heart of Hitler's Bayreuth*, trans. Alan Bauce (London: Granta Books, 2005; orig. German 2002).

*Handbuch literarisch-kultureller Vereine, Gruppen und Bünde 1825-1933*, Wulf Wülfing, K. Bruns and Rolf Parr, eds. (Stuttgart; Weimar: J. B. Metzler, 1998).

*Handbuch zur "Völkischen Bewegung" 1871-1918*, Uwe Puschner, Walter Schmitz, Justus U. Ulbricht, eds. (Munich; New Providence; London; Paris: K. G. Saur, 1996).

Harman, Chris. *The Lost Revolution: Germany 1918-1923* (London: Bookmarks, 1982).

Hart, Julius. *Der neue Gott: Ein Ausblick auf das kommende Jahrhundert* (Florence and Leipzig: Eugen Diederichs, 1899).

— *Triumph des Lebens* (Florence and Leipzig: Eugen Diederichs, 1898).

Hartung, Günter. "Artur Dinter, der Erfolgautor des frühen deutschen Faschismus," in *The Attractions of Fascism: Traditionen und Traditionssuche des deutschen Faschismus*, ed. Günter Hartung (Halle a. d. S.: Martin-Luther-Universität/ Wissenschaftliche Beiträge, 1988), pp. 55-83.

Hauer, J. Wilhelm. "An Alien or a German Faith?" (lecture given to an audience of ten thousand at the Berlin Sportpalast in April 1933), in *Germany's New Religion: The German Faith Movement*, trans. T. S. K. Scott-Craig and R. E. Davies (London: George Allen & Unwin, 1937), pp. 36-70.

— *Deutsche Gottschau: Grundzüge eines deutschen Glaubens*, 4th edn. (Stuttgart: Kutbrod Verlag, 1935; 1st edn. 1934).

— "Die Anthroposophie als Weg zum Geist," *Die Tat*, 12, no. 11, February 1921, pp. 800-24.

Helmreich, Ernst Christian. *The German Churches under Hitler* (Detroit, MI: Wayne State University Press, 1979).

Henderson, Susan. "Böttcherstrasse: The Corporatist Vision of Ludwig Roselius and Bernhard Hoetger," *Journal of Decorative and Propaganda Arts*, 1994, 20: 165-81.

Herbert, Robert L., Eleanor S. Apter, Elise K. Kenney, eds. *The Société Anonyme and the Dreier Bequest at Yale University: A Catalogue Raisonné* (New Haven, CT, and London: Yale University Press, 1984).

Hervé, Florence. *Geschichte der deutschen Frauenbewegung* (Cologne: Pahl-Rugenstein, 1983).

Hickethier, Knut, Wilhelm H. Pott, Kristina Zerges. *Franz Pfemfert: Die Revolutions G.m.b.H.* (Wissmar and Steinbach: Anabas Verlag Günter Kampf, 1973).

Hieronimus, Ekkehard. "Zur Religiosität der völkischen Bewegung," in Cancik, ed., *Religions- und Gestesgeschichte der Weimarer Republik*, pp. 159-75.

Hinz, Thorsten. *Mystik und Anarchie: Meister Eckhart und seine Bedeutung im Denken Gustav Landauers* (Berlin: Karin Kramer Verlag, 2000).

Hitler, Adolf. *Reden, Schiften, Anordnungen: Februar 1925 bis Januar 1933*, 6 vols., ed. for Institut für Zeitgeschichte (Munich: K. G. Saur, 1992-2003).

— *Mein Kampf*, trans. Ralph Mannheim (Boston MA: Houghton Mifflin Co., 1943).

Himmler, Heinrich. *Geheimreden 1933 bis 1945*, ed. Bradley F. Smith and Agnes Peterson, introduction by Joachim Fest (Berlin: Propyläen Verlag, 1974).

Hübinger, Gangolf. "Der Verlag Eugen Diederichs in Jena," *Geschichte und Gesellschaft*, 1996, 22: 31-45.

Hundt, Walter. *Bei Heinrich Vogeler in Worpswede: Erinnerungen* (Worpswede: Worpsweder Verlag, 1981).

Hutton, Christopher M. *Race and the Third Reich: Linguistics, Racial Anthropology and Genetics in the Dialectic of 'Volk'* (Cambridge: Polity Press, 2005).

Jefferies, Matthew. "*Lebensreform* – a Middle-Class Antidote to Wilhelminism?," in Geoff Eley and James Retallack, eds., *Wilhelminism and its Legacies*, pp. 91-106.

Jeziorkowski, Klaus. "Empor ins Licht: Gnostizismus und Licht-Symbolik in Deutschland um 1900," in *Eine Iphigenie rauchend: Aufsätze und Feuilletons zur deutschen Tradition* (Frankfurt a. M.: Suhrkamp, 1987), pp. 152-80.

Jonas, Hans. *The Message of the Alien God and the Beginnings of Christianity: The Gnostic Religion*, 3rd edn. (Boston: Beacon Press, 2001).

Jonas, Klaus W. *Der Kronprinz Wilhelm* (Frankfurt a. M.: Heinrich Scheffler Verlag, 1962).

Jungbluth, Rüdiger. *Die Quandts: Ihr leiser Aufstieg zur mächtigsten Wirtschaftsdynastie Deutschlands* (Frankfurt and New York: Campus Verlag, 2002).

Jünginer, Horst. "Sigrid Hunke: Europe's New Religion and its Old Stereotypes," in Hubert Cancik and Uwe Puschner, eds., *Antisemitismus, Paganismus, Völkische Religion / Anti-semitism, Paganism, Voelkish Religion* (Munich: Saur, 2004) pp. 151–63; also http://homepages.uni-tuebingen.de/gerd.simon/hunke.htm

Junker, Daniel. *Gott in uns! Die Germanische Glaubens-Gemeinschaft: Ein Beitrag zur Geschichte völkischer Religiosität in der Weimarer Republik* (Hamburg: Verlag Daniel Junker, 2002). Self-published through www.bod.de (Hamburg University Master's Thesis, 1997).

Kamenetsky, Christa. *Children's Literature in Hitler's Germany: The Cultural Policy of National Socialism* (Athens, OH, and London: Ohio University Press, 1984).

Karrer, Otto, ed. *Gott in uns: Die Mystik der Neuzeit* (Munich: Verlag 'Ars Sacra' Josef Müller, 1926).

Kater, Michael H. *Das "Ahnenerbe" der SS 1935-1945: Ein Beitrag zur Kulturpolitik des Dritten Reiches* (Stuttgart: Deutsche Verlagsanstalt, 1974).

— "Die Artamenen: Völkische Jugend in der Weimarer Republik," *Historische Zeitschrift*, 1971, 213: 577-638.

Kauffeldt, Rolf. "Die Idee eines 'Neuen Bundes' (Gustav Landauer)," in Manfred Frank, ed., *Gott im Exil: Vorlesungen über die Neue Mythologie*, 2. Teil (Frankfurt a. M.: Suhrkampf, 1988), pp. 131-79.

Kersten, Felix. *The Kersten Memoirs 1940-1945*, introd. H. R. Trevor-Roper, transl. Constantine Fitzgibbon and James Oliver (London: Hutchinson, 1956).

Kessler, Harry, Graf. *Walther Rathenau: His Life and Work* (New York: Harcourt Brace and Company, 1930).

— *Das Tagebuch 1880-1937*, ed. Roland S. Kamzdak and Ulrich Ott, 7 vols. in progress (Stuttgart: Cotta, 2004 -).

— *Berlin in Lights: the Diaries of Count Harry Kessler 1918-1937*, trans. and ed. Charles Kessler (New York: Grove Press, 2000).

Kirchbach, Wolfgang. *Ziele und Aufgaben des Giordano Bruno-Bund* (Schmargendorf bei Berlin: Verlag Renaissance - Otto Lehmann, 1905).

Klabunde, Anja. *Magda Goebbels*, trans. Shaun Whiteside (London: Little Brown, 2001; German orig. 1999).

Klönne, Arno. "Eine deutsche Bewegung, politisch zweideutig," in K. Buchholz, ed., *Die Lebensreform: Entwürfe zur Neugestaltung von Leben und Kunst um 1900*, vol. 1, pp. 31-32.

Köhler, Joachim. *Wagner's Hitler: The Prophet and his Disciple*, trans. Ronald Taylor (Cambridge: Polity Press, 2000).

Konopath, Hanno. *Ist Rasse Schicksal? Grundgedanken der völkischen Bewegung*, 3rd edn. (Munich: J. F. Lehmann, 1931; 1st edn. 1926).

Koonz, Claudia. *The Nazi Conscience* (Cambridge, MA, and London: Harvard University Press, 2003).

Korotin, Erika. *"Am Muttergeist soll die Welt genesen": Philosophische Dispositionen zum Frauenbild im Nationalsozialismus* (Vienna; Cologne; Weimar: Böhlau Verlag, 1992).

Krabbe, Wolfgang R. *Gesellschaftsveränderung durch Lebensreform* (Göttingen: Vandenhoek & Ruprecht, 1974).

Kratz, Peter. *Die Götter des New Age* (Berlin: Elefanten Press, 1994).

Kratzsch, Gerhard. *Kunstwart und Dürerbund: Ein Beitrag zur Geschichte der Gebildeten im Zeitalter des Imperialismus* (Göttingen: Vandenhoek & Ruprecht, 1969).

Krause, Gerhard and Gerhard Müller, eds. *Theologische Realenzyklopädie*, 36 vols. (Berlin; New York: Walter de Gruyter, 1976-2004).

Krüger, Arndt. "Breeding, Rearing and Preparing the Aryan Body," in J. A. Mangan, ed., *Shaping the Superman: Fascist Body as Political Icon* (London and Portland, OR: Frank Cass, 1999), pp. 42-68.

Kuckuk, Peter. *Bremen in der deutschen Revolution 1918-1919* (Bremen: Bremen Verlagsgesellschaft Steintor, 1986).

Lagarde, Paul de. *Deutsche Schriften*, ed. Wilhelm Rössle (Jena: Eugen Diederichs Verlag, 1944; 1st edn. 1878).

Landauer, Gustav, trans. *Meister Eckharts Mystische Schriften in unsere Sprache übertragen von Gustav Landauer* (Berlin: Karl Schnabel [Axel Junckers Buchhandlung], 1903).

Lane, Barbara Miller. *Architecture and Politics in Germany 1918-1945* (Cambridge, MA: Harvard University Press, 1968).

Langbehn, Julius. *Rembrandt als Erzieher* (Leipzig: C. L. Hirschfeld, 1891).

— "Niederdeutsches," *Volk und Rasse*, 1926, 1: 257-62 (extracted from Langbehn's posthumously published *Niederdeutsches: Ein Beitrag zur Völkerpsychologie*, ed. Benedikt Momme Nissen [Buchenbach-Baden: Felsen Verlag, 1926]).

Laqueur, Walter. *Young Germany: A History of the German Youth Movement* (New York: Basic Books, 1962).

Leuschner, Udo. "Walther Rathenau: Ein Dissident seiner Klasse, seiner Rasse und seines Geschlechts," in his *Zur Geschichte des deutschen Liberalismus* (http://www.udo-leuschner.de/liberalismus/liberalismus0.htm.)

Lienhard, Friedrich. *Das Harzer Bergtheater* (Stuttgart: Greiner & Pfeiffer, 1907).

— *Der Meister der Menschheit*, 3 vols. (Stuttgart: Greiner und Pfeiffer, 1919-21).

Linse, Ulrich. "Völkisch-rassische Siedlungen der Lebensreform," in *Handbuch zur "Völkischen Bewegung" 1871-1918*, ed. Uwe Puschner, Walter Schmitz, Justus U. Ulbricht (Munich: K. G. Saur, 1996), pp. 397-410.

— *Zurück, o Mensch zur Mutter Erde: Landkommunen in Deutschland 1890-1933* (Munich: Deutscher Taschenbuch Verlag, 1983).

Lippe-Biesterfeld, Friedrich-Wilhelm, Prince zur. *Vom Rassenstil zur Staatsgestalt* (Berlin-Neu Finkenkrug: H. Paetel, 1928).

Lipstadt, Deborah E. *Denying the Holocaust: The Growing Assault on Truth and Memory* (New York: The Free Press, 1993).

Loewenstein, Hubertus, Prince zu. *Conquest of the Past: An Autobiography* (Boston: Houghton Mifflin Company, 1938).

Lovin, Clifford R. "*Blut und Boden*: The Ideological Basis of the Nazi Agricultural Program," *Journal of the History of Ideas*, 1967, 28: 279-88.

Lutzhöft, Hans-Jürgen. *Der Nordische Gedanke in Deutschland 1920-1940* (Stuttgart: Ernst Klett Verlag, 1971).

Maasdorff, W. *Die Religion und die Philosophie der Zukunft*, 2nd edn. (Lorch-Württemberg: Karl Rohm, 1914).

Malinowksi, Stephan. "From King to Führer: The German Aristocracy and the Nazi Movement," *Bulletin of the German Historical Institute of London*, 2005, 27: 5-28. [Summary version in English of his 2003 book].

— *Vom König zum Führer* (Berlin: Akademie Verlag, 2003).

Mangan, J. A., ed., *Shaping the Superman: Fascist Body as Political Icon* (London and Portland, OR: Frank Cass, 1999).

Marchlewska, Zofia. *Eine Welle im Meer: Erinnerungen an Heinrich Vogeler und Zeitgenossen* (Berlin: Buchverlag Der Morgen, [1968]).

Marten, Heinz-Georg. "Racism, Social Darwinism, Anti-Semitism and Aryan Supremacy," in J. A. Mangan, ed., *Shaping the Superman: Fascist Body as Political Icon* (London and Portland, OR: Frank Cass, 1999), pp. 23-41.

Martens, Gunter. "Stürmer in Rosen: Zum Kunstprogramm einer Straßburger Dichtergruppe der Jahrhundertwende," in *Fin de Siècle: Zur Literatur und Kunst der Jahrhundertwende* (Frankfurt a. M.: Vittorio Klostermann, 1977), pp. 481-507.

Mases, Werner. *Adolf Hitler: Eine Biographie* (Munich and Berlin: Herbig Verlag, 1978; orig. Munich: Bechtle Verlag, 1971).

Matheson, Peter, ed. *The Third Reich and the Christian Churches* (Edinburgh: T. & T. Clark, 1981).

Mecklenburg, Jens, ed. *Handbuch deutscher Rechtsextremismus* (Berlin: Elefanten Press, 1996).

Mees, Bernard. "*Germanische Sturmflut*: From the Old Norse Twilight to the Fascist New Dawn," *Studia Neophiloligica*, 2006, 78: 184-98.

— "Hitler and *Germanentum*," *Journal of Contemporary History*, 2004, 39: 255-70.

Meier, Kurt. *Die Deutschen Christen: Das Bild einer Bewegung im Kirchenkampf des Dritten Reiches* (Göttingen: Vandenhoeck & Ruprecht, 1964).

Merker, Reinhard, *Die bildenden Künste im Nationalsozialismus* (Cologne: DuMont, 1983).

Mommsen, Hans. *The Rise and Fall of Weimar Democracy*, trans. Elborg Forster and Larry Eugene Jones (Chapel Hill, NC, and London: University of North Carolina Press, 1996; orig. German 1989).

Mosse, George L. *Germans and Jews: The Right, the Left, and the Search for a 'Third Force' in Pre-Nazi Germany* (New York: Howard Fertig, 1970).

— *Nazi Culture: Intellectual, Cultural and Social Life in the Third Reich* (New York: Grosset & Dunlap, 1978; 1st ed. 1966).

— *The Crisis of German Ideology* (New York: Schocken Books, 1981; 1st edn. 1964).

Nanko, Ulrich. "Religiöse Gruppenbildungen vormaliger 'Deutschgläubiger' nach 1945," in Hubert Cancik and Uwe Puschner, eds., *Antisemitismus, Paganismus, Völkische Religion*, pp. 121-34.

— *Die Deutsche Glaubensbewegung: Eine historische und soziologische Untersuchung* (Marburg: Diagonal-Verlag, 1993).

Neteler, Theo. *Heinrich Vogeler: Buchgestalter und Buchillustrator; Mit einer Bibliographie* (Fischerhude: Galerie-Verlag, 1991).

Niekisch, Ernst. *Widerstand: ausgewählte Aufsätze aus seinen "Blätter für sozialistische und nationalrevolutionäre Politik*, ed. Uwe Sauermann (Krefeld: Sinus-Verlag, 1982).

Nipperdey, Thomas. *Religion im Umbruch: Deutschland 1870-1918* (Munich: C. H. Beck, 1988).

Nowak, Kurt. "Deutschgläubige Bewegungen," in *Theologisches Realenzyklopädie*, ed. Gerhard Grause and Gerhard Müller, 36 vols. (Berlin and New York: Walter de Gruyter, 1976-2004), 8: 554-59.

Odenwald, Florian. *Der nazistische Kampf gegen das 'Undeutsche' in Theater und Film 1920-1945* (Munich, 2006) Münchner Universitätsschriften, Theaterwissenschaft, 8.

Osterkamp, Ernst. *Lucifer: Stationen eines Motivs* (Berlin and New York: Walter de Gruyter, 1979).

Osterrieder, Markus. "Völkische 'Niebelungei': Das Wiederaufleben der 'Nibelungenströmung' in der deutschen Kultur des 19. Jahrhunderts," *Erziehungskunst*, 2002, 66: 3-10; also http://www.celtoslavica.de/bibliothek/nibelungelei.html

Paetel, Karl O. *Reise ohne Uhrzeit: Autobiographie*, ed. Wolfgang D. Elfe and John M. Spalek (London: The World of Books; Worms: Verlag Georg Heinz, 1982).

Paret, Peter. *An Artist against the Third Reich: Ernst Barlach 1933-1938* (Cambridge: Cambridge University Press, 2003).

Parr, Rolf. "Werdandi-Bund (Berlin)," in *Handbuch literarisch-kultureller Vereine, Gruppen und Bünde 1825-1933*, ed. Wulf Wülfing, pp. 485-95.

Paul, Gustav. *Grundzüge der Rassen- und Raumgeschichte des deutschen Volkes* (Munich: J. F. Lehmann, 1935).

Paungarten, Ferdinand Freiherr von., ed. *Das Eheproblem im Spiegel unserer Zeit* (Munich: Ernst Reinhardt Verlag, 1913).

Petropoulos, Jonathan, *Royals and the Reich, the Princes von Hessen in Nazi Germany* (New York: Oxford University Press, 2006).

Petzet, Heinrich Wiegand. *Von Worpswede nach Moskau: Heinrich Vogeler – Ein Künstler zwischen den Zeiten* (Cologne: M. DuMont Schauberg, 1972).

Picker, Henry. *Hitlers Tischgespräche im Führerhauptquartier* (Stuttgart: Seewald, 1977; 1st edn. 1963).

Pittwald, Michael Michael. *Ernst Niekisch: Völkischer Sozialismus, nationale Revolution, deutsches Endimperium* (Cologne: PapyRossa Verlag, 2002).

Poewe, Karla. *New Religions and the Nazis* (New York and London: Routledge, 2006).

Poliakov, Leon and Josef Wulf. *Das Dritte Reich und seine Diener: Dokumente* (Berlin-Grünewald: Arani-Verlag, 1959).

Pool, James and Suzanne Pool. *Who Financed Hitler: The Secret Funding of Hitler's Rise to Power 1919-1933* (New York: Dials Press, 1978).

Przbysczewski, Stanislas. "Das Geschlecht," *Der Sturm*, no. 32, 6 October 1910 (Kraus reprint I, pp. 251-52).

Puschner, Uwe. "Weltanschauung und Religion: Ideologie und Formen völkischer Religion," *Zeitenblicke* 2006, 5 (1), www.zeitenblicke.de/2006/1/Puschner

— "Die Germanenideologie im Kontext der völkischen Weltanschauung," *Göttinger Forum für Altertumswissenschaft*, 2001, 4: 85-97.

— *Die völkische Bewegung im wilhelminischen Kaiserreich: Sprache, Rasse, Religion* (Darmstadt: Wissenschaftliche Buchgesellschaft, 2001).

Rathenau, Walther. *Gesamtausgabe*, ed. Hans-Dieter Hellige and Ernst Schulin (Munich: G. Müller; Heidelberg: Lambert Schneider), vol. 2 (*Hauptwerke und Gespräche*, 1977); vol. 4 (*Walther Rathenau-Maximilian Harden Briefwechsel 1897-1920*, 1983).

Rauschning, Hermann. *The Voice of Destruction* (New York: G. P. Putnam's Sons, 1940).

Reichold, Helmut. *Der Streit um die Thronfolge im Fürstentum Lippe 1895-1905* (Münster [Westf.]: Aschendorffsche Verlagsbuchhandlung, 1967).

Reider, Frédéric. *The Order of the SS* (Tucson, AZ: Aztex Corporation, n.d. [1981]).

Reuter, Ernst. *Schriften, Reden*, ed. Hans E. Hirschfeld and Hans J. Reinhardt, 4 vols. (Berlin: Propyläen Verlag, 1972-75).

Richard, Lionel. *Le Nazisme et la culture* (Brussels: Editions Complexe, 2006).

Roselius, Ludwig. *Reden und Schriften zur Böttcherstrasse in Bremen* (Bremen: Verlag G. A. v. Hallem, 1932).

— *Briefe* (Bremen: H. M. Hauschild, 1919).

Rosenberg, Alfred. *The Myth of the Twentieth Century*, trans. Vivian Bird (Torrance, CA: Noontide Press, 1982; orig. German 1930).

Schaumburg-Lippe, Friedrich Christian, Prinz zu. *Als die golden Abendsonne: Aus meinen Tagebüchern der Jahre 1933-1937* (Wiesbaden: Limes-Verlag, 1971).

— *Verdammte Pflicht und Schuldigkeit: Weg und Erlebnis 1914-1933* (Leoni am Starnberger See: Druffel-Verlag, 1966).

— ed. *Wo war der Adel?* (Berlin: Zentral Verlag, 1934).

Scheuer, Helmut. "Zur Christus-Figur in der Literatur um 1900," in *Fin de Siècle: Zur Literatur und Kunst der Jahrhundertwende* (Frankfurt a. M.: Vittorio Klostermann, 1977), pp. 378-402.

Schlender, Ida H. *Germanische Mythologie: Religion und Leben unserer Urväter*, 4th edn. (Dresden: Alexander Köhler, 1925).

Schmidt, Friedrich. *Das Reich als Aufgabe* (Berlin: Nordland Verlag, 1940).

Schnurbein, Stephanie von. "Die Suche nach einer 'arteigenen' Religion in 'germanisch' - und 'deutschgläubigen' Gruppen," in *Handbuch zur "Völkischen Bewegung" 1871-1918*, pp. 172-85.

Schoenbaum, David, *Hitler's Social Revolution: Class and Status in Nazi Germany 1933-1939* (New York. W.W. Norton, 1980; orig. 1966).

Scholder, Klaus. *The Churches and the Third Reich*, vol. 1: *Preliminary History and the Time of Illusions 1918-1934*, trans. John Bowden (London: S. C. M. Press, 1987; orig. German, 1977).

Schwaner, Wilhelm. *Germanen-Bibel*, 2nd edn., 2 vols. (Berlin-Schlachtensee: Volkserzieher-Verlag, 1904-05).

Schwarzenwälder, Herbert. *Das Grosse Bremen-Lexikon* (Bremen: Edition Temmen, 2002).

— *Berühmte Bremer* (Munich: Paul List Verlag, 1972).

Segal, Joes. *Krieg als Erlösung: Die deutsche Kunstdebatten 1910-1918* (Munich: Scaneg, 1997).

Seidel, Gill. *The Holocaust Denial: Antisemitism, Racism and the New Right* (Leeds: Beyond the Pale Collective, 1986).

Siemsen, Hans. *Hitler Youth*, trans. Trevor and Phyllis Blewitt (London: Lindsay Drummond, 1940).

Siewert, Sylvia. *Germanische Religion und neugermanisches Heidentum* (Frankfurt; Bern; Berlin; Brussels; NewYork; Oxford; Vienna: Peter Lang, 2002).

Sommer, Andreas U. "Weltanschauung, Skepsis und Modernitätskritik. Arthur Schopenhauer und Franz Overbeck," *Philosophisches Jahrbuch*, 2000, 107: 192-205.

Speer, Albert. *Inside the Third Reich*, trans. Richard and Clara Winston (New York: Avon Books, 1971; orig. German 1969).

Speit, Andreas. "Fieses unterm Findling: Der Nazi-Kultort 'Ahnenstätte Conneforde' hat einen prominenten Grabredner: Bundeslandwirtschaftsminister Karl-Heinz Funke," *Jungle World*, 21 April 1999, http://www.nadir.org/nadir/periodika/jungle_world/_99/17/12b.htm

Spinoza, Benedict de. *Tractatus Theologico-Politicus* [Gebhardt Edition, 1925], trans. Samuel Shirley (Leiden; New York; Copenhagen; Cologne: E. J. Brill, 1989).

Spohr, Wilhelm. *Bilder und Stimmungen: Gedichte* (Berlin and Leipzig: Modernes Verlagsbureau-Curt Wiegand, 1909).

Stadler, Ernst. *Dichtungen, Schriften, Briefe, Kritische Ausgabe*, ed. Klaus Hurlebusch and Karl Ludwig Schneider (Munich: C. H. Beck, 1983).

Stark, Gary D. *Entrepreneurs of Ideology: Neoconservative Publishers in Germany, 1890-1933* (Chapel Hill: University of North Carolina Press, 1982).

Steigmann-Gall, Richard. *The Holy Reich: Nazi Conceptions of Christianity 1919-1945* (Cambridge: Cambridge University Press, 2003).

Steiner, Rudolf. *Earthly and Cosmic Man* (Blauvelt, NY: Spiritual Science Library, 1986).

Stenzig, Bernd. *Heinrich Vogeler: Eine Bibliogaphie der Schriften* (Worpswede: Worpsweder Verlag, 1994).

— *Worpswede Moskau: Das Werk von Heinrich Vogeler*, exhib. cat. (Worpswede: Worpsweder Verlag, 1989).

— *Heinrich Vogeler: Vom Romantiker zum Revolutionär; Ölbilder, Zeichnungen, Grafik, Dokumente von 1895-1924*, exhib. cat., Bonner Kunstverein, 23 June-1 August 1982).

Strohmeyer, Arn. *Parsifal in Bremen: Richard Wagner, Ludwig Roselius und die Böttcherstrasse* (Weimar: Verlag und Datenbank für Geisteswissenschaften, 2002).

— "Kunst im Zeichen der germanischen Vorfahren und der Wiedergeburt Deutschlands: Ludwig Roselius und Bernhard Hoetger," in Arn Strohmeyer, Kai Artinger, Ferdinand Krogman, *Landschaft, Licht und niederdeutscher Mythos: Die Worpsweder Kunst und der Nationalsozialismus* (Weimar: Verlag und Datenbank für Geisteswissenschaften, 2000), pp. 43-110.

Susser, Bernard. "Ideological Multivalence: Martin Buber and the German Volkish Tradition," *Political Theory*, 1977, 5: 75-96.

Thalmann, Rita. *Être femme sous le IIIe Reich* (Paris: Robert Laffont, 1982).

Tidl, Georg. *Die Frau im Nationalsozialismus* (Vienna: Europa-Verlag, 1984).

Tödt, Heinz Eduard. *Komplizen, Opfer und Gegner des Hitlerregimes: zur „inneren Geschichte" von protestantischer Theologie und Kirche im "Dritten Reich"* (Gütersloh: Chr. Kaiser, 1997).

Trimondi, Victor and Victoria. *Hitler-Buddha-Krishna: Eine unheilige Allianz vom Dritten Reich bis heute* (Vienna: Verlag Carl Ueberreuter, 2002).

Tschirschky, Fritz Günther von. *Erinnerungen eines Hochverräters* (Stuttgart: Deutsche Verlagsanstalt, 1972).

Tumasonis, Elizabeth. "Berhard Hoetger's Tree of Life: German Expressionism and Racial Ideology," *Art Journal*, 1992, 51: 81-91.

Ulbricht, Justus H. "'Cogito ergo credo': Religionswissenschaftliche Argumente für ein Museum der Lebensreform," in *Unweit von Eden: Tagung der Konzeption des Museums der deutschen Lebensreform im Fidushaus Waltersdorf*, ed. Ute Grund (Potsdam: Verlag für Berlin-Brandenburg, 2000), pp. 39-54.

— "'Theologia deutsch': Eugen Diederichs und die Suche nach einer Religion für moderne Intellektuelle," in *Romantik, Revolution und Reform: Der Eugen Diederichs Verlag im Epochenkontext 1900-1949* (Göttingen: Wallstein Verlag, 1999), pp. 156-74.

— and Meike G. Werner, eds. *Romantik, Revolution und Reform: Der Eugen Diederichs*

*Verlag im Epochenkontext 1900-1949* (Göttingen: Wallstein Verlag, 1999).

Ullstein, Hermann. *The Rise and Fall of the House of Ullstein* (New York: Simon and Schuster, 1943).

Vermeil, Edmond. *Hitler et le Christianisme* (Paris: Gallimard, 1939).

Vogeler, Heinrich. *Werden: Erinnerungen, mit Lebenszeugnissen aus den Jahren 1923-1942*, new edn. by Joachim Priewe and Paul-Gerhard Wenzlaff (Berlin: Rütten und Loening, 1989).

Vollnhals, Clemens. "Völkisches Christentum oder deutscher Glaube: Deutsche Christen und Deutsche Glaubensgemeinschaft," *Revue d'Allemagne*, 2000, 32: 205-17.

von Oven, Wilfrid. *Finale Furioso: Mit Goebbels bis zum Ende* (Tübingen: Grabert-Verlag, 1974).

Waite, Robert G. L. *Vanguard of Nazism: The Free Corps Movement in Postwar Germany 1918-1923* (Cambridge, MA: Harvard University Press, 1952).

Walter, Marianne. *The Poison Seed: A Personal History of Nazi Germany* (Lewes, Sussex: The Book Guild, 1992).

Weindling, Paul. *Health, Race and German Politics between National Unification and Nazism* (Cambridge: Cambridge University Press, 1989).

Weiss, Volkmar. "Die Vorgeschichte des arischen Ahnenpasses," Part III, *Genealogie*, 2000, 50: 615-27.

Werner, Meike G. *Moderne in der Provinz: Kulturelle Experimente in Fin de Siècle Jena* (Göttingen: Wallstein, 2003).

Wienfort, Monika. "Gesellschaftsdamen, Gutsfrauen und Rebellinnen. Adelige Frauen in Deutschland 1890-1939," in *Adel und Moderne*, ed. Eckart Konze and Monika Weinert (Cologne; Weimar; Vienna: Böhlau, 2004), pp. 181-203.

Werner, Uwe. *Anthroposophen in der Zeit des Nationalsozialismus (18933-1945)* (Munich: R. Oldenbourg, 1999).

Wiggershaus, Renate. *Frauen unterm Nationalsozialismus* (Wuppertal: Hammer, 1984).

Wille, Bruno, ed. *Deutscher Geist und Judenhass* (Berlin: Kultur-Verlag, 1920).

Wilser, Ludwig. *Die Germanen: Beiträge zur Völkerkunde* (Eisenach and Leipzig: Thüringischer Verlags-Anstalt, 1903).

Wirth, Herman. *Der Aufgang der Menschheit: Untersuchungen zur Geschichte der Religion, Symbolik und Schrift der Atlantisch-Nordischen Rasse* (Jena: Eugen Diederichs, 1928).

Wistrich, Robert. *Who's Who in Nazi Germany* (London: Weidenfeld and Nicolson, 1982).

Wolf, Friedrich. *Briefwechsel: Eine Auswahl* (Bonn and Weimar: Aufbau Verlag, 1968).

— *Kolonne Hund*, in *Gesammelte Werke*, ed. Else Wolf and Walther Pollatschek, 16 vols. (Berlin: Aufbau Verlag, 1960-68), vol. 2, pp. 83-175.

Wolfschlag, Claus. *Ludwig Fahrenkrog: Das goldene Tor* (Dresden: Verlag Zeitenwende, 2006).

# Index

Achterberg, Eberhard, 108
*Ahnenerbe* [*Ahnenerbe Forschungs- und Lehrgemeinschaft*], Himmler's Research Institute, 11, 46, 111-12, Intr. n. 21, Ch. 3 n. 1
*Ahnenstätte Conneforde*, pagan burial ground, 111-12, Ch. 8 n.8
*Alldeutscher Verband*, 28
Anarchist movement, 6, 18, 35, 85-86, 129, Ch. 1 n. 26, 31, Ch. 3 n. 2
Angelsachsen Verlag, 1, 8-9, 127, Intr. n. 1
Artamans, 20, 80, 101, Ch. 5 n. 53
*Aktion, Die*, fig. 2, 1, 58, Intr. n. 2, Ch. 4 n. 1
Anthroposophy, 17, 24, 32, 57, Ch. 1 n. 49. *See also:* Steiner, Rudolf
Anti-Semitism, 28-29, 33, 43-44, 69-71, 74, 80, 107, Intr. n. 11, Ch. 1: nn. 7, 10, 26, 31, 37, 49, 57, 62, Ch. 2 n. 2, Ch. 3 n. 2, Ch. 5: nn. 4, 8, 23, 53, 83, Bibl. n. 1. *See also:* Jews and Judaism; Christianity; Religion; *völkisch*
*Arbeitsgemeinschaft deutscher Glaubensbewegung*, 75, 79, Ch. 5 n. 47
*Arische Freiheit*, Ch. 1 n. 37. *See also: Monatsschrift für arische Gottes- und Welterkenntnis*
Aristocracy, 12, 67-69, 75, 81, 82, 112, Ch. 5 n. 13; idea of a "neuer Adel", 53, 65-66, 82, 112. *See also:* Darré, Richard Walter; Günther, Hans F.K.; German princes; NSDAP;
*Armanen-Orden*, 28, Ch. 5 n. 53
Aryan, Aryanism, 16, 28-34, fig. 18, 47, 58-59, 70-72, 77, 90, 112, Ch. 1: nn. 34, 50, 57, 59, Ch. 3 n. 1, Ch. 5: nn. 8, 17, 53, 83, Ch. 8 n. 11
Atlantis, 9, 29, Ch. 1 n. 16, Ch. 8 n. 11
Atlantis House, 9, fig. 11, 58, Intr. n. 21
August, Wilhelm (Auwi), son of Kaiser Wilhelm II, 67, 84, Ch. 5 n. 70
*Aus meinem Blute*, 22, Ch. 1 n. 21. *See also:* Bruns, Max

Avenarius, Ferdinand, 18, 25, 27, 45-46, Ch. 1 nn. 13, 31, 53, Ch 2 n. 12. *See also: Kunstwart, Der*

Bahr, Hermann, 18-19
*Baldur*, play by Ludwig Fahrenkrog, fig. 12, 19-21, fig. 13.
Baldur, 70, Intr. n. 17, Ch. 1 n. 16, Ch. 5 n. 47
Barkenhoff, 5-6, Intr.: nn. 10, 11, 15
Barnes, Harry Elmer, 111-12, Ch. 8 n. 12. *See also:* Historical Revisionism
Bartels, Adolf, 43, Ch. 1 n. 31, Ch. 5 n. 56
*Bauernschaft, Die*, 113-14. *See also:* Christophersen, Thies
Bauhaus, 72, 84, 85
Bäumler, Alfred, Ch 1 n. 49, Ch. 6 n. 3
Bavarian Socialist Republic [Bavarian Workers' and Soldiers' Council Republic, January-February, 1919 or *Räterepublik*], 2, 5, 17, 29, 85-86
Bayreuth, 21, Ch. 4 n. 11, Ch. 5 n. 26. *See also:* Wagner, Richard
Bechstein, Helene, Ch. 5 n. 68
Becher, Johannes, 5
Bell, Gertrude, Ch. 5 n. 4
Bergmann, Ernst, 61, Ch. 6 n. 1
Bernstein, Eduard, Ch. 1 n. 31
Blavatsky, Helena Petrowna, 17, 24, 32
Blut und Boden ideology, 1-2, 82, 84-85, 114. *See also:* Darré, Richard-Walter
*Blut und Boden: Monatsschrift für wurzelhaftes Bauerntum, für deutsche Wesensart und die nationale Freiheit*, 80
*Bodenreform*, 80, Ch. 1 n. 31
Böhme, Herbert, 108
Böhme, Jacob, 17, 34, 43-44, Ch. 1 n. 58
Bölsche, Wilhelm, 24-25, 45, Ch. 1 n. 31. *See also: Giordano Bruno-Bund*
Bonus, Arthur, 43, 60-61, Ch. 1: nn. 31, 69
Böttcherstraße, 58, Intr. nn. 17, 21, Ch. 6 n. 6

Bremen, 1, 5, 8, 9, 58, 65, 75, 102, 107, 109, 110, 111, Intr. nn. 5, 15, 17, 21, 23, Ch. 1, n. 16, Ch. 6, n. 1. *See also*: Böttcherstraße
Bruns, Max, 22, Ch. 1 n. 21.
Buber, Martin, 17, 43-45, Intr. n. 15, Ch. 1: nn. 7, 31, Ch. 2: nn. 2, 3, 4, 7, Ch. 5 n. 23
Buddha, Buddhism, 8, 30, 47, Intr. n. 13, Ch. 3 n. 1
Bülow, Friedrich von, Ch. 5 n. 13
Busoni, Ferruccio, 5
Büttner, Herman, 24, 38-39

Chamberlain, Houston Stewart, 27, 33, 34, 70, 90, Ch. 1 n. 59, Ch 2.: nn. 2, 9, Ch. 5 n. 83
Chasidism, 43, Ch. 2 n. 2
Christianity, 15-17, 54; Christian Churches, 17, 31, Ch. 5 n. 66; Roman Catholic Church, 25-25, 31, 33, 58, 59, 91, 100, Ch. 1 n. 32, Ch. 5 n. 66; relation to Judaism and Old Testament, 16, 30, 34, 47, 58, 59, 70, 90, Ch.: 1 nn. 7, 32, Ch. 4 n. 11; religion of subservience, alien to German *Volk*, 22-24, 27, 28, 30-33, 34-37, 39, 47, 57-61, Ch. 4, 89-92; *Deutsche Christen*, 33-34, 39, 61, 90-91, Ch. 1 n. 50, Ch. 5 nn. 35, 78
Clauß, Ferdinand, 67, 77, 90-91, Ch. 5: nn. 7, 8, 23, 36
Communism, 85-86, 89, 101, Intr. n. 11, Ch. 1 n. 49, Ch. 5 n. 70; German Communist Party (KPD), 5, 6, 9, Intr. n. 15, Ch. 3 n. 2. *See also: Spartakus*
Conn, Alfred, 61, Ch. 1 n. 32
Cunard, Nancy, Ch. 5 n. 4
Christophersen, Thies, 113-14, Ch. 8 n. 13, Bibl. n. 1

Damaschke, Adolf, Ch. 1 n. 31
Darré, Richard-Walter, 1-2, 53, 65-66, 73, 80, 85, 87, 88, 111; ideologist of *Blut und Boden*, 81-83, 84, 114, Ch. 5: nn. 54, 55, 58, 59; Minister of Food and Agriculture, 1, 73; wins rural support for NSDAP, 80-81; *Neuadel aus Blut und Boden*, Ch. 5: n. 3, 58; *Neuordnung unseres Denkens*, Ch. 5 n. 57; critique of *Lebensreform*, Ch. 5, n. 54; high place of women in Nordic cultures, 82. *See also: Odal*
Darwinism, 23-27, 45, 60, Ch. 2 n. 11; biologism, Ch. 5 n. 79
Dauthendey, Max, 22
Decadence, degeneration, 11, 18, 58, 60, 69, 128-29, Intr. n. 21
Dehmel, Richard, 22, 57
*Deutsch-gläubige Gemeinschaft*, 79
*Deutsch-Religiöse Gemeinschaft*, 148, Ch. 1 n. 57, Ch. 5 n. 47
*Deutsche Adelsgenossenschaft*, Ch. 5, n.4
*Deutsche Christen. See under:* Christianity
*Deutsche Freiheit*, 77, Ch. 1 n. 37
*Deutsche Glaubensbewegung*, 16, 33, 39, 44-45, 79-80, 108, 128, Ch. 2 n. 9, Ch. 5: nn. 47, 48
*Deutsche Kolonialgesellschaft*, Ch. 5, n. 4
*Deutsche Unitarier Religionsgemeinschaft (DUR)*, 107-09, 111
*Deutsche Vaterlandspartei*, 11
*Deutscher Freidenkerbund*, 24
*Deutscher Monistenbund*, 24, 27
*Deutscher Orden*, Ch. 1, n. 57
*Deutsch-religiöse Gemeinschaft*, Ch. 1 n. 57, Ch. 5 n. 47
*Deutscher Widarbund*, 71
*Deutsches Kulturwerk Europäischen Geistes*, 108
*Deutschbund*, 28. *See also*: Lange, Friedrich
*Deutschlands Erneuerung* (periodical), 72, 83. ch. 5, n. 43
*Deutschvolk*, 39, 111
Diederichs, Eugen, 17, 18, 24, 35, 38-39, 43, 45, 77-78, fig. 19, Ch. 1: nn. 7, 20, 50, Ch. 2: nn. 1, 14, Ch. 5: nn. 17, 30, 44, 56
Dinter, Arthur, 32, 61, Ch. 1 n. 46, Ch. 5: nn. 66, 83
Dirksen, Viktoria, Freifrau von, 68, 69, 71, 83, 86, Ch. 5: nn. 9, 68; *See also*: National Club
Dix, Otto, 85
Dreier, Katherine, 6, 8
*Dürer-Bund*, 27-28, Ch. 1: nn. 10, 31

Index 197

Ebert, Friedrich, 85
Eckart, Dietrich, 39, Ch. 1 n. 49
Ebert, Friedrich, 85
Eckhart, Meister, 17, 24, 32, 34, 86, Ch. 1: nn. 6, 24
*Edda*, 31, fig. 18, 77, 96, 97, Ch. 1: nn. 16, 37
*Edda Gesellschaft*, 72, 77
Epp, Franz Xaver, Ritter von; put down Bavarian *Räterepublik*, 84, 85-86, Ch. 5 n. 75

Fahrenkrog, Ludwig, 16 fig. 12, 19,-21, fig. 13, 37-38, fig. 17, fig. 18, 48-49, 54, 60, 79, 90, Ch. 1: nn. 2, 16, 57, 58, Ch. 5 n. 47
Fidus, See under: Höppener, Hugo
*Fraktur* (German typeface), 15, 114, Intr. n. 22, Ch. 1 n. 1
Frank, Hans, 74
Freemasons, freemasonry, 108, Ch. 1 n. 49, Ch. 4, n. 9
*Freikorps*, 5, 85-86, Ch. 5 n. 16
Frick, Wilhelm, 73; action against "degenerate art" in Thuringia, 84-86
Friedrich, Caspar David, fig. 16
Friedrich Wilhelm, Crown Prince, son of Kaiser Wilhelm II, 67, 79, Ch. 5 n. 80
*Friedrichshagener Kreis*, 25
Fritsch, Theodor, 28-29, Intr. n. 11, Ch. 1 n. 10, Ch. 5 n. 83. See also: *Der Hammer*
Frobenius, Leo, Ch. 1, n. 31

German Revolution of 1918-19, 5-6, 29-30, 31, 98-100, 115-17; Intr.: nn. 5, 7; Ch. 5 n. 13
*Germanen-Bibel*, 15-16, 33, 35-37, fig. 16, 60, Intr. n. 17, Ch. 1: nn. 2, 31, Ch. 5 n. 18
*Germanenbund*, 28
*Germanisch-deutsche Religionsgemeinschaft*, 37-38
*Germanen-Orden*, 28
German Princes, abdication of, 66, 68, 98-99
*Germanische Glaubensgemeinschaft (GGG)*, 19, 21, 38, 48, 52, 60, Intr. n. 17, Ch. 1: nn. 1, 2, 57, Ch. 5: nn. 18, 47, 66

Gerstenberg, Wilhelm, *Freikorps* commander, 5
*Glaubensbewegung deutscher Christen*, 74-75
Goethe, Johann Wolfgang, 1, 15, 43, 111, Ch. 1 n. 58
Gorsleben, Rudolf John, 77, Vh. 1 n. 37
*Giordano Bruno-Bund*, 24-27, fig. 15, 27, 45, Ch. 1 n. 31
Gnosticism, neo-Gnosticism, 17, 34-35, 47, 116, Ch. 3 n. 1
Gobineau, Arthur de, 72-73, 130, Ch. 5: nn. 29, 62
Goebbels, Joseph, 65-66, 68, 73, 74, 83-84, 85-87, Intr. n. 23, Ch. 5: nn. 13, 70, 79, 83, 84, Ch. 8 n. 4
Goebbels, Magda (Magda Friedländer; Magda Quandt), 84, Intr. n. 13, Ch. 5: nn. 4, 70
Goethe, Johann Wolfgang, von, 1, 15, 17, 43, 111, Ch. 1 n. 58
Göring, Hermann, 74, 84, 85, 86, Ch. 1 n. 37
Gorsleben, Rudolf John, 77, Ch. 1 n. 37
Grabert, Herbert, 108
Grotjahn, Alfred, 76-77
Gruenberg, Louis Theodore, 5
*Guido von List Society*, 28. See also: von List, Guido
Günther, Hans F. K., 71-72, 75-77, 82, 84, 85, 88, 90, Ch. 5: nn. 7, 15, 23, 36; *Ritter, Tod und Teufel. Der heldsiche Gedanke; Rassenkunde des deutschen Volkes; Rassenkunde Europas; Adel und Rasse; Der Nordische Gedanke unter den Deutschen; Führeradel durch Sippenpflege*, 75
Gurlitt, Ludwig, 58-59, Ch. 4 n. 1

Haeckel, Ernst, 26-27, Ch. 1 n. 30
*Hammer, Der*, 29, Ch. 1 n. 10
*Hammerbund*, 28-29
Harden, Maximilian, 69, Ch. 5: nn. 13, 16
Hart, Heinrich, 18, 27, 30, 86, 129, Ch. 1 n. 26, Ch. 4 n. 11
Hart, Julius *(brother of Heinrich)*, 18, 22-23, fig. 14, 27, 30, 86, 129, Ch. 1 n. 26
*Harzer Bergtheater*, 19, 59, Ch. 1, n. 57

## 198  Brownshirt Princess

Hauer, Wilhelm, 16, 32, 33, 39, 44-45, 75, 79-80, 90, 128, Ch. 1: nn. 3, 66, Ch. 2: nn. 7, 9, Ch. 5 n. 66
Hauptmann, Carl, 5, 25
Hauptmann, Gerhard (*brother of Carl*), 5, 71
Heidegger, Martin, 17, Ch. 1 n. 8
Heimatkunst, Ch. 1: nn. 17, 31
*Heimdall*, Ch. 1 n. 59
Helldorff, Wolf Heinrich, Count, 83, Ch. 5, n. 13
Henckell, Karl, 22
Hentschell, Willibald, Intr. n. 11
Heraclitus, 30
Hermann-Neisse, Max, 57
Heydrich, Reinhard, Ch. 5, n. 48
Hierl, Constantin, 73
Himmler, Heinrich, 11, 46, 78, 80, 81, 87, 109, 111-12, Intr.: nn. 13, 20, Ch. 1: nn. 18, 37, Ch. 3 n. 1, Ch. 4: nn. 9, 16, Ch. 5: nn. 59, 80, Bibl. n. 1
Hindenburg, Paul von, President of Germany, 83
Hirschfeld, Magnus, Ch. 1 n. 31
Historical Revisionism (Holocaust denial), 2, 112-14, Ch. 8: nn. 4, 12. See also: Barnes, Harry Elmer; Rassinier, Paul
Hitler, Adolf, 11-12, 39, 58, 68-69, 72, 74, 83-85, 106, 130, Intr.: nn. 17, 21, 22, 23, Ch. 1: nn. 1, 37, 49, 59, 62, Ch. 2 n. 6, Ch. 5: nn. 5, 13, 19, 33, 66, 68, 69, 70, 76, 84, Ch. 8 n. 14, Bibl. n. 1
*Hitler Youth*, 102-103, Ch. 5: n. 56,
Hoetger, Bernhard, 8, 9, fig. 11, 11, 58, Intr.: nn. 17, 21
Höppener, Hugo (Fidus), cover fig., 22, fig. 14, 25, 125, Intr. n. 17, Ch. 1: nn. 21, 31, Ch. 3 n. 2
Huch, Ridarda, Ch. 1 n. 31
Huizinga, Johan, Ch. 5, n. 6
Hunke, Sigrid, Ch. 8 n. 9
Hunkel, Ernst, Intr. n. 11

Jacobowksi, Ludwig, 22
Jews and Judaism, 2, 12, 16, 28-29, 33-34, 44-45, 47, 57-58, 59, 79, 91, 98, 113, Intr. n. 23, Ch. 1: nn. 7, 26, 31, 66 Ch.2: nn. 2, 9, Ch. 4: nn. 9, 11, Ch. 5 n. 8, Ch. 5: nn. 8, 23, 39, 60, Bibl. n. 1. See also: Anti-Semitism; Christianity; relation to Judaism and Old Testament
*Journal of Historical Review*, 113
*Jugendstil*, 1, 2, 51, 53, Intr. n. 2 See also: Vogeler, Heinrich
Jünger, Ernst, Ch. 8, n. 9
*Jungnordischer Bund*, 72

Kaffee HAG, p. 8, Fig. 10
Kaiser Wilhelm II. See under: Wilhelm II
Kandinsky, Wassily, 85
Kapp, Wolfgang (organizer of Kapp Putsch), 11 Kent, Rockwell, 9
Kirchbach, Wolfgang, fig. 15, 25, 26-27, Ch. 1 n. 31
Klee, Paul, 85
Klinger, Max, 143-44
Kokoschka, Oskar, 57, 85
Konopath, Hanno, 65-66, 71, 73; *Ist Rasse Schicksal?*, 72, Ch. 2 n. 2; head of *Abteilung Rasse und Kultur*, 74; head of NSDAP's *Abteilung Film und Radio*, 74; submits design for European flag (1952), Ch. 5 n. 35; See also: *Jungnordischer Bund*
Kossinna, Gustav, 77
Krannhals, Paul, 39, Ch. 9 n. 2
Krause, Reinhold, 34, 39, 44. See also: *Deutsche Christen* under Christianity
Krieck, Ernst, 44
*Kritik: Die Stimme des Volkes*, 114, Fig. 21, 115, Ch. 5 n. 10. See also: Christophersen, Thies
Kropotkin, Prince Peter, 6
*Kunstwart, Der*, 18, 25, 45
Kusserow, Wilhelm, 79, Ch. 4 n. 5, Ch. 5 n. 47

Lagarde, Paul de, 31, Ch. 1: n. 31, 58, Ch. 5 n. 83
Lamprecht, Karl, 144, Ch. 1 n. 31
Landauer, Gustav, 17, 21-22, 86, Ch. 1: nn. 6, 20, 26, 31, 38, Ch. 3 n. 2
Langbehn, Julius, 11, Ch. 2 n. 2, Ch. 5 n. 58
Lange, Friedrich, 28, Ch. 1 n. 33
Langeweyde, Georg Sluyterman von, 2, 114
Lanz von Liebenfels, Jörg, 28, 72, Ch. 5:

Index 199

nn. 15, 27, 53, Ch. 7 n. 2
Lasker-Schüler, Else, 57, Ch. 1 n. 31
*Lebensphilosophie*; 6, 45, Ch. 2 n. 11. *See also*: Darwinism
*Lebensreform* movement, 18-23, fig. 18, 47, 80, 129, Ch. 1: nn. 12, 18, 20, Ch. 5 n. 54
Lehmann-Verlag, 72
Leers, Johann von, Ch. 5, n. 6
Lenin, Vladimir Ilyich, 8
Levetzoff, Magnus von, 84
Liebenfels, Lanz von, 28, 72, Ch. 5: nn. 15, 27, 53, Ch. 7 n. 2
Liebermann, Max, Ch. 1 n. 31
Liebknecht, Karl, 100, Intr. n. 15
Lienhard, Friedrich, Ch. 1 n. 4
Lippe-Biesterfeld, Friedrich Wilhelm, Prince zur, 79, 87; author of *Vom Rassenstil zur Staatsgestalt*, 67, Ch. 5 n. 49
List, Guido von, 28-29, 59, Ch. 1 n. 63, Ch. 5 n. 53; *See also: Guido von List Society*
Loewenstein, Hubertus, Prinz zu, 61, Ch. 4: nn. 9, 13
Ludendorff, Erich and Mathilde von, 39, 60, 108, 111, Ch. 1 n. 49, Ch. 4: nn. 5, 9; *See also: Deutschvolk*
Luther, Martin, Ch. 6 n. 3
Luxemburg, Rosa, 100, Intr. n. 15

Male fraternity, or *Männerbund*, 28
Marc, Franz, 85
Marchlewska, Zofia ("Sonja"), 8, Intr.: nn. 10, 15
Marx, Karl; Marxists, 6, 79, Intr. n. 15, Ch. 1 n. 13, Ch. 4 n. 9, Ch. 5 n. 13, Ch. 9 n. 2
Materialism, 6, 17-18, 21-22, 129
Mc Cloy, John, American High Commissioner for Germany, 109, fig. 20, 112, Ch. 8 n. 7
Meinecke, Friedrich, Ch. 1, n. 31
Mitford sisters (Diana, Jessica, Unity), Ch. 5, n.4
Modernism, Modernity, 18-19, Intr. n. 6; critique of and opposition to, 21, 72, Ch. 1 n. 31; idea of "alternative modernity," 22, Ch. 1: nn. 20

Modersohn-Becker, Paula, 8, 11, Intr. n. 21, Ch. 6 n. 1
Monarchy, aim of restoring, 68-69, Ch. 5: nn. 5, 13, 69
*Monatsschrift für arische Gottes- und Welterkenntnis* [later renamed *Arische Freiheit*], 73, 77. *See also: Arische Freiheit*
Monism, 24-28, 30. *See also: Deutsche Monisten-Bund*
Mother Earth, myth of, 2, 95, 97, 100, 104
Munch, Edvard, 57
Mühsam, Erich, Ch. 1 n. 31
Münchhausen, Börries, Freiherr von, Ch. 1 n. 31, Ch. 2 n. 2, Ch. 5 n. 23

Natorp, Paul, Ch. 1, n. 31
*National Club*, 69
National Socialism, National Socialist Party, 11-12, 21, 22, 32, 69, 74-75, 79, 82, 86-87, 89-90, 107, 120, Intr.: nn. 21, 22, Ch. 1: nn. 31, 62, Ch. 3 n. 2, Ch. 5: nn. 1, 5, 8, 13, 19, 66, 78; *Abteilung Film und Rundfunk*, 74; *Abteilung Rasse und Kultur*, 74; and aristocracy, 66-69, 72, 75, 112, Ch. 5 n. 13; and class distinctions, 11, 17-18, 21-22, 29, 69, 96, 98-102, Ch. 1: nn. 10, 18, 32, Ch. 5: nn. 15, 53, 66; and death, 29-30, 43, 50-55, 92, 96-97, 102, 109, 111, 116-123, 128, 130, Ch. 4 n. 8, Ch. 5 n. 18, Ch. 8 n. 9; and nature/naturism, 8, 21-28, 38, 45-49, 59-61, 80, 89-93, 106, 111-12, 127-29, Ch. 1 n. 18, Ch. 4 n. 8, Ch. 6 n. 3; and orient, 16, 37, 44, 58-59, 70, 75, 82, 85, 90-91, 112, Intr. n. 17, Ch. 4 n. 8, Ch. 5: nn. 17, 18, 39, 49, Ch. 8 n. 11; and religion, 1-2, 8, 16-17, 19, 21, 23-28-39, 43-52, 58-61, 70, 77-79, 83, 90-93, 100-101, 103, 107-08, 112, 116, 117, 125, 128, Intr.: nn. 13, 22, Ch. 1: nn. 2, 12, 13, 20, 24, 37, 50, Ch. 3 n. 1, Ch. 4: nn. 5, 8, Ch. 5: nn. 17, 18, 19, 48, 49 78; Ch. 6 n. 1; and vegetarianism, 21, 28, Ch. 1 n. 18, Ch. 5 n. 54; and women, 33, 51, 52, 55, 58-59, 71, 72, 78, 82-84, 89-93, Ch. 7, 111, 127, Ch. 1 n. 31, Ch. 5: nn. 1, 4, 45, 53

NSDAP [*Nationalsozialistische Deutsche Arbeiterpartei*], 2, 12, 30, 55, 67, 73-74, 77, 78, 80-83, 85-90, 102-03, 108, 111, 130, Intr.: nn. 5, 17, Ch. 1: nn. 31, 37, 46, 49, Ch. 2 n. 6, Ch. 5: nn. 4, 23, 33, 56, 66, 70, 83, Ch. 9 n. 2
Nazi party, *see*: NSDAP
Neckel, Gustav, 77
Neo-nazi organization, 2, Ch. 8, 127, Ch. 5: nn. 10, 60, Ch. 8: nn. 3, 9, Bibl. n. 1
Neo-paganism, 2, 16, 19, 30-33, 59-61, 75-79, 107-108, 111, 115-17, Ch. 1 n. 1, Ch. 5: nn. 19, 47. *See also: völkisch; Germanische Glaubensgemeinschaft; Deutsch-religiöse Gemeinschaft*
*Neue deutsche Volksbühne*, 24
*Neue Gemeinschaft*, 27, 30, Ch. 1 n. 31
New Age ideas, 55
"New Man", 30, 35, 47, 129
Niedlich, Joachim Kurd, 31-32, Ch. 1 n. 44
Niekisch, Ernst, 35, Ch. 1 n. 62, Ch. 2 n. 6
Nietzsche, Friedrich, 6, 23-24, 35, 44, 45, 53, 54, 57-58, 60, 68, 112, 128, Ch. 1 n. 7, Ch. 2 n. 11, Ch. 4 n. 11, Ch. 6 n. 3
Nolde, Emil, 85
Nordicism, Nordic idea, 11-12, 19-21, 60, 67-88, 89, 107, 109-12, Intr.: nn. 21-22, Ch. 2 n. 9, Ch. 5: nn. 15, 17, 23, 24, 26, 27, 44, 45, 47, 58, 83, Ch. 6 n. 1, Ch. 8 n. 11; *Aufnordung, Entnordung*; Goebbels' reservations; history of decline of Nordic race, 9-12, 23-24, Ch. 4 n. 13; place of women in Nordic cultures contrasted with subordinate role in "Oriental" or "Semitic" cultures, 82, 91-93; *Nordische Vermittlungsstelle*; and race, 11, 43, 46, 72; and religion, 2, fig. 11, 16, 29-32, 47, 70-71, 73, 79, 90-91, Ch. 1 n. 31, Ch. 3 n. 1, Ch. 5: nn. 19, 49; *Thing*, 73. *See also under*: race
*Nordische Glaubensbewegung*, 79, 89, Ch. 5: nn. 47, 51
*Nordischer Ring* [later renamed *Bogenklub München; Deutscher Widar-Bund*], 69, 71-72, 81-82, Intr. n. 22, Ch. 5 n. 76

*Nordische Vermittlungsstelle*, 72
November Revolution, *see:* German Revolution

*Odal. Monatschrift für Blut und Boden*, Ch. 5: nn. 54, 60. *See also:* Darré, Richard-Walter
Odin, 8, 9, fig. 11, 19, 50, 58-60, 70, Ch. 1 n. 16
*Ordo novi Templi*, 28, Ch. 1 n. 37, Ch. 7 n. 2
Ostwald, Wilhelm, 27, Ch. 1 n. 30

Paetel, Karl O., Ch. 2 n. 6
Pantheism, 24, Ch. 3 n. 1
Petri, Egon, 5
Pfemfert, Franz, 1, 58, Intr. n. 2, Ch. 1 n. 16. *See also: Die Aktion*
Pfitzner, Hans, Ch. 1 n. 31
Ploetz, Alfred, 71, Ch. 5 n. 23; plan for *Pacifica*, a racially pure commune, 71. *See also: Ring der Norda*
Pohl, Hermann, founder of *Germanen-Orden*, 28
Przybyszczewski, Stanislas, 57-59

Race, 44-46, 67, 83-85, 89-93, 97, 101, 114, 128, Intr.: nn. 17, 20, Ch. 1 n. 49, 50, 57, 63, Ch. 3 n. 1, Ch. 4 n. 16, Ch. 5: nn. 8, 13, 15, 17, 24, 39, 47, 55, 80; *Aufnordung*, 72, 76-77, 87, Ch. 2 n. 57; the "call of blood", 96; biological bases of, 59, 69; Department for "Judentum und Freimaurerei", 108 Department of Race and Culture, 74; disagreements about race in NSDAP, 86-87, Ch. 5 n. 83; racial materialism, 86-87; study of, 46, 75-80; Nordic, 9-11, 23-24, 32, 46, 47, 69, 75-77, 80-81, 90-92, Ch. 5: nn. 17, 19, 23, 27, 83; purity and preservation of, 11, 28-29, 59-61, 69-72, 76-77, 85, 87, 112, Ch. 5: nn. 19, 23, Ch. 7 n. 2; and religion, 16, 30-41, 58-59, 75-76, Ch. 5: nn. 4, 79
Rassinier, Paul, 2, 113
Rathenau, Walther, 69-70, Intr. n. 17, Ch. 5: nn. 16, 18; advocate of *Aufnordung*, 69-70; antithesis of *Mutmenschen* and *Furchtmenschen*, 70; relation to

Wilhelm Schwaner; Intr. n. 17
Reger, Max, Ch. 1, n. 31
Reuß zur Lippe, Marie Adelheid, Prinzessin, 68-75, 77, 78, 82-93, Ch. 9; author of *Gott in mir*, Part I, 66-67, 75, 79, 80, 82, 88, 98; neo-Nazi activities post 1945, 2, 113, Ch. 9; revolt against her class, 22, 65-66, Ch. 3 n. 2; works: *Die Overbroocks*, 55, 66, 68, Ch. 7, 80; *Freundesgruß*, 2, 114-15; *Mutter Erde*, 2, 55; *Nordische Frau und Nordischer Glaube*, 2, 88, Ch. 6, 95, 96, 98, 107, 109, Ch. 5, n. 51, Ch. 6 n. 1; *Weltfrömmigkeit*, 2, 112, 114, 125; translator of Holocaust-denying literature, 2, Bibl. n. 1; family background, 65-69, 75, 79, 87; Arbeitsleiterin für Frauenkultur, 82;
Reuß, Heinrich XLV, Erbprinz, 67-68
Reuter, Otto Sigfrid, 59, 79, Ch. 1 n. 57, Ch. 5 n. 47
Reventlow, Franziska von, Ch. 5, n. 4
Rilke, Rainer-Maria, fig. 4, 5, Ch. 8 n. 9
*Ring der Norda*, 71. See also: *Nordischer Ring*
Rohde, Erwin, Ch. 4 n. 11
Roselius, Hildegard, Intr. n. 23
Roselius, Ludwig, 1, 8-12, 29, 46, 58-59, 77, 107, 112, 127, Intr.: nn. 11, 18, 20, 21, 23, Ch. 6 n. 1
Rosenberg, Alfred, 32, 34, 39, 74, 79, 87, 108, Intr. n. 13, Ch. 1: nn. 37, 58, 59, Ch. 5: nn. 83, 84
*Rote Hilfe*, 5
Runic signs, 111, 125, Intr. n.17, Ch. 5 n. 44

Saalack, 85, Ch. 5 n. 74 *Saaleck-Kreis*, 85
Saxony, Lower (Niedersachsen), 8, 75, 80, 95-96, 99, 102, 111, 114
Schäfer, Wilhelm, Ch. 1 n. 31
Schaumburg-Lippe, House of, Ch. 5: nn. 11, 12
Schaumburg-Lippe, Friedrich Christian, Prinz zu, 68, Ch. 5 n. 12, Bibl. n. 1
Schenkendorf, Max von, Ch. 8 n. 7
Schickele, René, 57
Schiele, Egon, Intr. n. 2
Schmidt-Rottluff, Karl, Intr. n. 1

*Index* 201

Schmitt, Carl, 77
Schmitt, Eugen Heinrich, 35-37, Ch. 1 n. 64
Schopenhauer, Arthur, Ch. 4 n. 11
Schultze-Naumburg, Paul, 72, 84-85, 87, Ch. 1 n. 31, Ch. 5 n. 74; *Kunst und Rasse*, 84-85 *Kunst aus Blut und Boden*, 85. See also: Saaleck
Schwaner, Wilhelm, 16, 19, 31, 33, 35, fig. 16, 44, 60, Intr. n. 17, Ch. 1: nn. 2, 10, 16, 31, Ch. 2 n. 4, Ch. 5 n. 18; editor of *Volkserzieher*, 37, 60. See also: Germanen-Bibel; Germanische Glaubensgemeinschaft
Sebottendorf, Rudolf von, 29-30
*Sera-Kreis* [Sera Circle], Ch. 1 n. 7, Ch. 2 n. 1, Ch. 5 n. 30
Silesius, Angelus, 17, 34, Ch. 1 n. 58
Socialism, 6, 11, 12, 17-18, 22, 57, 71, 85-86, 89, 98, 100, 113, 129, Intr. n. 6, Ch. 1: nn. 31, 32, Ch. 2 n. 6, Ch. 3 n. 2
Social Democratic Party of Germany (SPD), 12, Intr.: nn. 5, 17
Sombart, Werner, 70; antithesis of *Helden* and *Händler*, 70
*Sonne, Die* (periodical), 72, 73, 83, Ch. 5. n. 30
Spaak, Paul-Henri, Ch. 5 n. 35
*Spartakus*, communist league, 100, Intr. 15
Spinoza, Benedict de, 30, Ch. 1: nn. 24, 66
Spohr, Wilhelm, Ch. 3 n. 2
Stadler, Ernst, Ch. 1 n. 16
Stassen, Franz, Ch. 1 n. 31, Ch. 5 n. 76
Steiner, Rudolf, 17, 24-25, 32, Intr. n. 15, Ch. 1: nn. 26, 31, 49
Strasser, Gregor, 73, Intr. n. 17
Strindberg, August, 57, 58
*Sturm, Der*, fig. 10, 57
Syndicalist Press, 6

Tacitus, 24, 44,
Tappert, Georg, Intr. n. 1
*Tat, Die* (periodical), 32
Tesserow, Heinrich, Ch. 1 n. 31 Thale *Volkstheater*, 19-21
Thale *Volkstheater*, see: *Harzer Bergtheater*
Theosophy, 17, 24, 32

Thode, Henry, Ch. 1 n. 31
*Thule, Thule-Gesellschaft*, 29-30, Ch. 1, n. 37

Van den Bruck, Moeller, 27, 68
Vogeler, Heinrich, fig. 1, fig. 2; artistic career and politics, 1, 2-9, 25, 50-55, 58, 127, 129, Intr.: nn. 2, 3, 6, 8, 13, 17, 18, Ch. 3 n. 2, Ch. 8 n. 9; Barkenhoff, 5-6, Intr.: nn. 11, 15; "Das Märchen vom Lieben Gott: Brief eines Uneroffiziers an den Kaiser im Januar 1918", Intr. n. 7; *Zukunft*, 69
*Volk und Rasse*, 81, Ch. 5 n. 43
*Völkisch*, 17, 20-21, 25, 72, Ch. 1: nn. 1, 21, 22, 24, 31; definition, 28, Ch. 1 n. 32, 43, 49; marginalising of *völkisch* groups under National Socialism; relation to National Socialism, 87, Ch. 2 n. 2, Ch. 5 n. 18, Ch. 5: nn. 47, 53, 56, 66, 83, Ch. 8: nn. 2, 14, Ch. 9 n. 2; religion, 24, 30-33, 35, 43-45, 47, 52, Ch. 4, 75, 79-80, 82-83, 107-08, 111, 128, Intr.: nn. 17, 22, Ch. 1 n. 66, Ch. 4 n. 13, Ch. 6 n. 3
*Völkischer Beobachter*, 86, Ch. 1, n. 49
*Volkserzieher, Der* (periodical), Ch.1 n. 10, Ch. 5, n. 18

Wachler, Ernst, 20-21, 59, Ch. 1: nn. 17, 57

Wagner, Richard, 21, 73, Ch. 1 n. 31, Ch. 4 n. 11, Ch. 5 n. 76
Walden, Herwarth, fig. 10, 57
*Wandervögel*, 21, 101, Ch. 1 n. 21, Ch. 5 n. 24
Weber, Max, 18, Ch. 1 n. 31
Webern, Anton von, Ch. 1 n. 31
*Werdandi-Bund zur Förderung jungdeutscher Kunst*, 27-28, Ch. 1 n. 31
*Werkbund für deutsches Volkstum und Rassenforschung*, 72
Wilhelm II, Kaiser, 67
Wille, Bruno, 24-25, Ch. 1 n. 26
Wirth, Herman, 9-10, 11, 29, 43, 46, 77, 111, Intr. n. 21, Ch. 2 n. 13, Ch. 5 n. 83
Wolf, Friedrich, 6, Intr. n. 8
Wolzogen, Ernst Ludwig, Freiherr von, 60, Ch. 4 n. 11
World War I, 11, 12, 39, 55, 60, 69, 85, 109, Intr. n. 15, Ch. 1 n. 16, Ch. 5 n. 30, Ch. 7 n. 2, Bibl. n. 1
World War II, 2, 9, fig. 11, 38, 39, 55, 66, 68, 108-09, 111, 114, 130, Intr. n. 20, Ch. 1 n. 57
Worpswede, 2, 5, 8, 25, Intr.: nn. 2, 15, 17
Wotan, *see:* Odin

Zarathustra, 30, 45
Zur Mühlen, Hermynia, Ch. 3 n. 2, Ch. 5, n. 4

Open Book Publishers is an independent community interest company set up and run by academics for academics and for readers of academic work. We publish high quality, peer-reviewed monographs, collected volumes and lecture series in the humanities and social sciences.

Open Book speeds up the whole publishing process from author to reader by applying three recent technological advances: digital medium, the internet and print-on-demand. We thus offer all the advantages of digital texts (speed, searchability, updating, archival material, databases, discussion forums, and links to institutions' websites) together with those of the traditional printed medium.

Works accepted for publication, after the rigorous peer-review process, are published within weeks.

All Open Book publications are available online to be read free of charge by anyone with access to the internet, a point of high importance for those who wish to reach colleagues, students, and other readers around the world with poor access to research libraries.

For further information on our publishing enterprise, additional digital material related to our titles and to order our books please visit our website: www.openbookpublishers.com

or contact the Managing Director, Dr. Alessandra Tosi: a.tosi@openbookpublishers.com

www.ingramcontent.com/pod-product-compliance
Lightning Source LLC
Chambersburg PA
CBHW050558170426
43201CB00011B/1738